TRANSLATION AND POWER

TRANSLATION
and Power

EDITED BY
MARIA TYMOCZKO
AND
EDWIN GENTZLER

University of Massachusetts Press
Amherst and Boston

Copyright © 2002 by University of Massachusetts Press
All rights reserved
Printed in the United States of America

LC 2002008285
ISBN 1-55849-358-1 (library cloth ed.); 359-X (paper)
Designed by Milenda Nan Ok Lee
Set in Galliard by Binghamton Valley Composition
Printed and bound by Thomson-Shore, Inc.

Library of Congress Cataloging-in-Publication Data
Translation and power / edited by Maria Tymoczko and Edwin Gentzler.
      p. cm.
      ISBN 1-55849-358-1 (lib. cloth : alk. paper) — ISBN 1-55849-359-X
(pbk. : alk. paper)
   1. Translating and interpreting—Social aspects.   2. Power (Social
sciences)   3. Language and culture.   I. Tymoczko, Maria.
II. Gentzler, Edwin, 1951–
   P306.97.S63 T7 2002
   418'.02—dc21

                                                            2002008285

British Library Cataloguing in Publication data are available.

In memory of André Lefevere

Contents

Translation as Testimony: On Official Histories and
Subversive Pedagogies in Cortázar

Translating Woman: Victoria Ocampo and the Empires of
Foreign Fascination

Germaine de Staël and Gayatri Spivak: Culture Brokers

Spanish Film Translation and Cultural Patronage: The
Filtering and Manipulation of Imported Material during
Franco's Dictatorship

Translation as a Catalyst for Social Change in China

Translation, *Dépaysement,* and Their Figuration

Translation, Poststructuralism, and Power

Acknowledgments

We would like to express our gratitude to all the participants in the Translation Center's International Visitors Program, especially those who contributed to this anthology. Special thanks go as well to Lee Edwards, dean of the College of Humanities and Fine Arts, who had great vision regarding the future of translation studies, and to the cosponsoring departments at the University of Massachusetts, including the departments of Comparative Literature, French and Italian, Spanish and Portuguese, German, Judaic and Near Eastern Studies, Asian Languages, and English. We also wish to acknowledge other sponsors, including the Five College Faculty Seminar on Literary Translation and Five Colleges, Inc. Thanks go also to all the students in Maria Tymoczko's courses on the theory and practice of translation and Edwin Gentzler's courses on translation and postcolonial studies and translation techniques and technologies, who attended the lectures and participated in discussions. We are indebted to the University of Massachusetts Press, particularly Bruce Wilcox, director, for support of this project, as well as Carol Betsch, managing editor, and Marie Salter, copy editor, for their help in the production phase. Finally, we are grateful to Marilyn Gaddis Rose and Douglas Robinson for their careful readings of the manuscript and their many valuable suggestions.

EDWIN GENTZLER AND MARIA TYMOCZKO

Introduction

A focused examination of questions pertaining to power and translation can be dated from 1990, when Susan Bassnett and André Lefevere wrote in the introduction to *Translation, History and Culture* that although empirical historical research can document changes in modes of translation, to *explain* such changes a translation studies scholar must go into "the vagaries and vicissitudes of the exercise of power in a society, and what the exercise of power means in terms of the production of culture, of which the production of translations is a part" (1990a:5). Although this call from Bassnett and Lefevere initiated more searching examinations, the interest in power and translation has deep roots, roots that reach back more than a quarter of a century, both to historical events in the second half of the twentieth century and to their reflection in the emerging discipline of translation studies.

In the 1950s and 1960s, as Madison Avenue tightened its grip on the United States and the world and pioneered techniques for using mass communications for cultural control, practicing translators began consciously to calibrate their translation techniques to achieve effects they wished to produce in their audiences, whether those effects were religious faith, consumption of products, or literary success. In short, translators began to realize how translated texts could manipulate readers to achieve desired effects. Such functionalist techniques soon led, in turn, to early descriptive approaches to translation, exemplified in the work of James R. Holmes, who was among the first to analyze those translation techniques. Holmes, himself a gifted translator, showed that a reader could dissect translations to discern the effects that they would have on audiences and to determine the literary, but also the political, commitments of their translators. Using a range of translations of the same text, he and scholars such as Anton Popovič contrasted the varied purposes and impacts that diverse translation techniques would achieve. The result was nothing short of a revolution in the field of translation studies: the realization that a normative approach was tantamount to an implicit allegiance to a given but unspecified range of values commonly shared by those in power in any given culture. It was obvious that practicing translators and the profession would be better served by becoming flexible and proficient in a number of translation techniques and approaches that could be deployed in context-specific situations.

Even as these shifts were happening in the domain of translation, however, historical events deepened the understanding of power as a motivating factor in cultural domains. In the 1960s somewhat naive ideological frames of reference—whether based on materialist theories or more diffuse political theories—began to implode. For two decades after World War II, the breakup of colonial empires brought huge geopolitical shifts and realignments to the world. Moreover, the opposition to the Vietnam War challenged expansionist ideologies of all sorts. Within virtually all cultures, disenchantment with dominant ideologies resulted in reconceptualizations of society and power. Motivated by Civil Rights movements in the United States and elsewhere, by the activities of the generation of 1968 in Europe, by resistance to Soviet occupation in central Europe, and by feminism worldwide, the result was a growing consensus that however important materialist issues might be, more fundamental were the structures of power in societies, both implicit and explicit, formal and informal. These interests have accelerated since the disintegration of the Soviet Union, the end of the Cold War, the rise of postcolonialism, and the globalization of the economies and cultures of the world.

The changes in translation studies and the field's interest in power thus take their place within the larger political trajectories since the 1960s. This is the context within which we can situate the contributions of various important movements in translation studies since 1975, when many scholars worldwide began to explore issues of power and translation—movements that this survey can only delineate briefly, perforce omitting many whose work made important contributions to the trajectory we are tracing. Our work is greatly informed by scholars, predominantly from the Low Countries and Israel, whose explicit interest in the topic of translation and power had its beginnings in the late 1970s and early 1980s. They outlined a program of descriptive studies of translation that would connect literary translation norms and goals with extraliterary translation contexts. A new stage was reached in 1985 with the essays in the anthology *The Manipulation of Literature*, edited by Theo Hermans. The group of scholars who participated, including Gideon Toury from Israel; José Lambert, Raymond van den Broeck, Theo Hermans, and André Lefevere from Belgium; Susan Bassnett from the United Kingdom; and Maria Tymoczko from the United States, among others, demonstrated that translations, rather than being secondary and derivative, were instead one of the *primary* literary tools that larger social institutions—educational systems, arts councils, publishing firms, and even governments—had at their disposal to "manipulate" a given society in order to "construct" the kind of "culture" desired. To do so, however, the source text itself was manipulated to create a desired representation. The writers in Hermans's anthology and their followers demonstrated that churches would commission Bible translations, governments would support translations of national epics, schools would teach translations of great books, kings would be patrons for translations about heroic conquests, and socialist regimes would underwrite translations of social realism, all for their own purposes pertaining to ideology and cultural power.

The manipulation theses posited in 1985 evolved into the "cultural turn" in translation studies in the next decade, a movement that had ramifications in every branch of the discipline. Within descriptive approaches, it coalesced in 1990 with the publication of Bassnett and Lefevere's anthology *Translation, History and Culture*. That collection of essays redefined the object of inquiry in descriptive translation studies as a text within the networks of literary and extraliterary signs, in both the source and target cultures. Frustrated that translation studies scholarship was spending so much effort analyzing minute literary and linguistic differences, such that often the forest could not be seen for the trees, Bassnett and Lefevere wanted to *explain* the shifts that occur in translation, not just by poetic devices but by ideological forces as well. They argued in their introduction that "the student of translation/rewriting is not engaged in an ever-lengthening and even more complex dance around the 'always already no longer there,' " but that studies of translation should deal "with hard, falsifiable, cultural data, and the way they affect people's lives" (1990a:12).

An explosion of scholarship ensued in every branch of translation studies in the 1990s. Within the strand of descriptive studies, Lefevere published three books on translation in 1992, including *Translation, Rewriting, and the Manipulation of Literary Fame*. From an Anglo-American critical theory perspective, Lawrence Venuti brought out his important anthology entitled *Rethinking Translation: Discourse, Subjectivity, Ideology* that same year, and in 1993 Edwin Gentzler's *Contemporary Translation Theories* appeared. New journals such as *Target* and *The Translator* were launched. Conference activity increased all over the world. New publishing firms got into the market. Old series were revived, notably the Rodopi Series in Holland. Encyclopedias of translation studies were developed in England, Germany, China, and elsewhere. Perhaps most significantly, translation studies expanded in academia, with new master's and doctoral programs starting at a number of universities.

Though many of the early descriptive studies of translation tended to employ structuralist methodologies and approaches, after the cultural turn, publications in translation studies that dealt with questions of power increasingly had a poststructuralist basis. In *Rethinking Translation*, for example, Venuti insisted that the study of translations be submitted to "the same rigorous interrogation that other cultural forms and practices have recently undergone with the emergence of poststructuralism and its impact on such theoretical and political discourses as psychoanalysis, Marxism, and feminism" (1992:6). In many studies of translation since 1990, translation scholars have thus made their comparisons less to unified meanings in individual source texts and more to the long chains of multiple meanings and the pluralities of language that lie behind any textual construct. This strand of the cultural turn has produced significant individual works that foreground issues of power, notably Venuti's *The Translator's Invisibility* (1995) and *The Scandals of Translation* (1998), as well as anthologies such as Román Álvarez and M. Carmen-África Vidal's *Translation, Power, Subversion* (1996).

But, more important, whole schools of translation and translation scholarship can be connected with this turn in translation studies. The translators and translation scholars who work on the literature of Quebec—including Annie Brisset, Barbara Godard, Susanne de Lotbinière-Harwood, and Sherry Simon—form such a group, translating and theorizing translation with poststructuralist and postmodernist techniques. They have become involved in the negotiation of meanings in Canada, challenging both implicit and explicit structures of power in their culture. Similarly, a "postmodern translational aesthetics" (Vieira 1994) has arisen since the 1960s in Brazil, where a group of translators, including the eminent Haroldo de Campos and Augusto de Campos, has developed assertive translational methods based on the modernist principles of the *movimento antropófago* ('cannibalist movement') initiated in 1928 by Oswald de Andrade (cf. Johnson 1987). Such translators—and the scholars who write about them—have been intimately engaged in the renegotiation of Brazilian language, culture, and nation, both at home and within the power structures of the wider world.

Perhaps the most significant of these movements is the diverse group of translators and scholars who have independently yet simultaneously applied postcolonial theory and practices to translation. This is one of the exciting growing edges of translation studies at present, and numerous studies focused on questions of power and colonialism have appeared, all incorporating to a greater or lesser extent poststructuralist perspectives. Notable here are the collection of essays edited by Anuradha Dingwaney and Carol Maier, *Between Languages and Cultures* (1995b); the anthology edited by Susan Bassnett and Harish Trivedi, *Post-colonial Translation: Theory and Practice* (1999); Maria Tymoczko's *Translation in a Postcolonial Context* (1999); and the collection edited by Sherry Simon and Paul St-Pierre, *Changing the Terms: Translating in the Postcolonial Era* (2000).

Meanwhile, outside the realm of translation studies, scholars from many fields have articulated the central importance of translation in establishing, maintaining, and resisting imperialist power structures. Postcolonial scholars have turned to translation studies for new ideas, terminology, and metaphors with which to express their views. Homi Bhabha has gone so far as to coin the term *translational culture* to refer to all those migrants and hybridized identities he finds characteristic of the postmodern world; translation, according to Bhabha, has become *the* site for cultural production, the space where "newness" enters the world (1994:212). Tejaswini Niranjana in *Siting Translation* (1992), Eric

Cheyfitz in *The Poetics of Imperialism* (1997), and Vicente Rafael in *Contracting Colonialism* (1993) connect the use of translated texts to colonizing and postcolonial cultures in India, North America, and the Philippines, respectively. Of this group perhaps the most notable is Gayatri Spivak who has turned to translating the Bengali tribal writer Mahasweta Devi and has theorized translation in terms of its politics, using materialist feminist theory in addition to her earlier work in deconstruction. Spivak's seminal essay, "The Politics of Translation" (1992) and her translation and introduction of Devi in *Imaginary Maps* (1995) are landmark contributions to these developments.

The key topic that has provided the impetus for the new directions that translation studies have taken since the cultural turn is *power*. In poststructuralist and postcolonial fields, discussions have increasingly focused on the question of *agency*: given that we are always already formed by the discourses of the age in which we live, how can anyone effect cultural change? How can we bridge cultural gaps so as to experience anything new or different? How can we penetrate reified worldviews, particularly in the West, to allow real cultural difference to enter? Although in translation studies all now agree that translations are never fully homologous to the original—always containing shifts, errors, and subjective interpretations—it is also agreed that translations do nevertheless import aspects of the Other to the receiving culture. What sort of impact does translation have on cultural change? Under what circumstances do translations have the most impact? What forms of translation are most successful? And how does all this relate to cultural dominance, cultural assertion, and cultural resistance—in short to *power*? In a sense such questions as these have meant that the "*cultural* turn" in translation studies has become the "*power* turn," with questions of power brought to the fore in discussions of both translation history and strategies for translation.

Attempting to cultivate this fertile ground, the Translation Center at the University of Massachusetts, Amherst, has sponsored an international visitors series, inviting translation studies scholars and translators from around the world to come and give talks on the topic of translation and power. The series has been extremely successful, with presentations from numerous scholars and translators, including Else Vieira, Adriana Pagano, and Neusa da Silva Matte from Brazil; Annie Brisset, Suzanne de Lotbinière-Harwood, and Sherry Simon from Canada; Jin Di and Lin Kenan from China; André Lefevere, Susan Bassnett, and Michael Cronin from Europe; and Carol Maier and Lawrence Venuti from the United States, among others. Despite having a wide variety of perspectives and methodologies, all have made significant contributions to the discourse of power and translation. We found the quality of the talks so impressive that we decided to publish an anthology based on the subject, and this decision was the genesis of the present publication. The first talk in this series was presented by the late André Lefevere, who spoke impromptu and without interruption for more than an hour on the topic, giving the audience a stream of examples ranging over a broad spectrum of languages and cultures. It is our hope that this anthology will be seen as a continuation of his pioneering research.

Before continuing, it is worthwhile to look at the culturally accepted meanings of the word *power*. It is a complex term, with the entry in the *Oxford English Dictionary* extending across four pages. Ranging from the first meaning, the "ability to do or effect something . . . , or to act upon a person or thing," to "might; vigour, energy," to "possession of control or command over others; dominion, rule; government, domination . . . ; influence, authority," to "legal ability, capacity, or authority to act," the word can refer to persons, things, spiritual beings, or fighting forces. *Power* also has various technical meanings, including mathematical (i.e., "the product obtained by multiplying a number . . . onto itself a number of times") and mechanical ones ("any form of energy or force available for application to work" and the "capacity for exerting mechanical force"). The word enters into many idioms as well, not the least of which are *in power* and *power of life and death*. The essays that follow instantiate and explore many of these meanings of power in relation to translation, from questions of influence and authority in the nineteenth century, bolstered by changing meanings of the word *democracy* in translation, to the legal capacity of the British and the establishment of dominion over the Maori by the Treaty of Waitangi, to the vigor and energy of translation in the transformation of cultures ranging from China to Latin America. At the same time, the essays illustrate that translation is not simply associated with the "possession of control or command over others" and, hence, with colonization or oppression, but also with "the ability to act upon" structures of command, such that translation becomes a means to resist that very colonization or exploitation.

Translation is associated with power in all these senses, in part, because translation is a metonymic process as well as a metaphoric one.

Translations are inevitably partial; meaning in a text is always over-determined, and the information in a source text is therefore always more extensive than a translation can convey. Conversely, the receptor language and culture entail obligatory features that shape the possible interpretations of the translation, as well as extending the meanings of the translation in directions other than those inherent in the source text (cf. Tymoczko 1999: chapters 1, 10, and sources cited; Tymoczko 2000). As a result, translators must make choices, selecting aspects or parts of a text to transpose and emphasize. Such choices in turn serve to create representations of their source texts, representations that are also partial. This partiality is not to be considered a defect, a lack, or an absence in a translation; it is a necessary condition of the act. It is also an aspect that makes the act of translation partisan: engaged and committed, either implicitly or explicitly. Indeed partiality is what differentiates translations, enabling them to participate in the dialectic of power, the ongoing process of political discourse, and strategies for social change. Such representations and commitments are apparent from analyses of translators' choices, word by word, page by page, and text by text, and they are also often demonstrable in the paratextual materials that surround translations, including introductions, footnotes, reviews, literary criticism, and so forth. The very words associated with politics and ideology used here (i.e., *partiality, partisan, participate*) suggest that the partial nature of translations is what makes them also an exercise of power.

The concept of power as used by early studies of translation in some cases needs to be critically analyzed. One of the weaknesses of the early stages of the cultural turn in translation studies was at times an uncritical application of power dichotomies. Scholars were inclined to see an either/or situation with regard to translation: either the translator would collude with the status quo and produce fluent, self-effacing translations, or oppose a particular hegemony and use foreignizing strategies to import new and unfamiliar terms to the receiving culture. In Canada, within a perceived polarization of power, some women translators aggressively "womanhandled" translations in order to critique and challenge Western patriarchal discourse. Some of this absolutist and dichotomous thinking may derive from fairly monolithic theories of power and various micro-politics of resistance aimed at dismantling institutions of power, whether capitalist or communist, West or East, typical of the 1960s and 1970s.

Power was typically seen as a form of repression, and those who wielded power did so at the expense of "the people."

The essays collected here challenge such dichotomous and absolutist views, in part because of increasingly complex and divergent views of power from those of earlier decades. The study of translation in charged political contexts illustrates the relationship between discourse and power, and shows that, as a site where discourses meet and compete, translation negotiates power relations. But the workings of power are not simply "top down," a matter of inexorable repression and constraint; instead, translation, like other cultural activities, can be mobilized for counterdiscourses and subversion, or for any number of mediating positions in between. Moreover, having power or not having power is not necessarily good or bad in and of itself. Whereas institutions of power historically have marginalized many groups—including religious groups, women, gay men and lesbians, ethnic groups, and, as can especially be seen in the papers that follow, cultural and linguistic minorities—translators, as is the case with many community leaders, often find themselves simultaneously caught in both camps, representing both the institutions in power and those seeking empowerment. Indeed, often a certain ethics of translation limits the amount of advocating a translator can do on behalf of either party, which puts the translator in a nearly impossible situation—similar to a lawyer having to represent both the plaintiff and the defendant in the same case. Often with divided allegiances, representing the status quo while simultaneously introducing new forms of representation, the translator acts as a kind of double agent in the process of cultural negotiation.

Rather than see this as a necessarily compromised position, we see the translator's double role as a strength, one perhaps indicative of the complex communications found in the hybridized conditions characteristic of many cultures today. Many formerly colonized peoples find themselves empowered, participating in the construction of new nation-states and negotiating across borders with other emerging nations. Many minority groups find themselves increasingly represented in formerly monolithic institutions, with growing power to effect change. And many groups in power are more open to new interpretations and change, thereby increasing diversity and community access. Translation can be valuable in this shifting terrain, but such cultural complexity makes the analysis of translation difficult, particularly the analysis of whom the translation best serves. Translations often face two ways at once, depending on context. Thus, most contemporary translation studies scholars view the process of translation as heterogeneous, with different issues addressed by different translations and different translators at different times and different places, depending on the specific historical and material moment. These shifts in translation strategies are often palpable in the translation record, as the writers in this collection demonstrate. No single translation strategy can be associated with the exercise of oppression or the struggle for resistance; no single strategy is *the* strategy of power.

This multiplicity in the interpretation of translated texts is related to a view of discourse interactions as being fragmentary and incomplete (cf. Mills 1997:153), an approach that is particularly compatible with an understanding of translation as metonymic and partisan. As with other discursive practices, texts to be translated must be seen as embodying a range of discourses, all of which impinge on the choices of the translators, thus contributing to the gaps, inconsistencies, and fragments that can be found in translations. Here we might compare Dennis Porter's (1983) critique of Edward Said's view of Orientalist discourse as a homogeneous representational system stifling resistance and opposition. Porter stresses the gaps, contradictions, and inconsistencies in writing about other cultures, the destabilizing elements that turn such a colonialist production from a unified discourse to a series of fragments. Translation and other writing practices that respond to such fragmented discourses also generate fragmented texts. Attention to the fragmentary aspects of translations and the processes of translation constitutes a thread linking the essays that follow.

For translation scholars, the analysis of translation is made increasingly difficult by the acknowledgment of the fragmentary nature of discourses and the configuration of the power that they exert. One must analyze not only the parts of the source text and source culture that are present in translated texts, but also the parts that are left out. Lawrence Venuti offers a model for such an approach, calling for an analysis of the "remainder," a term he has borrowed from Jean-Jacques Lecercle's *The Violence of Language* (1990). The *remainder* is that part that exceeds the transparent use of language and that may in fact impede communication (Venuti 1995:216). Analysis of translations must therefore attend to sounds, archaic references, erotic impulses, puns, and all sorts of multiple, often contradictory, referents. Contemporary translation scholars are increasingly open to both the parts translated and the leftovers, including the literal omissions and the absence of translations in the historical record, and, contextualizing translation in its historical moment, they are always aware of how a dominant cultural form or power marginalizes certain other forms and interpretations. Thus, silences, whether the silence of zero translation or the silencing of the remainder, are often critical in understanding the workings of power in translation and in culture, a topic that is also taken up in the current collection.

In traditional models for the analysis of translation, scholars assumed that the translator had knowledge of both the languages and cultures in question and that the translator translated in a linear fashion from the source to the target text. Scholars who have taken the power turn, however, have come to realize that in polyvalent and multicultural environments, knowledge does not necessarily precede the translation activity, and that the act of translation is itself very much involved in the creation of knowledge. Colonialism and imperialism were and are made possible not just by military might or economic advantage but by knowledge as well; knowledge and the representations thus configured are coming to be understood as a central aspect of power. Translation has been a key tool in the production of such knowledge and representations. Yet this cultural domain is not uncontested: through translation can be used by colonizers as a kind of intelligence operation to interrogate subjects and maintain control, it can also be used by opponents of oppression as counterespionage, to conspire and rebel, for the ultimate goals of self-definition and self-determination in both the political and epistemological senses (cf. Tymoczko 1999:294). Translation thus is not simply an act of faithful reproduction but, rather, a deliberate and conscious act of selection, assemblage, structuration, and fabrication—and even, in some cases, of falsification, refusal of information, counterfeiting, and the creation of secret codes. In these ways translators, as much as creative writers and politicians, participate in the powerful acts that create knowledge and shape culture.

In this anthology, we have selected translation studies scholars who have begun the often difficult work of analyzing the selection, assemblage, and fabrication of translated texts, thereby exposing institutions of power at work, not based on abstract philosophical concepts or ideal linguistic structures but instead on *actual translated documents*. Alexandra Lianeri in "Translation and the Establishment of Liberal Democracy

in Nineteenth-Century England: Constructing the Political as an Interpretive Act" looks at the concept *democracy* as understood in Victorian
England, showing that rather than referring simply to a Greek word or
to a "universal" Greek ideal, the term is part of a complex sociohistorical
struggle, in which translation played an active role in the word's cultural
evolution. Writers such as John Stuart Mill and Matthew Arnold engaged
in the political discourse of the period and helped to lead the way to a
radical transformation of the meaning of the term *democracy*, one which
was so politically charged at the time that it threatened the regimes of
various European monarchies. After looking at negative interpretations
of the term *democracy* by seventeenth- and eighteenth-century translators
including Thomas Hobbes, Lianeri then reviews a new conceptual landscape in the nineteenth century, one much influenced by liberal thought
in France and the Americas. She documents how translators participated
in constructing new definitions of democracy that were much more in
tune with newly emerging British cultural and economic goals.

In "The Translation of the Treaty of Waitangi: A Case of Disempowerment," Sabine Fenton and Paul Moon discuss a treaty signed in
1840 that has come to represent the birth of the New Zealand nation.
They show the role that translation of the treaty played in the British
colonization of the Maori. The translator, Anglican missionary Henry
Williams, had little experience in translation, but he was well versed in
the strategic goals of colonization, for missionaries had colluded with the
colonizers by creating the orthography and the dictionaries of the Maori
language and then translating a host of religious documents from the
West into Maori. In the treaty in question, the manipulation through
translation of crucial terms led to Maori acceptance of the treaty. Though
some argue that the British offered the translation in the spirit of generosity, the confusion resulting from this founding document has not
been resolved to this day, and current Maori activists maintain that the
treaty has been used to rob them of their land, resources, and right to
self-governance. Fenton and Moon show how a translation more than a
century old is one reason for revolutionary unrest today.

In "The Empire Talks Back: Orality, Heteronomy, and the Cultural
Turn in Interpretation Studies," Michael Cronin looks at power relations
within the field of interpretation studies, demonstrating that the field, by
and large, has been dominated by research on conference interpreting,

just a minor sector in the overall field. Interpreting for minority groups, including refugees, immigrants, and ethnic minorities—much of which does not operate within the academy—is excluded. As translation studies took a cultural turn in the 1990s, so too, Cronin argues, should interpretation studies take a cultural turn; he suggests a more comprehensive model that will examine all forms of interpreting, particularly those serving and reflecting cultural domains that still have an oral basis. Turning to travel writing and materials from the age of Western imperialism, Cronin questions the neutrality of interpreters, showing that interpreters' views are complicated by their social position within their respective communities. Interpreters, like translators of written documents, have vested interests, economic goals, and political ends, and they frequently find themselves in between power groups, often with mixed or ambivalent feelings and divided loyalties about their role. He argues that, for these reasons, interpreters are in some sense "monsters" with both horrible and wonderful traits, and he calls for a "new cultural teratology" of interpretation to better analyze this complex behavior.

Translation scholars from Latin America have been acutely aware of the power dimension of translation and its monstrous nature, and we are pleased to present several essays that engage the reader in the best of translation theory from Brazil and Argentina. Rosemary Arrojo in "Writing, Interpreting, and the Power Struggle for the Control of Meaning" analyzes fiction by Franz Kafka, Jorge Luis Borges, and Dezso Kosztolányi in terms of a Nietzschian "will to power" or, in this case, an author's will to construct and control meaning, and a translator's will to reconstruct someone else's meaning. She focuses on the use of architectural metaphors, especially the theme of translation or reproduction as it occurs in fiction, to raise questions about definitions of translation, to illustrate the potential tensions between author and translator. In Kafka's "The Burrow," Borges's "Death and the Compass," and Kosztolányi's "The Kleptomaniac Translator," translators/narrators often find themselves in a struggle to construct the impossible perfect text or edifice. Arrojo's analysis destabilizes essentialist notions of language and translation. Instead, she suggests that every translation (and every act of creation) deconstructs and decanonizes an earlier creation, stealing or appropriating that creation in a kind of power struggle with the object the translation intends to represent. Arrojo calls this the dark side of translation, one

perhaps more closely aligned with crime and thieves, yet she suggests that
the translation theorist needs to include this aspect of translation that
practicing translators and creative writers know only too well.

The use of translation as a central theme in fiction is further explored by Adriana Pagano in her essay "Translation as Testimony: On
Official Histories and Subversive Pedagogies in Cortázar." Julio Cortázar,
who with Jorge Luis Borges has shaped the concept of embedding literary
theory within his fiction, has also foregrounded the topic of translation
in several works, including *Hopscotch* (*Rayuela*), "Blow-Up" (a short
story originally entitled "Las babas del diablo"), *62: A Model Kit* (*62-
Modelo para armar*), and *A Manual for Manuel* (*Libro de Manuel*), the
novel in which translation is most explicitly thematized and the primary
subject of Pagano's essay. Cortázar himself worked as a translator for
UNESCO and other Parisian agencies for many years while in exile during the Peron regime in Argentina, and Pagano's essay interweaves Cortázar's displacement with the movement of translation. In *A Manual for
Manuel*, the main characters translate a variety of documents, including
news reports, prisoners' records, and police interviews, for the child Manuel, who comes to represent the future of the country. The sociohistorical period documented was turbulent and includes the escape of guerrillas, the kidnapping of the West German ambassador, and the dispute
between Argentina and Britain over the Malvinas/Falkland Islands. The
translation efforts by the protagonists become a kind of pedagogy for the
future: fearing that Manuel would only receive a diluted version of the
historical facts, their work aims to preserve a historical record before it is
covered up or banned by the authorities. Translation for Latin America,
thus, becomes a means of survival, a method of preserving memory, and
a way to subvert official histories.

In "Translating Woman: Victoria Ocampo and the Empires of Foreign Fascination," Christopher Larkosh continues to explore the theme
of translation and pedagogy in Latin America. In his discussion of Victoria Ocampo's translation, fiction, editorial work, and travel, Larkosh
shows how Ocampo, though shaped by her colonialist upbringing,
sought cross-cultural communication to better realize and translate her
own identity. As editor of *SUR* and a person of privilege, Ocampo en-
joyed a degree of freedom and mobility that few women shared, coming
to embody Argentine literature in her editorial work and her life. Shaped
by translation from an early age—her nannies taught her English and

French—Ocampo developed a love/hate relationship with those foreign-language cultures that dominated her education. For Ocampo, translation is viewed as much more encompassing than transposing words across linguistic boundaries; it involves a physical and spiritual translation of oneself. In his analysis of Ocampo's interactions with the Bengali poet Rabindranath Tagore, Larkosh illustrates her desire to share a common language, to be able to communicate not just in an intermediary language but to translate directly without the need for an "imperial" language. Larkosh suggests that only in taking into consideration Ocampo as a woman and a kind of literary migrant can her form of translation/auto-biography/testimonio be understood. By diffusing the boundaries of translation, Larkosh suggests new openings for translation theorists to transgress the limits of knowledge in a field that continues to efface women writers and translators.

In a similar vein Sherry Simon analyzes two prominent women and cross-cultural communicators in "Germaine de Staël and Gayatri Spivak: Culture Brokers." By linking these two women translators and literary theorists across time and space, Simon shows how translation can be used in both the development and the decay of national identities. Whereas translation in de Staël's world helped contribute to the creation of strong national languages and identities, today in Spivak's world it is being used to destabilize those very notions and to offer a way to think about identity beyond the concept of nation-states. In de Staël's translations, which were more summaries rather than extended translations, Simon notes a liberal, quasi-Romantic view of translation, one which complemented notions of a modern free exchange of ideas and goods by leading European intellectuals of the time. Spivak's work, especially her translations of the Bengali tribal writer Mahasweta Devi, displaces even the most liberal notions of the concept of nation. Yet in both figures Simon finds not self-effacing language mediators, but strong-willed, forceful culture brokers, well aware of the pedagogical role of translation, participating in and shaping relations between disparate cultures, and promoting their own agendas as they wield their influence. Simon shows that by promoting certain literary values, by forging partnerships, women can use translation as a powerful tool to participate in the creation of new cultural dynamics.

In "Spanish Film Translation and Cultural Patronage: The Filtering and Manipulation of Imported Material During Franco's Dictatorship," Camino Gutiérrez Lanza focuses on two powerful institutional forces—

the Franco regime and the Catholic church—which jointly set up a strict set of guidelines to control imported material and to maintain a kind of cultural uniformity. While giving the illusion of allowing intercultural transfer, the church and state in Franco's Spain attempted to block many foreign topics and ideas. Yet by looking at the translation of film during Franco's dictatorship, Gutiérrez shows how international pressure and internal subversion destabilized even the strictest efforts to impose national cultural standards. Though Spanish censorship boards attempted to promote codes of sexual practice through cuts and modifications, the results were full of contradictions. In a more extended analysis of Billy Wilder's 1957 film *Love in the Afternoon*, translated as *Ariane*, a movie that contains an explicit adulterous relationship between Ariane and a rich American, Gutiérrez shows how strictures of the church and state were based on moral and political principles, as well as negotiated public opinion and economic interests. When obscenity laws in Hollywood relaxed and the range of sexual activities on the American screen broadened, film translators and distributors in Spain heeded implicit public resistance to the tenets of *nacionalcatolicismo*. As translators and script writers worked around the guidelines of the censorship code, and as the public refused to attend films that had been too radically altered, the power of church and state censorship gradually diminished, and those who dreamed of completely displacing the Franco regime were gradually empowered.

Likewise focusing on the role of translation in cultural transformation, in "Translation as a Catalyst for Social Change in China," Lin Kenan analyzes the long history of translation in China and its transformative role at certain key periods of Chinese history. He focuses on five major periods in which translation played a key role in Chinese culture: the translation of Buddhist scriptures into Chinese during the first millennium of the common era; the translation of Western documents, including sciences and technology, by Western missionaries at the end of the Ming dynasty and the beginning of the Qing dynasty (during the sixteenth and seventeenth centuries); the translation of Western materials, particularly Western humanities and social sciences, at the end of the Qing dynasty after China was forcibly opened by the Opium Wars; the translation movement focused on Soviet materials following the establishment of the People's Republic of China; and the current translation boom in China. Lin shows how translation during each of these periods was powerfully deployed to shape its era.

What do all these insights into translation, power, rising nationalism, dissolution of empire, exile, and displacement mean for the practicing translator? In a strikingly candid piece entitled "Translation, *Dépaysement*, and Their Figuration," Carol Maier gives us insight into how unsettling such paradigm shifts are. In an analysis of her work translating the essay of Cuban poet Octavio Armand, entitled "Poetry as *Eruv*," Maier reveals her shifting and often contradictory feelings. Armand's essay and poetry conceive of exile as a kind of an illness, a disease, but one that can be cured through poetry and translation. Armand suggests that poetry and translation might build and enclose community, as does *eruv*, the word used by orthodox Jews to name an area designated as private though communal by encircling it with wire on the Sabbath. Maier's personal experience involved at first assent to the message, followed by ambivalence and even abrasion. Having grown up in a family in which German and English were spoken almost interchangeably, in a cultural convergence that she experienced as a refuge, she initially felt at home with Armand's world where poetry of exile was to be a joint refuge. As she reflected further on his vision of exile and his voice as a poet, however, she felt growing discomfort with Armand's provocative and contestatory poetic gestures, resulting in her own sense of *dépaysement*, interfering with her ability to translate Armand. Rethinking the issues yet again led her in turn to reevaluate her own estimation of the cultural convergence in her family. Connecting her thoughts to those of translators and translation scholars such as Naomi Lindstrom, Suzanne Jill Levine, Lawrence Venuti, and Peter Bush, as well as writers such as Eva Hoffman, Maier raises questions with regard to any idealistic notion of translation and relocates the activity in the messy world of multiple discourses, with all their prejudices, complexities, and competitions.

In the final essay, "Translation, Poststructuralism, and Power," Edwin Gentzler expands on his earlier work, trying to make sense of what it means to translate in a world of "posts"—postmodernism, poststructuralism, postfeminism, and postcolonialism. If old definitions of translation no longer serve, how are the new ones working? He reviews some of the contributions of poststructural thinkers such as Michel Foucault and Jacques Derrida, and then looks at North American translators, including Lawrence Venuti and Suzanne Jill Levine, who have attempted to integrate poststructural thought into their translation practices and theories. Gentzler suggests that their attempts to integrate translation with current complex cultural theory have been largely problematic. Instead, like Sherry Simon before him, he turns to the work of Gayatri Spivak, who combines poststructural theory and translation practice in a form she calls "selective essentialism," as a way out of the labyrinth. Gentzler reviews Spivak's work, in particular her translation of "The Hunt" by Mahasweta Devi, demonstrating that the translator is never neutral in the translation process but is always already involved in the process of textual production. He argues that translation is not a neutral place of free and open exchange, but a site contested by powerful individuals and institutions, involving the translator in any number of gender, ethnic, and class discourses. By way of conclusion, he juxtaposes the United States translators with Canadian feminist and Brazilian "cannabalist" translators, suggesting that the process of translation is one of gathering and staging information that can be used for powerful social ends.

These groundbreaking essays thus range widely. They include the more familiar cases in which translation figures in the assertion of political and military power, as well as cultural and economic dominance, ranging from nineteenth-century imperialism to the twentieth-century fascism of Franco's Spain and the oppression of Latin American military dictatorships. They explore the way that translations are implicated in the construction of discourses of power, not least of which are the discourses of democracy, nation, and Western racism. Over and over again the writers in this collection show the power—in the sense of efficacy and vigor—of translation in cultural transformation and change. And finally, writers touch on the dimensions of power inherent in the translation process itself—in the relationship of the translator to author, source text, and translated text. These different perspectives and views cannot be neatly stitched together, reconciled, or abstracted, but in their very diversity and richness they represent the many facets of translation and power.

ALEXANDRA LIANERI

Translation and the Establishment of Liberal Democracy in Nineteenth-Century England: Constructing the Political as an Interpretive Act

The representation of other cultures in the signifying codes of a historical community is increasingly described by contemporary theorists as a process of interpretation or cultural translation.[1] The idea that our knowledge of cultures is neither unmediated nor neutrally articulated in scientific discourses, but remains contingent on the conceptual potential and social conditions of its own historical production, has resulted in the use of a metaphorical conception of translation as a theoretical alternative to the notion of representation as faithful reproduction of an original semiotic unit. Within the framework of this "interpretive turn" manifested in philosophy, as well as in cultural and social theory, Clifford Geertz described anthropological writings as "interpretations" of cultures, "fictions," not in the sense that they are imaginative thought experiments but in the sense that they are "something made," "fashioned," within the conceptual structures of the target community (1973:15). Starting from a more politicized theoretical perspective, James Clifford not only drew attention to the inherently translational character of disciplines, such as ethnography and anthropology, but also emphasized the transient, socially constructed truthfulness of their interpretive meaning, whose objectivist claims are in the full sense of the word ideological and "made possible by powerful 'lies' of exclusion and rhetoric" (1988:38–44, 1986:7). Such works have problematized traditional conceptions of transparency and the scientific neutrality of cultural representations by arguing both theoretically and through empirical studies that "writing" about other cultures necessarily takes place from a cultural and social perspective and on behalf of a political one.

A parallel discussion in the field of literary theory and cultural studies has employed the notion of interpretation in order to challenge the univocality of textual and, more particularly, literary meaning. Already anticipated by Mikhail Bakhtin's concept of *heteroglossia*,[2] which pointed out the plurality of social voices inscribed in literary texts, the idea that meaning cannot be reduced either to the individual intentions of its author or to the linguistic codes of a one-dimensional and static original context has been argued by theorists as diverse in their methodological and ideological positions as Fredric Jameson, Stanley Fish, and Jacques Derrida. Although it is not the intention of this work to impose a false unity among theoretical agendas ranging from Marxism to poststructuralism, it must be emphasized that what these writers suggest—if only as an initial theoretical presupposition—is a negative postulate: that meaning cannot be determinatively and finally defined, but exceeds definitions by being constantly (re)interpreted and (re)constructed within the diversified conceptual frameworks and sociocultural conditions of its constituting communities.

A postulate as revolutionary as this did more than disperse the romantic notion of interpretation as the revelation and empathetic reexperiencing of individual world perspectives. It was also directed against a fundamental hermeneutic assumption, prevalent as much in Friedrich Schleiermacher's romanticism and Wilhelm Dilthey's historicism, as in the radicalization of hermeneutic theories articulated by Martin Heidegger and Hans-Georg Gadamer: that intercultural interpretation can create the potential for true disclosures of historical meaning through a process of acquiring new conceptual frameworks, systems of relevance, and semantic relations, and hence by rising to "a higher universality that overcomes [one's] own particularity but also that of the other" (Gadamer 1989: 305). The idea of hermeneutic fidelity, which was intended to provide the human sciences with an interpretive method that would claim equal authority and validity with the explanatory methods of natural sciences, was deemed to be equally idealist as its Cartesian predecessors. The valorization of a totalizing conception of meaning inscribed in the idea of historical truthfulness, the assertion of the social and political neutrality of cultural languages, and the prioritization of a universalized tradition of world conceptions, as both the presupposition and the ultimate end of the hermeneutic process, became the focus of a rigorous critique, predominantly inspired by the work of poststructuralism, Marxism, feminism, and postcolonial theories.

While this critique was taking place within the fields of philosophy, anthropology, cultural studies, and literary theory, the hermeneutic model, as Edwin Gentzler has pointed out, became in the 1970s one of the basic targets of historically oriented translation research (1993:76–77). In this framework, a wide range of scholars, including James Holmes, Gideon Toury, André Lefevere, Theo Hermans, Susan Bassnett, Lawrence Venuti, and José Lambert, developed a theoretical vocabulary that called into question notions of interpretive faithfulness and sought to relate translation production to the cultural systems and norms, social institutions, and ideological convictions of historical communities.[3] What is more, translation studies introduced into this vocabulary a radicalized notion of interpretation, whose roots can be traced to the historicization of understanding effected by Gadamer's thought since the 1960s but whose development was dissociated from the idealism of the hermeneutic tradition, by seeking to relate conceptual and interpretive choices to the broader historical conditions of the target society.

Thus translation studies scholars employed the hypothesis that the understanding of a text does not entail the elimination but the use of historical presuppositions and "prejudices,"[4] in order to describe the determinative role played by the translator's conceptual horizon, cultural position, and social context in the process of rewriting the source text. This process was no longer assumed to imply the rediscovery of a univocal original meaning, but to manifest, as Bassnett indicates, the multiplicity of the source text's meanings and the need for a disengagement from the idea of the translator as a betrayer of an already given original (1996:11). The absence of a static and ahistorical meaning of a text was further explored by José Lambert and Clem Robyns in relation to the translated text itself. In an article that advances a productive dialogue between translation studies and the problematic of contemporary philosophy and semiotics, Lambert and Robyns suggest that translation can be understood as a historical product of a chain of interpretations. The translated text, they argue, should not be seen as the final component of a static dichotomy but as a sign in itself, subjected to other interpretations, whose formation is related to the interaction of different codes and normative models in the target society (Lambert and Robyns, forthcoming).

This dual function of interpretation, at both the level of production of translation and the level of its reception and reproduction by subsequent readership, is examined here on the basis of translations of the ancient Greek concept of *democracy* in nineteenth-century England. This case study demonstrates that translation can be described as the actualization of a series of interpretive acts, which include at once past translation choices and present historiographic accounts of translation writing.[5] These acts are neither reducible to a mere conceptual construct nor the direct and predictable outcome of social structures, which are established in themselves, irrespective of the ways in which their very reality is linguistically perceived and conceptualized in the target context. As a constitutive part of historical social formations, rather, translations develop as both a product of social realities and a means to make sense of, endorse, or seek to transform these realities. They delimit a space in which social agents can understand, defend, justify, control, but also criticize historical social structures and relations, and pursue alternatives to them. From this perspective, translations, as the following case study indicates, stand as much in a relation of accordance with, as in a relation of tension and opposition to, the social context that constitutes their precondition.

Translations of the concept of *democracy* in England developed from the sixteenth century onward as a reaction to absolutist forms of politics and as an endorsement of the liberal-democratic ideals that sustained the establishment of England as a modern bourgeois society. Translations acted to legitimize an emerging political system that was intimately related to the historical advancement of industrial capitalism. Particularly in the late eighteenth and early nineteenth centuries, socioeconomic changes—including the Industrial Revolution, the establishment of capitalist production, urbanization, and the shaping of the bourgeois and working classes—created the potential for Britain's transition from a feudal, predominantly religious society that believed in the aristocracy and the God-given power of kings, to a modern industrialized nation-state.

Challenging previous social structures, translations provided new social models for an audience that was ideologically heterogeneous and that still lacked a sense of its social and political identity. The process entailed transformation and manipulation of the source texts, relating democracy to an abstract ideal of individual freedom and equality (employed as an equivalent of the Greek notion of citizenship), and defining democratic politics as a system of contestable social hierarchies. This ostensibly consistent ideological discourse was, however, simultaneously interrupted and fragmented by conceptual gaps, tensions, and contradictions that are inscribed in the translated texts and related to their historical context. Translation became the symbolic code for the representation of an imaginary historical tradition that connected nineteenth-century politics to Athenian democratic institutions. It altered preexisting systems of ethical and political judgment and reconceptualized, thereby actualizing, nineteenth-century political reality on the basis of new structures, norms, and models of political thought. Far from being an impoverished reproduction of the "real" original meaning of *democracy*, translation contributed to the constitution of a new political order and its stabilization as a social and political unity.

Translation and the Shifting Image of the Concept of Democracy

One of the most significant images of Athenian democracy was included in Thucydides' *History*. As Thucydides writes, when fifth-century Athens came to the end of the first year of the Peloponnesian war, Pericles, political and military leader of the city, delivered his famous "Funeral Speech," which presented a glorifying image of the Athenian polity. The speech began by defining the name and features of this polity:

καὶ ὄνομα μὲν διὰ τὸ μὴ ἐς ὀλίγους ἀλλ' ἐς πλείονας οἰκεῖν δημοκρατία κέκληται. (Book 2, section 37)

Charles Foster Smith translates this passage in the following fairly literal way:

> It is true that our government is called a democracy, because its administration is in the hands, not of the few, but of the many. (1956: 323)

Smith's translation suggests that in a democracy, government is administered not by a privileged minority, but by the majority of the people,
"the many." It therefore relates democracy to what Anthony Arblaster
has described as the basis of democratic institutions: "the idea of popular
power, or a situation in which power and perhaps authority too, rests
with the people" (1993:8).[6]

From such a perspective, a different translation of Thucydides' *History*, written by Thomas Hobbes in 1629, appears to distort the real
image of the Athenian polity:

> We have a form of government . . . which, because in the *adminis-
> tration* it hath *respect not to a few, but to the multitude*, is called a
> democracy. (1843:8.191, my emphasis)

The essence of democracy in this translation is found not in the power
of the people but in the fact that government has regard to the multitude
("hath respect . . . to"), that is, it has consideration for the majority in
the administration of social issues.[7] In other words, people do not govern
themselves but their views and interests are taken into account by the
government. A translation mistake, one might argue, if one could afford
to ignore its constant repetition until at least the end of the nineteenth
century.

Hobbes's work, which was reprinted three times from the seventeenth to the mid-eighteenth century, was succeeded in 1753 by William
Smith's translation. Smith suggested the following rewriting of the passage:

> . . . our form [of government] as committed not to the few, but to
> the whole body of the people is called a democracy. (1831:1,167)

Smith does not relate democracy to the multitude but to the society as
a whole, that is, to the well-being and interests of both the social elite
and the majority. This choice does not, however, entail a conception of
democracy as a form of self-government, insofar as it establishes again a
strict division between the government of a society and the people.

This denial of what many of us would tend to recognize as the core
of Athenian democracy, namely the sovereignty and equality of the people, becomes more meaningful when related to conceptions of democracy

before the twentieth century, when political consensus in Western thought was based, as Crawford Brough Macpherson notes, on negative appraisals of democratic constitutions: "Democracy used to be a bad word. Everybody who was anybody knew that democracy, in its original sense of rule by the people or government in accordance with the will of the bulk of the people, would be a bad thing—fatal to individual freedom and to all the graces of civilized living" (1966:1). For the translators in question, democracy—defined as a form of government bestowing power and authority on the majority—was not an institution that established political liberty and social justice but, rather, a menace to social order and coherence, threatening prosperity and cultural development alike.

A series of negative appraisals of democracy dating back to the sixteenth century constituted a significant political heritage for this interpretive tradition, which was first manifested in Thomas Elyot's 1531 description of Athenian democracy as a "monster with many heads," lacking stability and social coherence (1883:1.9–10), and later consolidated by Hobbes's translation of Thucydides. Hobbes described the ancient author as "most hostile to democracy," noting that social order and consistency would be damaged by following the demagogically susceptible political judgment of the common people (1843:xvi–xvii). The same position underwrote the translations of the Scottish historian John Gillies. More specifically, Gillies's 1797 translation of Aristotle's *Politics* was introduced as an attack on government based on consent, even as Aristotle's description of man as a "political animal" was interpreted as an indication of the "natural" disposition of men to form political societies based on the authoritative power of monarchy and the strict separation between the main body of citizens and their government (1813:2.3–6). In the same spirit, Gillies's translations of Lysias and Isocrates claimed to present an illustration of the unhappiness generated by republican polity and the turbulent life in "democracies" (1778:1.lxii–lxiii), and his *History of Ancient Greece* (1786) pointed out "the incurable evils inherent in every form of Republican polity" and "the inestimable benefits" of "hereditary Kings and the steady operations of well-regulated Monarchy" (1792:1.iii). Likewise, William Mitford's *History of Greece* (1778) stressed the "uncertainty and turbulence of democratic rule" and the evident undermining of the Athenian democracy by the "want of one supreme authority" whenever the city encountered serious problems and difficulties (1835:1.326, 2.104–5).

Translations and rewritings of classical democracy from the sixteenth until the late eighteenth century seem to have been defined by the denial of any value to democracy, as well as the tendency to dissociate classical culture from institutions establishing the liberty, equality, and sovereignty of the Athenian citizens. Though none of these works bestowed a definitively positive value on the concept of *democracy*, the central issue regarding the period following Hobbes's translation is that representations of classical Athens provided a context, within which democracy was spoken about—a field for discussion, which sought to illuminate the political features of Athenian society through historical writings and to reproduce the cultural and intellectual voices that grew out of democratic institutions through the translation of classical texts. Such a proliferation of discourses, as Michel Foucault (1990) has emphasized, cannot merely be examined as a negation of democratic principles. For apart from asserting the dangers of democracy or, more accurately, irrespective of the expression of negative or positive appraisals, these writings acted to introduce *democracy* into the political thought of their time and determined, among other factors, its subsequent range of meanings and significance. In this sense these writings constituted the conceptual frameworks within which democracy was revived and accepted as a positive concept and a legitimate form of government during the next centuries.

One can identify two interrelated notions evoked by these works: that of the individual and that of social hierarchies. Hobbes's translation, which was considered to have a deep and lasting influence on the development of the philosopher's thought and language,[8] expressed a concept that was scarcely established in his contemporary political discourses but that was to become the central assumption of liberal democratic thought in the next centuries: the concept of the *subject*, who is able to contemplate and discuss social matters and has the right to be a *citizen* of a state. This idea was most clearly conveyed by the translation of the debates that took place in the Athenian Assembly and that constitute a significant part of Thucydides' books. These debates portray a model for political organization based on reasoned discussion and deliberation among (male) citizens, who are given full freedom to speak and decide on issues of public concern, while being considered in this context as moral and political equals. The translation of these passages did not simply record the speeches and dialogues of the source text. Rather it functioned metonymically, as an evocation of the broader social and political life of classical Athens.[9] In other words Hobbes's translation did not merely transfer the source text as a historical document but presented a model for political institutions and social organization as well.

In this capacity Hobbes's work became an integral part of a wider seventeenth-century problematic about the legitimacy of religious authorities, the status of monarchic power, and the feudal system of property rights. Written only thirteen years before the outbreak of the English civil war in 1642, in a context that was marked by radical economic and social changes (including the passage from feudalism to a capitalist mode of production and the subsequent constitution of the bourgeois classes, represented in the House of Commons), this evocation of democratic polity set up the traits of a political model that could fulfill the needs of the newly emergent bourgeoisie to contest previously established hierarchies and articulate a range of values and ideals that would legitimize its social position and power. The key concept in this process was that of the *individual*: the "self-conscious" human being, who does not automatically subject himself [sic] to a social condition prescribed by God (and materialized by the representatives of God on earth) but can freely formulate his own political opinion and will. It was because of this radical idea of "individuality," which was further elaborated in the *Leviathan*, that Hobbes can be described, in Foucault's terms, as a "founder of discursivity," who set up, in conjunction with his main theoretical opponent, John Locke, the "rules of formation" of liberal democratic discourses (Foucault 1977b:131).

Hobbes's individuals were essentially self-interested, uncultivated, and unable to solve by themselves social conflicts and oppositions. Hence their freedom had to be surrendered to the power of a sovereign governor. Yet this move of subjection could only be legitimized once individuals *decided* to establish this power and *agreed* to obey it.[10] What is more, this form of sovereign government was no longer the expression of the will of God. It was described in the *Leviathan* (1651) as "representative" of the will of the people (Hobbes 1968:220). This conception of representation, which bestowed controlled political freedom on the social body but implied simultaneously the exclusion of the people from political constitution and government, dictated the transformation of one of the most renowned features of Athenian democracy in Hobbes's translation: the direct participation of all citizens in the public affairs of the city. The Athenian citizens, as Thucydides writes, were all equally responsible for the political government of the city:

> ἔνι τε τοῖς αὐτοῖς οἰκείων ἅμα καὶ πολιτικῶν ἐπιμέλεια καὶ ἑτέροις πρὸς
> ἔργα τετραμμένοις τὰ πολιτικὰ μὴ ἐνδεῶς γνῶναι· μόνοι γὰρ τόν τε μηδὲν
> τῶνδε μετέχοντα οὐκ ἀπράγμονα, ἀλλ' ἀχρεῖον νομίζομεν, καὶ αὐτοὶ ἤτοι
> κρίνομέν γε ἢ ἐνθυμούμεθα ὀρθῶς τὰ πράγματα. (Book 2, section 40)

A "literal" translation of this passage by Charles Foster Smith reads as follows:

> And you will find united in the same persons an interest at once in
> private and in public affairs, and in others of us who give attention
> chiefly to business, you will find no lack of insight into political mat-
> ters. For we alone regard the man who takes no part in public affairs,
> not as one who minds his own business, but as good for nothing;
> and we Athenians decide public questions for ourselves or at least
> endeavour to arrive at a sound understanding of them. (1956:329)

Hobbes translated the passage as follows:

> Moreover there is in the same men, a care both of their own and the
> public affairs; and a *sufficient knowledge* of state matters, *even in those
> that labour with their hands.* For we only think *one that is utterly
> ignorant therein,* to be a man, not that meddles with nothing, but is
> good for nothing. *We likewise weigh what we undertake, and appre-
> hend it perfectly in our minds.* (1843:8.194, my emphasis)

The most striking transformation of the source text by Hobbes is found in the rendering of the phrase "μόνοι γὰρ ... νομίζομεν," which says that the Athenian people considered a man who did not participate in politics to be worthless and incompetent, into a much milder renunciation of apolitical men as "utterly ignorant" of public affairs. Hobbes's position was further sustained by the translation of the phrase "καὶ ἑτέροις ... γνῶναι," which says that people who are chiefly involved in work (πρὸς ἔργα) have "no lack of insight into political matters," (Smith 1956:329) by the statement that there is "sufficient knowledge of state matters, even in those that labour with their hands." Hobbes's translated phrase not only diminishes the involvement of the Athenian people in politics by suggesting that citizens have merely "sufficient knowledge" of political issues but also introduces the idea that those "that labour with their hands"—thus presumably those least likely to be involved in politics—are in possession of this knowledge. A final change can be found in the translation of the last phrase of the passage, which says that "we Athenians decide public questions for ourselves" (Smith 1956:329). Hobbes's translation does not bestow a political connotation on this statement. It describes, instead, a process of intellectual evaluation and apprehension, which is not related to "public questions" and political decisions, as is the case in the source text.

If Hobbes was reluctant to recognize individual sovereignty, Locke, at the end of the seventeenth century, employed the concept of *man* to celebrate the rationality of individuals as well as their natural property of "Lives, Liberties, and Estates" and the obligation of political government to protect this property (Locke 1988:350). The work of both of these thinkers was appropriated by the founders of the American constitution and became the basis of the ambivalent disposition of American revolutionary thought toward Athenian democracy. Despite some general appeals to classical antiquity, the founding of the United States of America manifested a self-distancing of republican thought from "purely" democratic affiliations, on the grounds that the exercise of political power by the commons would violate the principle of mixed government and endanger individual liberty and rights. "Pure democracies," as Madison wrote in *The Federalist* in 1788 (no. 10), "have ever been spectacles of turbulence and contention; have ever been found incompatible with personal security or the rights of property; and have in general been as short in their lives as they have been violent in their deaths" (Hamilton, Madison, and Jay 1970:45). The notion of *republic* was thereby explicitly distinguished from the idea of bestowal of power on the people. As Russell L. Hanson has argued, "whereas a democracy represented rule *by* the 'commons' or *demos*, a republic was ruled *in* common *for* the commonweal" (1985:77). The establishment of this semantic distinction allowed for the dissociation of the American Revolution from the connotations of anarchy and political instability related to democratic polity,[11] and it also determined the subsequent reconceptualization of democracy as a form of government whose power is established by and should be accountable to the governed, but whose main aim is not the realization of the self-institution of a social community but the protection of the rights of *individuals* to life, liberty, and the pursuit of happiness. This was a conception of happiness that was more identified with narrow individualistic interests than with collective prosperity or a condition of social equality.

Democracy began to be described in positive terms once it ceased to evoke ideals of materialized social equality and was, instead, related to a liberal form of polity: a political system that established basic civil rights (freedom of speech and political association, and security of life and property), formal legal equality, and parliamentary representation.[12] These newly evoked rights, which had already been asserted during the French Revolution in 1789 by the *Déclaration des droits de l'homme et du citoyen* (*Declaration of the Rights of Man and the Citizen*), gave voice to contemporary bourgeois demands by evoking Man as the ontological hallmark and ultimate end of political practice. Although inspired in certain respects by the ideals of the American Revolution, the promise of the *Declaration* for liberty, equality, and justice was novel. It favored the establishment of a fully extended liberal democracy and implied the formal dissociation of social and cultural distinctions from the right to political participation. The French conception of the nation as identified with the whole of the people was not merely radical, it was revolutionary. Yet it was simultaneously an ideal that was rendered unrealizable by those very principles that enabled its formulation: an understanding of democracy as a matter of legal and political administration that was presumably strictly dissociated from the unequal positions from which social agents were able to participate in social institutions and politics. That is to say, a conception of democracy that subsumed freedom and equality to an ideological attempt at securing and strengthening the hierarchical social structures of modern bourgeois societies.

Altering Norms, Translations, and Politics: The Establishment of Liberal Democracy

From the beginning of the nineteenth century, British interest in classical culture and politics was remarkably intensified.[13] Hobbes's translation was reprinted five times and Smith's translation six times during the century. A significant proportion of these publications were initiated and/or endorsed by utilitarian thinkers, although several of Hobbes's translations were edited under the auspices of Jeremy Bentham, the political philosopher who together with James Mill, formulated the basic principles of nineteenth-century English liberalism (Held 1996:95), in Macpherson's terms the "founding model for democracy for a modern industrial society" (1977:43). Bentham, James Mill, and the utilitarians in general, as David Held suggests, developed one of the clearest justifications for the liberal democratic state, which creates the conditions necessary for individuals "to pursue their private interests without the risk of arbitrary political interference, to participate 'freely' in economic transactions, to exchange labour and goods on the market and to appropriate resources privately" (1996:95). In the context of this turn, the meaning of *democracy* no longer evoked the notions of equality and political sovereignty. Liberal democracy, as Macpherson explains, has been a system "by which people can be *governed*," that is, made to do things they may not otherwise do and refrain from things they otherwise may have done. So long as this government is not controlled by the people themselves, "democracy . . . is then a system by which power is exerted by the state over individuals and groups." Most significant, a democratic government exists to uphold and enforce a certain kind of society and, therefore, a certain range of relations among individuals, a certain set of rights and claims that people have on each other, both directly and indirectly through their rights to property. These relations, as Macpherson argues, are relations of power: they stem from the conditions of social, economic, and cultural inequality that are established in capitalist societies, while acting, in turn, to nourish and strengthen these conditions (1966:4, cf. 35–45).

Parallel and interrelated to the change in political theorizing in nineteenth-century England was the development of a wider interest in classical Greece,[14] which was sustained by the increasingly dominant position of Greek studies in the educational institutions of the period. Oxford and Cambridge shifted the emphasis of classical learning from Latin to Greek and established the study of Greek literature as an educational requirement for every degree, while schoolmasters such as Samuel Butler, B. A. Kennedy, and Thomas Arnold advanced a new conception of Greek culture in the public schools by emphasizing the need to relate classical learning to contemporary interests, instead of pursuing a traditional study of texts only as models of style (Clarke 1959:74–127). This idea was explicitly expressed in Thomas Arnold's statement that fifth-century Athens belonged more to modern than to ancient history, that "the history of Greece . . . is not an idle inquiry about remote ages and forgotten institutions, but a living picture of things present, fitted not so much for the curiosity of the scholar, as for the instruction of the statesman and the citizen" (1835:3.xviii, xxii).

In this framework translators of classical Greek texts advanced an endorsement, but also a transformation, of classical conceptions of democracy, which oscillated between authoritarian social ideals and the convictions of an enlightened and liberal politics. The first translation of Thucydides' *History* during this period was written by S. T. Bloomfield in 1829. Unlike both Hobbes and Smith, Bloomfield was not directly opposed to democratic politics. He rather presented his work as an endorsement of the "*happily-attempted mixture* of aristocracy and democracy . . . embodied" in the British constitution (Bloomfield 1829:vi, original emphasis). From this perspective, his translation rewrote Pericles' definition of democracy as follows:

> From the government being administered, not for the few, but for the many [our institution] is denominated a democracy. (1829:366–67)

Hobbes's rendering of "the many" by the term *multitude* is missing from this translation and will not appear again in translations of the passage. What is more, Bloomfield did not describe democracy in Smith's terms, as a government that makes political decisions in accordance with the interests of the society as a whole. In Bloomfield's work, a democratic government is claimed to be administered "*not* for the few, but for the many." That is to say, democracy is not only posited in a social context in which the aims of the few are opposed to those of the many but also seeks to prioritize the latter over the former.

Bloomfield's emphasis on this opposition expresses a significant change in European conceptions of society and politics, which was crystallized in the English context after the French Revolution. Before 1789, English intellectuals and political theorists were able to perceive and represent their immediate reality in terms of social conflict but, nevertheless, believed that it would be possible to resolve this conflict by moderate reforms, which would establish a political alliance between the traditional aristocracy and the middle classes without being threatening to the existing status quo. The outbreak of the French Revolution, the September massacres of 1792, the execution of Louis XVI in 1793, and the images of the Terror dispersed this idea.[15] From the beginning of the nineteenth century, conceptions of democracy indicated an understanding of Western societies as fragmented and divided; as structured on the basis of conflictual rather than harmonious and reconcilable interests. This realization did not, however, entail an immediate acceptance of democratic ideas. Quite the contrary: Bloomfield's translation repeated the distinction between the government and the governed established by the works of Hobbes and Smith, and it further denied that classical Athens was *really* a democratic polity. The translation of the passage in question was qualified by a footnote, which suggested that Pericles' description "might be a good definition of the Athenian government as far as it was *supposed* to be" (original emphasis). Yet the Athenian polity was only "a democracy in name." "In fact" it was "a modification of aristocracy called elective monarchy" (Bloomfield 1829:367).

As the century progressed, the fear of the people and of revolution became weaker and Bloomfield's characterization of the Athenian polity was not repeated until the end of the century. Classical democracy instead became the central reference for liberal and utilitarian thinkers, in whose writings Athenian society was transformed from an object of fear and denial into a model for imitation. This turn was substantially advanced by *A History of Greece*, a significant publication written by George Grote (1846–56). In this work Grote presented extensive translated passages in order to sustain his appraisal of democratic Athens, and he also employed translation in the formation of his historical vocabulary, describing, for example, Pericles as the "prime minister" of the Athenian Assembly and Athenian politics as characterized by oppositions between the "conservative party" and the party of "reformers" (1888:4.454). As a result Athenian democracy was perceived as the equivalent of English society and politics and lost its previous connotations of anarchy and injustice. John Stuart Mill wrote two eulogizing reviews (1846, 1853) of Grote's *History*. He praised Grote for representing democracy as the real basis of Athenian progress and further described the Greeks as the "originators of political freedom and the grand exemplars and sources of it to modern Europe." "The battle of Marathon," Mill argued, "even as an event in English history is more important than the battle of Hastings" (1978: 316, 273).

But what did democracy mean for these writers? And how did translations of ancient Greek texts serve to sustain its meaning? J. S. Mill's appraisal of Athens was justified by the quotation of a further translation of Thucydides, which had been made by Grote himself and had been included in his *History*. This work defined democracy as follows:

> It [our constitution] is called a democracy, since *its permanent aim tends towards the Many and not towards the Few*. (Grote 1888:5.67, my emphasis)

The translation transforms the original phrase "καὶ ὄνομα . . . κέκληται" into the rather vague assertion that democracy is a form of government whose "permanent aim tends towards the Many and not towards the Few." This translation differs from Hobbes's work because it recognizes the majority as the "aim" of democratic government, whereas Hobbes restricted democratic processes to a government's "consideration" of the needs of the multitude. Yet it also follows its predecessors, by suggesting that this "aim" would not be sought by "the many" but by a social institution that is strictly separated from the social body of citizens: that is, the government. In the middle of the nineteenth century, Henry Dale wrote a similar translation of the source text: "In name, from its not being administered for the benefit of the few, but of the many, it [our form of government] is called a democracy" (1848:112). Subsequently, Richard Crawley's translation defined the Athenian polity as founded on a government "whose administration . . . favours the many instead of the few" (1876:1.121).

Neither the source text nor the history of classical Athens could justify such a division. Athenian democracy was administered on the basis of direct participation of citizens in the Assembly, which decided all significant political issues, from legislation to finance and military matters. In the context of the Assembly, Athenian citizens were considered as moral and political equals, and were all responsible for the government of the city.[16] It follows that in the source context the concept of *democracy* conveyed the idea of direct, free, and equal participation of all citizens in the institution of public affairs. This meaning was not reproduced in the translations.

After the first decades of the nineteenth century, this transformation crystallized into a significant change in the meaning of the concept, which implied that democracy was at once dissociated from ideas of social equality and the collective self-institution of a society, and intrinsically related to the notion of individual liberty: the freedom to participate in elections and articulate political opinions publicly, as well as the liberty to pursue one's goals and secure one's rights in the context of civil society. These forms of liberty were described in Crawley's introduction to his translation as the main features of the Athenian democracy. As he stated, the reader of his work could find in the presentation of Athens "the *political freedom* which he glories in, and the *social liberty* which he sometimes sighs for" (Crawley 1876: l.xi, my emphasis). Equality thereby became understood as electoral equality (political freedom) and equality of opportunity (social liberty): the right of all people to compete for the attainment of social status, political power, and economic growth, irrespective of their initial social position or rank.

It was precisely this understanding of democracy that enabled Grote to state in his translation that the Athenian city did not bestow political and constitutional power on the people but, rather, enabled social advancement and chose only those citizens of "real worth" as governors. As the source text reads:

> . . . μέτεστι δὲ κατὰ μὲν τοὺς νόμους πρὸς τὰ ἴδια διάφορα πᾶσι τὸ ἴσον, κατὰ δὲ τὴν ἀξίωσην ὡς ἕκαστος ἔν τῳ εὐδοκιμεῖ οὐκ ἀπὸ μέρους τὸ πλέον ἐς τὰ κοινὰ ἢ ἀπ᾽ ἀρετῆς προτιμᾶται. (Book 2, section 37)

A "literal" translation of this passage by Charles Foster Smith reads:

> . . . yet while as regards the law all men are on an equality for the settlement of their private disputes, as regards the value set on them it is as each man is in any way distinguished that he is preferred to public honours, not because he belongs to a particular class, but because of his personal merits. (1956:323)

Grote translated the passage as follows:

> As to private matters and disputes, the laws deal equally with every man; while in regard to public affairs and to *claims of individual influence, every man's chance of advancement* is determined not by party favour *but by real worth*, according as his reputation stands in his own particular department. (1888:5.67, my emphasis)

Grote's translation maintained the meaning of the first phrase of the passage, which refers to the equality of citizens before the laws as regards private disputes. The rest of the passage was substantially transformed by the employment of the concept of *individual influence,* which is absent from the source text, and the use of the phrase "every man's chance of advancement is determined . . . by real worth," which rewrote the source-text idea that every man's chance of attaining a position of political responsibility is determined by his ability to perform the particular task. Both of these choices stem from an understanding of democracy as the establishment of freedom for competition and "social advancement." They could not have made sense in a context in which political participation was open to all citizens and entailed no special privileges or profit as was the case in the Athens of Thucydides' text.[17]

But more than this, Grote suggested the negation of the source text's idea that all members of a democratic community have both the right to and obligation of equal participation in politics. The Athenian political model was based on the assumption that men could fulfill themselves only in and through the *polis,* on the maxim that the "virtue of the individual is the same as the virtue of the citizen" (Jaeger 1965: 2.157). This decisive trait of classical democracy was testified, as has been argued, by Thucydides' description of the Athenian citizen as a man who "participates" in the institution of the city (Book 2, section 40). Grote translated this passage as follows:

> The private citizen, while engaged in professional business, *has competent knowledge on public affairs.* For we stand alone in regarding the man who keeps aloof from these latter not as harmless, but as useless. Moreover *we always hear and pronounce on public matters when discussed by our leaders, or perhaps strike out for ourselves correct reasoning about them.* (1888:5.69, my emphasis)

Unlike Hobbes, Grote maintained the idea that the Athenians regarded as useless any man who abstained from public affairs. Yet Grote's rewriting of the last phrase of the passage, which states that "we Athenians decide public questions for ourselves" (C. F. Smith 1956:329), effected a significant transformation of the source text. The Athenians were presented in the translation as having a passive role in the determination of political issues, as a community that listens and chooses but does not

actively plan a certain politics. It hears and endorses but does not participate in political discussions. No aspect of the source text could legitimize
such a division between the "leaders" of the city and the people who
abstain from political deliberation. Furthermore, even when Grote acknowledged that Athenian citizens could *perhaps* formulate for themselves correct political reasoning, he changed the source text by adding
the word "perhaps," which presented this case as a rather unlikely one
and acted to cast doubt on and qualify the role of the people in the
institutions of Athenian politics. To say that the body of citizens was
capable of advancing "correct" political reasoning implied that the appraisal of this correctness was made on the basis of standards that did not
originate within this social body. Yet for the Athenians, it was precisely
the Assembly, the main body of citizens, that was responsible for drawing
the line between "correct" and "incorrect" opinions on political matters.

The rewritings previously discussed did more than dispute the validity of negative appraisals of democratic institutions, they provided a
context for the construction of a liberal conception of democracy, which
emphasized the need for the hierarchical organization of social communities, the liberty of individuals from excessive state power, and the establishment of formal equality of opportunity, based on a presumably free
competition and meritocracy. This conception, which set up the key political features of modern bourgeois societies, contested the authoritarian
organization of feudal monarchies and asserted that human beings are
the only legitimate source of political judgments. Thus it ostensibly left
no room for the justification of inequality and power relations. At the
same time, however, it posited an abstract conception of these human
beings as individuals who stood for humanity, lacking specific social and
cultural characteristics. This abstraction enabled the ensuing qualification
of these individuals as cultured, educated, Western European, white,
middle-class, and male subjects. What followed was the ability of these
subjects to judge political matters "better" than the rest of the people,
have a rationally justified political authority, and impose their historically
declared civil rights—"liberty, equality, and estate"—as the indisputable
"democratic" values of humanity. These values silenced the historical dependence of liberty and equality on the actual economic, social, and cultural inequalities of modern bourgeois societies, and they constructed a
new conception of secular authority as the necessary and desirable complement of democratic processes. It was precisely this interrelation of

democracy and authority that created the context for a final turn in translations of democracy after the middle of the nineteenth century. This new line of interpretation was profoundly influenced by Matthew Arnold's thought and represented classical culture as an alternative to individualistic ethics, excessive commercialism, and lack of authoritative power.

A Model for Social Assent: Ancient Greek Culture as a Unifying Social Force

Arnold was not hostile to democracy. Along with many of his contemporary thinkers, he had realized its inevitable establishment and its compatibility with the political interests of the nineteenth-century bourgeoisie, which for him was the only potential successor of a corrupt, politically incapable, and culturally degraded aristocracy. Yet he did not visualize a society based on social equality and self-institution. Instead, he described inequality as a "natural" feature of societies and sought to establish the presuppositions for an explicitly authoritative model of government, which could harmonize social conflicts and oppositions under the unifying power of the state. The latter was not, however, defined by him as a source of oppression and unjustifiable power relations but as the embodiment of a higher cultural authority, which was presumably dissociated from partisan interests and was able to guide the society as a whole (Arnold 1993:102–25; 1962:7–8, 20–21).

Two main aspects of Arnold's thought seem to have influenced the translation of Pericles' description of classical democracy toward the end of the nineteenth century: (1) the conviction that the majority could possibly attain a ruling political position and (2) the creed that such a prospect should be controlled by the intervention of a higher political authority. Hence Benjamin Jowett's translation of the passage in question reads as follows:

> *It is true* that we are called a democracy, for the administration is in the hands of the many and not of the few. *But* while the law secures equal justice to all alike in their private disputes, *the claim of excellence is also recognised*; and when a citizen is in any way distinguished, he is preferred to the public service, not as a matter of privilege but as the reward of merit. (1881:1.117–18, my emphasis)[18]

Unlike all previous translations, Jowett renders the source-text idea that democracy is a polity by which political power is "in the hands of the many and not of the few." Yet his work immediately disputes the existence of democracy in classical Athens ("it is true that we are called a democracy . . . but . . ."). A democracy, in Jowett's view, lacks the means to recognize excellence, whereas the classical city only established equality before the law, simultaneously electing an "aristocracy of merit" that was put at the service of the state.

Jowett proceeds to translate Pericles' assertion that all citizens "participate" in politics, suggesting that an Athenian citizen is fairly aware of political issues. As he writes,

> An Athenian citizen does not neglect the state because he takes care of his own household; and even those of us who are engaged in business have a *very fair idea of politics*. . . . and if *few are originators, we are all sound judges of a policy*. (1.119, my emphasis)

This translation changes the source text's representation of Athenian citizens as actively engaged in the political institution of the city and introduces a rigid distinction between "originators" of a policy and "judges" of political matters. Both ideas, as has been demonstrated, are absent from the source text.

Jowett's translations did not evolve in opposition to Mill's and Grote's conceptions of liberal democracy. Mill's initial doubt regarding the political ability of the "common" people was bound to be transformed into an idealization of secular authority in the context of the late nineteenth century. By then, the liberal promise of endless social and cultural progress, unrestricted pursuit of individual interests, and unprecedented maximization of human happiness seemed to many unrealizable and incompatible with the establishment of basic civil rights, equality, and social coherence in the context of bourgeois societies. This promise was crushed under the weight of its own presupposition that democracy implies the liberty to pursue "individual interests" in a society constructed by social inequalities and power relations. It was eroded and undermined by its own internal contradictions and inconsistencies: the glorification of human subjects that was paired with their immediate division into political authorities and "the common people"; the idealization of cultural progress and the simultaneous reduction of culture into a means for individual advancement; and the exaltation of political justice and moral values in a discourse that recognized no other human purpose or value apart from the accretion of private profit, growth of social status, and accumulation of capital.

Did the polity of ancient Athens contain an illusory potential? Was the radicalness of translating Greek democracy as a positive concept a deceiving political promise? Was translation simply a means for justifying a society structured on the basis of injustice, actual inequality, and power differentials? The answer to these questions cannot be one-dimensional. Classical political thought itself resists final concretizations by being variably interpreted and transformed throughout modern European history. Nineteenth-century English translators played a determining role in this process by articulating the optimistic enchantment of the period with the ideal of political reason and the belief in human progress. Their view challenged a long tradition of monarchic politics and endorsed at once the values of freedom, equality, and political justice, and an idealization of social inequality, human exploitation, and asymmetrical power relations. Their interpretation of the concept of democracy had a historical afterlife that continued to form Western political thought until World War I and entered a process of semantic alteration only after the actual collapse of humanist idealism materialized in Berlin and Hiroshima. This afterlife, which witnessed colonialism, political totalitarianism, and the imperialistic discourses of advanced capitalism, often turned back to the nineteenth-century liberal concepts of *natural human divisions, civil rights,* and *secular authority* for its own ideological legitimization. Yet, it was precisely the liberal interpretive framework that also established the value of democratic ideals, thus providing the means for radical critiques of its ideology and the conception of political alternatives to it. If nineteenth-century conceptions of classical democracy established a historical "interpretant" that claimed a unique validity in modern political discourses, this interpretant was not internally coherent and unified.[19] Its semantic concretization was the product of plural and internally opposed conceptualizations of democracy, which cannot be reduced to a single and unitary "original" meaning but established a sequence of differentiated interpretations that constituted the contemporary complexity and contestability of the concept.

Notes

1. I am very much indebted to Maria Tymoczko, Susan Bassnett, Joanne Collie, and Yorgos Avgoustis for valuable suggestions and comments on this work.

2. On Bakhtin's use of the concept, see especially the chapter "Discourse in the Novel" in *The Dialogic Imagination* (1981:259–422).

3. For a historical account of the work of these writers in the context of contemporary translation research, see Gentzler 1993.

4. On the issue, see Gadamer 1989:277–307.

5. For a further discussion of historiographic translation analysis as a form of interpretation and translation, see Hermans 1999:68–69.

6. Smith's translation of this passage and the ones that follow are offered more as a guideline to the reader with no knowledge of Classical Greek, rather than as an ultimate accurate rendering or as a translation that manages to escape interpretive bias. The translation of Pericles' definition of democracy continues to be a highly debated issue among contemporary scholars and continues to give rise to a wide range of interpretations. An indicative example of this disparity of readings is offered by comparing Smith's translation of this passage to that of Rex Warner: "Our constitution is called a democracy because power is in the hands not of a minority but of the whole people" (1972:145).

7. On the negative connotations of the word *multitude*, see Williams 1988: 192–97.

8. On the issue, see Rossini 1987:303.

9. For a discussion of the metonymic function of translation, see Tymoczko 1999:41–61.

10. For a further discussion of this issue, see Held 1996:76–78.

11. For a further discussion of this issue, see Roberts 1994:186.

12. As Raymond Williams points out, this move involved a substantial de-radicalization of democratic thought. It implied the dissociation of democracy from connotations of popular power and thus its distancing from a political system in which the interests of the majority are both exercised and controlled by the majority itself (Williams 1988:96).

13. The increase of translations from ancient Greek into English after the late eighteenth century is striking. As the bibliographical survey of F.M.K. Foster (1918) indicates, the total number of translations up to 1780 was 312, whereas book-length translations published from 1780 to 1900 reached 1259.

14. As Frank Turner points out, the extensive nineteenth-century concern with ancient Greece was a relatively novel phenomenon in European thought, for until the late eighteenth century, most Europeans thinkers conceived their culture as Roman and Christian in origin, having only an indirect relation to classical Greece. The search for new cultural roots in Greek antiquity assumed major intellectual significance in both Europe and America during the nineteenth century. It was manifested as an unprecedented enthusiasm for Greek cultural production

and exercised a deep influence on the development of literature, arts, scholarly discourses, and—I would add—translation (Turner 1981:1–14).

15. For a further discussion of the impact of the French Revolution on British scholarly and literary circles, see Dawson 1993:50–53.

16. This point does not imply that classical democracy was not formed on the basis of an exclusionist politics. "The many" in classical Athens were still the minority of the population of the city because women and slaves were deprived of any political rights. Slaves were not citizens, and Athenian free women were regarded as "citizens" only in order to legitimize their citizen-sons, having no right to participate in politics themselves. For a further discussion of "citizenship" and "participation" in classical Athens, see Sinclair 1988:24–135.

17. For the Athenians, to be in positions of political responsibility was not equivalent to the idea of *personal* advancement or influence. The members of the Athenian *Voulē*, a body of five hundred citizens who were responsible for the administration of issues that were not discussed in the *Ecclēsia*, were elected by lot. Their position was considered as predominantly administrative, had a relatively low salary, and did not entail the attainment of political power, since all important decisions on public matters had to be endorsed by the *Ecclēsia*. Participation in the supreme court of justice, the *Hēliaia*, was open to every Athenian citizen over the age of thirty. The *Ecclēsia* had the absolute right to force citizens to leave public positions, if they were deemed to be unfit for their responsibilities. What is more, no citizen had the right to attain a position in the public administration more than once or—in the case of participants in the *Voulē*—twice in his lifetime. This law prohibited the association of such positions with the fulfillment of political ambitions of individuals. For further discussion of these issues, see Glotz 1929.

18. Jowett's point is made explicit in the notes accompanying the translation in which he explicates the meaning of the passage: "though we bear the name of democracy, this name is an *inadequate* description of the Athenian commonwealth. For before the law all men (including the [few]) are equal, while at the same time *there is an aristocracy of merit* at the service of the state" (1881: 2.106, my emphasis).

19. For the notion of "interpretant," see Lambert and Robyns forthcoming.

SABINE FENTON AND PAUL MOON

The Translation of the Treaty of Waitangi: A Case of Disempowerment

The Treaty of Waitangi was signed in 1840 by William Hobson, a representative of the British Crown, and more than five hundred Maori chiefs signed a translation of it into Maori. Over the years the treaty has come to symbolize the birth of the New Zealand nation. It was a remarkable document in an age that saw nothing wrong with a powerful nation simply walking in and taking over the government of indigenous people and their country. The Treaty of Waitangi expressed a new morality and ethics toward the rights of an indigenous people by a colonizing government and is one of the rare examples of the British Crown going beyond its normal practices in treaty arrangements.

The former Prime Minister of New Zealand, David Lange, has claimed that the treaty ". . . has the potential to be our most powerful unifying symbol" (qtd. in Orange 1989:80). In recent times, however, it has been condemned as a fraud by a growing number of Maori and Pakeha (New Zealanders of European origin). Serious concerns have been raised concerning what actually had been signed. Although the treaty had seemingly brought together two distinct cultural groups in an act of enlightened respect for and trust of each other, ironically, the translation to a large extent has managed to destroy both and has become the cause of much confusion and bitterness.

The translator, Anglican missionary Henry Williams, had some previous experience in translation and was aware of the strategic goals of colonizing translation. In order to secure Maori agreement, the wording he chose was obscure and ambiguous. He produced a translation that was successful in terms of getting the Maori chiefs to sign the document, but a true and faithful rendition of the English text it was not.[1] There is little evidence today indicating what motivated Williams to create a document that renders some crucial points ambiguous, even to the point of deception, and that completely omits others. In order to find an explanation and shed some light on why and how a translation came to disempower a free and sovereign nation, here we examine the historical context in which the translation occurred, the ideological context for the translation, the translation process, and the effect the translation still has on the New Zealand nation. Through this process we reveal some of the discursive and institutional forces that influenced the translators and helped shape the translation, illustrating André Lefevere's contention that "translations are not made in a vacuum. Translators function in a given culture at a given time. The way they understand themselves and their culture is one of the factors that may influence the way in which they translate" (1992:14). Our investigation adds to and extends the discussion of the role translations played in the history of colonialism (Cheyfitz 1997; Niranjana 1992; Robinson 1997a; Venuti 1998). We also demonstrate that the field of colonial and postcolonial studies clearly extends to New Zealand, a "white settler" colony. As today's New Zealand is coming to terms with the legacy of the Treaty of Waitangi, the conquered Maori culture is responding to and resisting the coercion of the past that created their disadvantaged status and the power differential in their own country.

On 29 January 1840 Captain William Hobson arrived in New Zealand, empowered by the British government to negotiate with the Maori for the transfer of their sovereignty to the British Crown. His arrival marked the culmination of seventy years of "mutually advantageous contact" between the Maori and the British (Orange 1987:7). Recent events in New Zealand seemed to have prepared the ground for the "formal climax of treaty-making" (Orange 1987:6). Initially the British attitude toward formal intervention in New Zealand had been one of reluctance because "New Zealand offered little scope for investment and a very limited market" (Sinclair 1991:55). Furthermore, the British government at the time did not wish to extend its empire. Moreover, the strong humanitarian conscience of the period and sensitivity toward foreign powers led to a preference by the Colonial Office to see British interests advanced by missionaries and private enterprise. Overworked officials of the Colonial Office had developed a policy of "minimum intervention" for New Zealand as they tried to cope with the demands for action by the motherland from around the world (Sinclair 1991:55). Wars and upheavals in South Africa, India, and Canada were stretching their abilities to the limit. Near the end of the 1830s, however, there was a marked shift in British attitudes toward New Zealand.

New Zealand affairs were passionately discussed in Parliament and in public, with the debate being fueled by two well-organized pressure groups: the colonizers on the one hand and the humanitarians and missionaries on the other. In the early nineteenth century, New Zealand was a non industrialized country, with virtually the entire population employed in farming or forestry. The indigenous Maori communities still practiced subsistence farming, and for years after 1840, while farms were being cleared and developed, most settlers were dependent on this Maori economy to sustain them.

The most powerful constituent among the colonizers, which in no small way contributed to the reversal of British policy, was the New Zealand Company. It had grown out of the New Zealand Association, founded like many other colonizing companies on the ideals of Edward Gibbon Wakefield (1796–1862). Wakefield was a colorful and controversial figure whose theories about colonization were a powerful influence on the settlement of New Zealand. For Wakefield colonization was noble work, benefiting not only the colony but also Britain, by relieving it from the pressure of overpopulation and poverty. Wakefield's theory hinged on land sales that would enable industrious laborers to become landowners and masters of servants in due course. The new colonial society would become a replica of English society. In many respects Wakefield's theories were simultaneously progressive and reactionary. His ideal colonial community was modeled on English society before industrialism. He pictured New Zealand as a white man's country with little regard for the natives, a view that stood in direct contrast to the ideals of the majority of British humanitarians and their hopes for the future of New Zealand.

English humanitarianism was at the height of its influence in the early nineteenth century. By 1833 the slave trade within the British Empire had been abolished, and a second, more difficult, phase was being embarked on by groups such as the Church Missionary Society, the Aborigines Protection Society, and the Society for the Civilisation of Africa. This second phase involved the "civilization" of primitive peoples within the empire. The new humanitarian imperative found its highest expression in the establishment of the 1837 House of Commons Select Committee on Aborigines to consider the best ways of improving the conditions of the natives in the colonies of the British Empire. One of the committee's recommendations was to avoid treaties with indigenous people unless adequate accommodation for their rights could be made:

> As a general rule, however, it is inexpedient that treaties should be frequently entered into between the local Governments and the tribes in their vicinity. Compacts between parties negotiating on terms of such entire disparity are rather the preparatives and the apology for disputes than securities for peace: as often as the resentment or the cupidity of the more powerful body may be excited, a ready pretext for complaint will be found in the ambiguity of the language in which their agreements must be drawn up, and in the superior sagacity which the Europeans will exercise in framing, in interpreting, and in evading them. The safety and welfare of an uncivilised race require that their relation with their more cultivated neighbors should be diminished rather than multiplied. ("Report of the House of Commons" 1837:622)

Such a stance was fine for senior churchmen and petty politicians in London, but it was far from politically expedient, as events in New Zealand created a need for urgent action on the part of the government.

In 1839 the New Zealand Company was making extravagant claims about land purchases it had made in New Zealand; speculators boasted that they had secured thousands of acres of land and were ready to sell it to the highest bidder. In January 1840 the missionary William Williams noted in a letter to E. Marsh both the eagerness and the ethical shortcomings of these buyers: ". . . Europeans are trying to buy the land in every direction, or rather to cheat the natives out of it by procuring their signatures to documents prepared by lawyers in Sydney, which without being duly explained to the natives are to wrest them from their land for a mere nominal consideration" (qtd. in Porter 1974:77). Added to the pressures from the colonizers and the humanitarians was a third concern:

the growing problems of lawlessness in New Zealand. Alcohol abuse, violence, and crime were rampant among the Europeans, but nothing could be done by Britain to rein in her subjects, as New Zealand was not under British rule.

Respectable settlers, missionaries, and Maori elders had petitioned the British government repeatedly for protection, imploring the British government to act to control the alarming situation. From 1837 onward British authorities came more and more to the realization that British intervention in New Zealand was no longer avoidable, and they began to contemplate the question of how this intervention would occur, taking into consideration the conditions and opinions in New Zealand, as well as heeding public opinion at home. The situation was finally brought to a head when the New Zealand Company sent Colonel William Wakefield to New Zealand to purchase land and prepare for settlement, forcing the government to act to seek full sovereignty over New Zealand in order to control British subjects on the one hand and to secure a safe place for the Maori on the other hand. Earlier more modest approaches were abandoned. Captain William Hobson was charged with establishing a treaty with the Maori, securing sovereignty for Britain in exchange for British citizenship and protection from foreign powers. He hoped to achieve these ends peacefully and with the "free and intelligent" consent of the chiefs (Orange 1987:14).

Hobson arrived in the Bay of Islands of New Zealand not with a carefully drafted document but with general instructions from his superiors on the nature and possible content of any treaty he would conclude with the Maori. Lord Normanby, the Colonial Secretary, issued instructions to Hobson that clearly showed that the humanitarian sentiments toward the Maori and their welfare were sincere but were tempered by an underlying dose of pragmatism when it came to details of policy on New Zealand. The message and intent of the instructions were quite contradictory: they left no doubt in Hobson's mind that British sovereignty had to be achieved by him, but they also stressed that all transactions were to be "conducted on the principles of sincerity, justice, and good faith" (Normanby 1839:271). In his introduction Lord Normanby talked about the "encroachment" of the British, yet stressed that the Maori "must not be permitted to enter into any contracts in which they might be the ignorant and unintentional authors of injuries to themselves" (Normanby 1839:272). The burden of overcoming these irrec-

oncilable contradictions and achieving his task may have contributed to
Hobson's falling ill immediately on his arrival in New Zealand. The treaty
was, nevertheless, composed within a few days. Hobson's background
had not prepared him for such a task; he had no legal training. Nevertheless, he could draw on the help and knowledge of James Busby, the
British Resident in the Bay of Islands, and Chief Clerk James Freeman.
The final version of the Treaty of Waitangi drew together Hobson's
knowledge of other treaties, the particular set of circumstances Hobson
believed prevailed in New Zealand at the time, and the considerable influence of Busby, who edited Hobson's notes. These elements combined
in a chaotic mix to form the Treaty of Waitangi.

On the afternoon of 4 February 1840, Hobson arranged for the
version of the treaty he had settled on to be translated into the Maori
language, the final version to be presented to the assembled chiefs the
next morning. The head of the Church Missionary Society in New Zealand, the Reverend Henry Williams, was entrusted with the task of translating the treaty. Hobson could not have asked for a better ally. He and
Williams were united in the cause of securing British sovereignty over
New Zealand, and each saw in the other the potential for achieving his
aim. Prior to his departure from England, Hobson had been advised to
regard the missionaries as allies who could use their influence with the
Maori people in favor of the treaty. Henry Williams, for his part, had
received instructions from his superior, the Bishop of Australia, to exercise his influence over the chiefs attached to him in order to "induce
them to make the desired surrender of sovereignty to Her Majesty"
(Rogers 1973:162).

Henry Williams was undoubtedly a dominant figure among the missionaries. In the twelve years since his arrival in New Zealand, he had
won the respect and admiration of many Maori. His name was known
and honored throughout much of New Zealand. A man of great commitment, courage, and strength, who had become "a father indeed to all
the tribes," Williams was driven by his desire to bring Christianity to the
Maori (Rogers 1973:24). His religious convictions completely dominated
his thoughts and actions, and these convictions, together with the considerable influence of the church, must be understood and taken into
consideration in the examination of Williams's role as the translator of
the Treaty of Waitangi.

The Church of England, through the Church Missionary Society, had established its first foothold in New Zealand in 1814. Samuel Marsden, the chaplain of the convict colony of New South Wales in Australia, established the first mission in the Bay of Islands in New Zealand. From the beginning the mission not only spread the gospel but also instilled the belief that the British Crown had a special, paternal interest in the welfare of the Maori. Missionary activities continually worked at promoting and nurturing the idea of this protective relationship. Marsden also introduced the first Maori leaders to government circles in Sydney and England. Maori chiefs were received in an audience by King George IV in 1812, and, according to their tradition, the Maori felt justified in believing that this reception had created a special, personal bond between the king and the Maori people. During the following decades many opportunities arose that confirmed the benevolent intentions of the Crown in the minds of the Maori chiefs.[2]

By 1840 the power of the church and its influence over all aspects of life in New Zealand were at their height. On the political scene the church played a dual role: missionaries advised and supported representatives of the Crown, including the British Resident James Busby, as well as the Maori chiefs. The introduction of Busby to Maori society by the missionaries, through their well-established network, was as crucial as their role in shaping the attitude of the Maori to the Crown. The social and ethical influence of the church preceded its spiritual influence; missionaries not only preached but also were actively involved in Maori life and society. They condemned cannibalism, slavery, and polygamy; they treated the sick; and they negotiated peace between warring tribes. They also created a written Maori language such that the Maori learned to read and write their language from the missionaries. Maori chiefs protected the missionaries who, in turn, increased the power and prestige of their hosts through this association. When the first books were introduced to Maori oral culture, they were translations: missionaries had created the orthography and the dictionaries of the Maori language and then embarked on the translation of religious and legal texts into Maori. Thus conversion and colonization went hand in hand, with translation the channel of both.

It was not until the 1830s that the first Maori were converted to Christianity. Many Maori who had become Christians blended their new beliefs with traditional Maori practices. One important reason for Maori conversion was the spread of literacy: they were keen to learn to read and

write. Their teachers were the missionaries, and the only materials the
Maori could read at that time were the Bible and other religious writings.
Their oral tradition had served them well before the arrival of the missionaries who created the Maori's written language, but through their
contacts with the Pakeha, the Maori came to understand the importance
Europeans attached to written documents. They were taught by the missionaries that the word of God as presented in the Bible was a covenant
between God and his Christian followers, and these teachings served as
a model for their later understanding of the Treaty of Waitangi as a new
covenant between the queen and the Maori people. The missionaries
actively promoted these views.

The spiritual influence of the church made itself increasingly felt
throughout the 1830s. By 1840, however, after the first flush of conver-
sions, missionaries began to fear for the steadfastness of their new flock
in the face of the increasing temptations and lawlessness of everyday life.
Although they were arguably guided by humanitarian concerns for Maori
rights, while promoting the existence of a New Zealand under their spiritual influence without official British rule, in the years just before 1840
missionaries became convinced "that a regularization of English intrusion
into the country would be much preferable to the haphazard influx of
settlers and transients that was proving increasingly detrimental to Maori
welfare" (Orange 1987:58).

Henry Williams was given the difficult task of translating in a few
hours of one night a treaty intended to link two different cultures. He
had mastered the Maori language such that he could speak reasonably
fluently and clearly, and he had been involved in the translation of the
Scriptures into Maori for many years. Although Williams was no scholar,
he was aware of certain aspects of translation theory; he later stated that
"in this translation it was necessary to avoid all expressions of English for
which there was no expressive term in Maori, preserving entire the spirit
and tenor of the treaty" (qtd. in Orange 1990:13).

Williams was assisted that night by his twenty-year-old son, Edward,
who had grown up in New Zealand and was familiar with the local dia-
lect. At his young age Edward would probably have had difficulties understanding some of the concepts of the treaty in English, let alone possessing the ability to translate them into the legal language of the Maori.
No record exists of whether an attempt was made to engage a native
Maori speaker in this task. The choices that fell on Williams and his son,

as translators of such an immensely important legal document, were dictated by circumstance. There were others eminently more skilled and experienced in translation, but they were absent from the mission. Because of the urgency of the occasion, Hobson was forced to turn to the personnel available and willing to help.

A first comparison of the English and the Maori texts establishes the translation strategy Williams used and confirms Williams's intent to avoid all terms that had no direct equivalents in the Maori language. The convoluted and technical English text is recast in simple Maori, with glaring omissions. Certain crucial terms were not translated into the closest, natural Maori equivalents but instead into Maori words and concepts employed to convey meaning in the missionary translations of the Bible, words and concepts that were generally understood by the Maori to mean something other than the sense in which they were used in the translation of the treaty.

A comparison of the translation and its source text on the key elements of sovereignty and land ownership illustrates how "treaty issues" have polarized Maori-Pakeha relations in New Zealand. The English preamble sets out the objectives: the queen's desire to protect the Maori people from the excesses of British settlement, to "obtain sovereign authority," and to establish a "settled form of Civil Government" so as to maintain order and peace. In article one it is stated that the chiefs of the Confederation and all independent chiefs cede to the queen of England "absolutely and without reservation all the rights and powers of sovereignty." The key concepts of "sovereign authority," "civil government," and "powers of sovereignty" were all translated by Williams with the same term: *kawanatanga*, 'governance'. The concept of sovereignty in English is complex in legal documents and includes the power of jurisdiction at national as well as international levels, meanings that the term *kawanatanga* did not cover.

It has been suggested that at that time the Maori had no understanding of the concept of sovereignty and therefore no equivalent term existed. History, however, proves this argument wrong: the Declaration of Independence, signed by thirty-four Maori chiefs in 1835, when French interests seemed to James Busby, the British Resident in the colony, to extend to New Zealand, is a clear expression of the chiefs' understanding and appreciation of their sovereignty over New Zealand. Moreover, the declaration was acknowledged and honored by the Colonial Office. Although the French presence in the South Pacific was seen by Busby as a threat to British interests in New Zealand, the Colonial Office viewed the French as nothing more than a minor irritation in the region.

The Declaration of Independence had been intended as an assertion of the Maori right to self-governance but was initiated by Busby without approval from his superiors and was signed by less than 10 percent of Maori chiefs. Within three years of it being signed, the Declaration of Independence was rendered virtually useless. It is interesting to note, however, that in the declaration the phrase "New Zealand's independence" was translated by the term *rangatiratanga* and accepted as such by Britain. There exists another term that the Maori feel would have conveyed the meaning of the complex concept of sovereignty and made the intention of the treaty absolutely clear; Ranginui Walker notes that "the word 'mana' [is] the only equivalent to the concept of sovereignty" (1972:2). Both *rangatiratanga* and *mana* are central to the Maori understanding of themselves in the world and their role within their own culture. *Rangatiratanga* implies the execution of jurisdiction, *mana* adding to this concept shades of meaning associated with authority and status. Both terms were current and frequently used in 1840.

Instead of using these Maori phrases and words, Henry Williams chose to express the crucial English concept of sovereignty with *kawanatanga*, a term created by the missionaries, derived from *kawa*, 'governor'. It was a neologism, one well known by the recently converted Maori, appearing in the scriptures and biblical texts translated by the Christian Missionary Society and distributed in great numbers during the previous decade. In the Bible the term *kawanatanga* was used with reference to Pontius Pilate and his governance, and *rangatiratanga* referred to the phrase "the Kingdom of God," as it appeared in the King James Version of the Bible. It must be assumed that the employment of the term *kawanatanga* in the Maori version of the treaty led the Maori chiefs to understand that they were agreeing to and signing a concession of limited power only, a viewpoint clearly expressed by the comment on events by the Kaitaia Chief Napera Panakareao: "the shadow of the land goes to Queen Victoria but the substance remains with us" (Adams 1977: 235). It has even been suggested that in agreeing to *kawanatanga* by the British, the Maori signatories of the treaty understood their sovereignty to be fully intact, confirmed, and even strengthened by virtue of the fact that the British appeared to have officially recognized it (Orange 1989:46).

Further difficulties arose from the translation of article two. In the English text, it is stated that the queen

> . . . confirms and guarantees to the Chiefs and Tribes of New Zealand and to the respective families and individuals thereof the full exclusive and undisturbed possession of their Lands and Estates Forests Fisheries and other properties which they may collectively or individually possess so long as it is their wish and desire to retain the same in their possession. (Treaty of Waitangi 1840:1)

In Maori the article reads:

> Ko te Kuini o Ingarangi ka wakarite ka wakaae ki nga Rangatira, ki nga Hapu, ki nga tangata katoa o Nu Tirani, te tino rangatiratanga o o ratou wenua o ratou kainga me o ratou taonga katoa. (Treaty of Waitangi 1840:2)

Backtranslated into English the article reads:

> The Queen of England agrees to protect the Chiefs, Subtribes and all the people of New Zealand in the unqualified exercise of their chieftainship over their lands, villages and all their treasures. (Orange 1987:386)

The Maori translation of the English text not only omitted the condition of collective and individual ownership but also failed to include forests and fisheries under the guarantee of possession, talking instead about the general and undefined *taonga katoa*, 'all treasures'. Confusion moreover arose from the translation of the "guarantee of possession" of land as *te tino rangatiratanga*, 'chieftainship', as this concept is much wider and deeper in Maori than the word *possession* in English. The Maori concept includes authority and the right to exercise control and approaches the English concept of sovereignty.

Traditionally the Maori did not own land. A tribe had authority over a given area, but the land belonged to the past, present, and future generations. It was not an alienable commodity. People were part of the land; they could not own it. These very same notions of land as place (as the Maori would have understood it) and land as property (as the English understood it) led to the impossibility of reaching a mutual understanding when translating the term merely linguistically; the case is similar to the situation the English encountered in relation to American Indians, as Eric Cheyfitz has indicated. Cheyfitz suggests that "the use of the *English* terms *property, possession*, and *ownership* to refer to the Algonquians' land usages in seventeenth-century New England risks collapsing the cultures and histories of these peoples into the English histories" (1997:48). Two hundred years later nothing had changed in the procedures of English imperialism. Maori cultural specificities and their understanding of place, which is so fundamental to the coherence of their culture, were all ignored. The Maori version of the Treaty of Waitangi was written to express solely British understandings; it was embedded entirely in British culture. Ironically, the effect the translation had on the Maori people was that the guarantee of *te tino rangatiratanga*, 'chieftainship', heightened the belief of the Maori in their own chieftainship and control over their land. Neither the term *kawanatanga* for "sovereignty" in article one nor the translation of *te tino rangatiratanga* for "guarantee of possession" in article two indicated in any way to the Maori that the document they were asked to sign implied the annexation of New Zealand by Britain.

Moreover, the second section of article two talks of the selling and buying of land. In English the article reads, "the Chiefs of the United Tribes and the individual Chiefs yield to Her Majesty the exclusive right of Preemption over such lands as the proprietors thereof may be disposed to alienate" (Treaty of Waitangi 1840:1). In this section the term *preemption* was translated as *hokonga*, a term commonly used by the Maori to describe the buying, selling, and bartering of goods, a very familiar concept to them. Nowhere in the translation is the Crown's exclusive right to handle all land transactions mentioned, yet it is safe to assume that Henry Williams must have been fully aware of the Crown's intention from an earlier proclamation to this effect made by Hobson (Orange 1987:37).

The translation of the third article is the least contentious. In English the text reads:

> . . . the Queen extends to the Natives of New Zealand Her royal protection and imparts to them all the Rights and Privileges of British Subjects. (Treaty of Waitangi 1840:1)

The Maori version reads:

> . . . Ka tiakina e te Kuini o Ingarangi nga tangata maori katoa o Nu
> Tirani. Ka tukua ki a ratou nga tikanga katoa rite tahi ke ana mea ki
> nga tangata o Ingarangi. (Treaty of Waitangi 1840:2)

This can be backtranslated into English as:

> . . . the Queen of England will protect all the ordinary people of New
> Zealand and will give them the same rights and duties of citizenship
> as the people of England. (Orange 1987:387)

Here again we have a correct linguistic or meaning-based translation that, nonetheless, fails to take the disparity of the two cultures into consideration. As with the concept of preemption in article two, here the implications of the text for the Maori becoming subject to British law were not clarified either in the English or Maori versions of the treaty and could therefore not be expected to be fully understood in this form by the Maori signatories.

The treaty, however, was not just a written document but also a spoken agreement. Pre-European Maori only heard words and had no conception of seeing them. After the introduction of literacy to the Maori by the missionaries during the early part of the century, the situation had changed slightly, but it would be impossible to assess precisely the prevailing level of literacy at the time the treaty was signed. The spoken word still had a strong appeal and authority. The ability to orate was and still is an important skill among Maori, and the traditional routes of knowledge transfer were still intact. Words spoken by elders were attended to closely and heeded because of the accepted fact that the elders had collective wisdom and experience. Because of the importance of the Maori oral tradition, Hobson had invited the Maori chiefs to hear the treaty text and have it explained to them by Henry Williams, the translator and trusted "father to all tribes," before Hobson asked the chiefs to sign the document.

On the morning of 5 February 1840, a large crowd had gathered at Waitangi. Soldiers, missionaries, old residents, new settlers, and many Maori chiefs and their entourages were present. Hobson explained briefly that the purpose of the meeting was to seek the chiefs' consent to a treaty.

He then proceeded to read the English version of the Treaty of Waitangi aloud. His reading was followed by Henry Williams's reading of the text in Maori. A deep silence fell over the crowd. Williams interpolated the text with oral explanations, clause by clause. However, records show that these explanations did not cover the important wider intent of the treaty, but instead concentrated on the power the treaty would give the British to rein in the lawless and excessive behavior of their own citizens (Rogers 1961:66). Williams, the trusted "father to all tribes," who had brought them God's message and Christian values, further stressed the personal bond between the queen and the Maori people, indicating as well his own approval of the treaty. After the chiefs had heard the text of the treaty in their own language, they were encouraged to debate the proposal. Passionate discussions were held until late into the evening, with the mood for and against Hobson and the treaty changing often. Henry Williams recollects:

> There was considerable excitement amongst the people, greatly increased by the irritating language of ill-disposed Europeans, stating to the chiefs, in most insulting language, that their country was gone, and they now were only *taurekareka* (slaves). Many came to us to speak upon this new state of affairs. We gave them but one version, explaining clause by clause, showing the advantage to them of being taken under the fostering care of the British Government, by which act they would become one people with the English, in the suppression of wars, and of every lawless act; under one sovereignty, and one law, human and divine. (qtd. in Orange 1987:51)

By the morning of 6 February 1840, the chiefs had decided to bring the deliberations to a close. Food was becoming short, and many had far to travel to return home. A formal signing ceremony was hastily prepared, and Hobson, who had been on his ship and unaware of the turn of events, rushed back to Waitangi. The treaty was again read out loud in Maori by Henry Williams. When their names were called out one by one, the majority of the chiefs stepped forward to sign the Treaty of Waitangi. With the spiritual dimension between them and the queen as head of the Church of England already existing, with the special, personal bond between the British monarch and the Maori people emphasized repeatedly during the two days of deliberations, it must have felt safe for the Maori chiefs to go one step further and accept also the temporal dimension of this special alliance. Hone Heke, one of the leading chiefs, encapsulated the feeling that the chiefs close to the missionaries shared at that moment: "The native mind could not comprehend these things, they must trust to the advice of the missionaries" (Colenso 1890:18).

The treaty then traveled to other parts of the North Island and more signatures were collected in ceremonies similar to the one at Waitangi. Hobson had been authorized to ignore the few Maori who inhabited the South Island, and the treaty was not taken across the Cook Strait that separated the two islands (Sinclair: 1991). Great care was taken to allow time for consultation with the chiefs. The negotiations were led in "the language of persuasive diplomacy" (Orange 1987:86). The missionaries' knowledge of Maori customs and their sensitivity to Maori culture were invaluable to the negotiators of the treaty. As at Waitangi, the paternal, protective relationship with the British Crown was emphasized. The trust the Maori chiefs showed in the missionaries and their recommendation to sign the treaty was an indication of the extent to which the treaty had taken on a spiritual dimension. On 21 May 1840, Hobson proclaimed full sovereignty over the North Island on the basis of cession by treaty and over the South Island on the basis of discovery.

Confusion surrounded the treaty and its translation from the beginning. When the Colonial Office received from Hobson several copies of the treaty in English, each with slight variations, it assumed that they were translations of the Maori text. One of the copies had attached to it a certification by the translator Henry Williams that the English text was "as literal a translation of the Treaty of Waitangi as the idiom of the language will admit of" (Orange 1987:85). This, however, was inaccurate. The text was not a backtranslation of the Maori treaty. History does not tell us what motivated Henry Williams to create this false impression and present the translation as the original. In the history of translation however, this is not an isolated case (Kálmán 1986:117). Translations have been and are still today presented as originals, and originals as translations for various reasons. Here it must be assumed that Williams, keenly aware of the new humanitarianism in Britain, including views embraced by his own Church Mission Society, gave in to these pressures by according to the Maori text the status of an original. His decision to give the Maori text priority over the English text when submitting both documents to the government must have been grounded in his ardent wish to find acceptance for the concluded treaty by the political and moral powers in Britain. Further confusion was added when Hobson finally sent the English version and the Maori version to London, with both carrying the heading "Treaty." When those two documents were printed for publication, however, the Maori text carried the heading "Treaty," and the English text the heading "Translation," thus consolidating further the idea and understanding in Britain that the Maori fully understood that they had signed away their country's sovereignty.

In 1869 in a climate of governmental and public anti-Maori feelings, the government, recognizing that the original translation had been executed in "execrable Maori," commissioned a new Maori translation in order to fully clarify for the Maori their position, their obligations, and their rights as British subjects (Orange 1987:182). The crucial phrase "rights and powers of sovereignty" was now translated into "all customary powers and *mana* of chieftainship." The word *possession* in the second article, originally rendered as *rangatiratanga*, 'chieftainship', now became *tuturutanga*, 'absolute guarantee'. This text, however, was not merely a new translation; it was a very different treaty from that to which the original signatories had given their consent. Through Maori members sitting in the New Zealand Parliament, an awareness of the change of the claims around the treaty began to spread slowly through the Maori community.

What was originally conceived in the spirit of generosity and enlightenment is today seen by a new wave of Maori activists as a conspiracy that has robbed them of their land, their resources, and their right to govern themselves. As Walker writes, "The blame for the faulty translation of the treaty must lie with Williams" (1972:5). But what is Williams to be blamed for? The translation environment of today would blame him for the fact that his translation failed to achieve informational equivalence, which consequently led to a lack of functional equivalence. Though the source text clearly states the cession of sovereignty, the translation in its written and oral form led to the perception of an "act of love" by the queen toward the Maori people. The source text is a legal document that was written in a climate in which some legal opinions asserted that only the acts and attitudes of "civilized" nations mattered, yet the translation was regarded by the Maori people as a covenant in which the various promises and conditions acquired an almost sacred force.

Modern translation studies would further blame Williams for mis-understanding the role of the translator as the mediator between two cultures. With both source and target texts embedded in cultures at a great distance from each other, the translator occupied a key position as a mediator between them. Instead of mediation, making the intention, perception, and expectation of each group clear to the other, we find in this instance manipulation seemingly aimed at hiding the true intention of the source text in order to achieve acceptance of it by the target group.

Williams was a product of his time, his religion, and the prevailing ideology. His translation reflected all three. He firmly believed that Maori interests would be best served under British rule, just as he believed that Maori souls would be saved by faith in a Christian God. Williams's translation illustrates the development of strategies by translators in the service of power. In Williams's case the worldly power he served was reinforced by the spiritual power. His view of the world and that of his own position in it were the dominant factors that determined his translation strategy. In the final analysis they turned Williams, the "father of all Maori," from *traduttore to traditore*, from translator to traitor. Two years after the treaty was signed, the *Bay of Islands Observer* of 7 July 1842 summed up what many settlers felt about the treaty at that time: "For the good people at home, the affair was made to assume the appearance of one of the purest of philanthropy on the part of England in favour of the Natives to protect them against European aggression: but the simple truth is, disguise it as we may, that under this cloak of benevolence, has been practised the greatest hypocrisy, to obtain possession of the country hon-estly, if possible, but never the less to obtain it" (qtd. in Orange 1987: 91).

This case study confirms the view that translations reflect the im-peratives of their context, their time, and their culture. Translators, caught in a web of often contradictory relationships, will resolve the ten-sions according to their understanding of their own position and role within their culture (Lefevere 1992:14). Moreover, the study demon-strates how translation becomes even more problematic when source and target cultural systems are substantially different. While in the polysystem approach of scholars like Itamar Even-Zohar, Gideon Toury, and Lefev-ere, it is possible to negotiate the values of one culture in terms of the values of the other, in a postcolonial context, however, this is no longer so palatable. Once the divide between two cultures includes great power disparities, culture becomes untranslatable. The translation of the Treaty of Waitangi from English, the dominant culture, into Maori, the indigenous culture, is a case in point. The untranslatability of culture of which Homi Bhabha (1994) speaks is demonstrated here in its most dramatic form: the merely semantic transfer resulting in the disempowerment of an indigenous nation.

The historic circumstances of the translating and signing of the Treaty of Waitangi constitute an example of the important role translations by missionaries have played in colonial projects and of the role played by translations in the imposition and reproduction of power structures. As Susan Bassnett has argued, "We are compelled now to recognise the role [translators] play in reshaping texts, a role that is far from innocent" (1996:23). In the case of the translator of the Treaty of Waitangi, his role was indeed anything but innocent. Henry Williams reshaped the text and changed one part of the world forever. The political impact this translation had at the time and still has today is so enormous that it has become the basis for the continued existence of two peoples within one nation. Recently it has pitted against each other the two nations that have built New Zealand. From the day the treaty was signed until recent times, it was the English version of the treaty that was interpreted and implemented by successive New Zealand governments. A burst of immigration from England saw the Maori population surpassed by the 1860s and it has declined steadily since then. Once the Maori were in control of their resources and their destiny, but since the signing of the treaty, every facet of their lives has become subordinate to the Pakeha. When in 1877 Chief Justice Prendergast declared the treaty a "legal nullity," it "blew the Treaty away into a judicial limbo for the better part of a century" (Kawharu 1995:x). Yet the voice of Maori protest against the unfulfilled provisions and principles of the Treaty of Waitangi was always there to be heard. The treaty in the Maori language became the uniting factor of a Maori protest movement and gradually the focus of considerable political activity. Between 1975 and 1985 New Zealand was shaken by Maori sovereignty and land claims, with the 1975 "land march" as the first of several confrontational events.[3] The land march was a response to the sentiment felt by many Maori that successive New Zealand governments had ignored their obligations to the Treaty of Waitangi, to the detriment of Maori development. By the time the land march reached Wellington, the country's capital, thousands had joined its ranks, indicating to the government in no uncertain terms that it had to face up to its responsibilities in relation to the treaty.

The culmination of more than one hundred years of struggle was the creation of the Waitangi Tribunal, constituted by the Treaty of Waitangi Act of 1975 and its amendment of 1985, enabling Maori to take claims back to 1840 in order to rectify past injustices. This was a courageous step, undertaken by the Labour government of the day to initiate a process of coming to terms with the trauma of the treaty. In the 1990s three major claims were settled in what the government planned would be full and final settlements of certain grievances arising from breaches of the treaty by the Crown. The first was the fisheries settlement, in which the Crown returned approximately 15 percent of the country's fishing resources to Maori control. The money this agreement intended to generate has yet to be distributed to the various tribes, however, because the settlement was made on a pan-tribal basis and contained within it no detailed provision for the allocation of profits on a tribe-by-tribe basis. The next two claims, settled between 1996 and 1998, were the Tainui and Ngaitahu claims. Valued at NZ172 million each, both were effected by legislation to be full and final settlements for all grievances claimed by both of these tribes against the Crown under the provisions and principles of the treaty. At present there are more than five hundred smaller claims waiting to be heard. With a delay often of decades in the processing of claims, there is growing frustration among some Maori that justice is not being done.

On the other side of the political spectrum, there are those who argue that the claims "business" has been dragging on for too long. Today there are voices gaining in strength[4] that want to put a stop to the ever-growing "Waitangi Tribunal industry" of lawyers, historians, researchers, and consultants, an industry that cost the taxpayers in 1998–99 an estimated NZ 46.2 million (Orange 1987:55). Enough is enough they cry, the treaty has never been adopted into law by Parliament and therefore does not have the force of law. The opposition in sectors of most of the main political parties argues that the settlement of all claims should be stopped, the treaty given the status of a historical document and replaced by a constitution based on today's realities. Whatever the decisions concerning the treaty's future, decision makers and stakeholders know that their actions will either jeopardize race relations in New Zealand or finally create the ideal that Hobson articulated to each chief as they shook hands after signing the Treaty of Waitangi: "*He iwi tahi ta-tou*," 'We are now one people' (qtd. in Orange 1987:55).

Notes

1. The version of the Treaty of Waitangi cited here is kept in the National Archives in Wellington, New Zealand. A printed version can be found in Orange 1987, appendix two.

2. For example, in 1817, 1823, and 1828, laws were enacted that empowered Australian courts to deal with crimes against Maori committed by British subjects. Although these had little or no effect on the situation in New Zealand, they served to promote the image of the Crown's continued personal interest in Maori welfare.

3. The land march involved several hundred Maori marching from various points in the country and converging at the parliament buildings in the capital, Wellington. Protests at Waitangi Day celebrations also became larger during this period.

4. These include members of the ACT (Association of Citizens and Taxpayers) and National political parties.

MICHAEL CRONIN

The Empire Talks Back: Orality, Heteronomy, and the Cultural Turn in Interpretation Studies

I n *The Twits* by Roald Dahl, the monkey Muggle-Wump and his family are prisoners of Mr. and Mrs. Twit.[1] They try to warn birds that wish to land on a tree in the Twits' garden that the tree is covered with glue and that the birds will end up encased in bird pie, but "these were English birds and they couldn't understand the weird African language the monkeys spoke" (Dahl 1982:56). It is only when the Roly-Poly bird turns up that the English birds are saved from their culinary fate, as he knows the language both of Muggle-Wump and of the birds, and thus is able to warn the latter. The Roly-Poly bird's indignant reply when asked whether he knows how to speak to the English birds is eloquent, "Of course I do," said the Roly-Poly bird. "It's no good going to a country and not knowing the language" (1982:56).

From the literature of children to the transactions of adulthood, traces of interpreting are everywhere. As an oral form of translation, interpreting predates written translation by millennia. Despite its historical antiquity and geographical spread, interpretation studies still remain very much a minority interest in academic studies in general and in translation studies in particular. Out of the twenty-six sessions at one major conference on translation studies, only one was explicitly devoted to interpreting, not an uncommon proportion at such conferences.[2] Yet interpreting, as an activity that goes on in courts, police stations, social welfare offices, conferences, coach tours, factory floors, journalism assignments, and airports, is arguably the most widespread form of translation activity in the world today and has been for tens of thousands of years. Why then this "minoritization" of interpretation? In a world of globalization, increased refugee and immigrant flows, and exponential growth in tourism, interpreting should be a leading area in cultural investigations of language contact, yet this is largely not the case. In addition, power is everywhere in the definition, context, and practice of interpreting, yet there has often been a reluctance to reflect on the consequences of power in interpretation studies.

In this essay, I begin by exploring the fundamentally oral nature of interpreting and the neglect by interpretation scholars of precious insights from literacy/orality studies. I argue that interpretation studies is characterized by a signal bias toward prestigious forms of interpreting practiced in developed countries and that this geopolitical partiality has to be challenged by a new "cultural turn" in interpretation studies. Similar to what has already occurred in translation studies, this turn would encourage scholars to address explicitly questions of power and issues such as class, gender, and race in interpreting situations. Examples are taken from colonial history and the development of tourism to illustrate areas that could be usefully investigated by a more explicitly material history of interpreting, guided by the "cultural turn" paradigm. Particular attention will be paid to ambivalent perceptions of the interpreter, to the particular role of the interpreter as returned native, to the shift from heteronomous to autonomous interpreting, and to the part played by interpretation in the emergence of the native as a hermeneutic subject. I suggest that a more materialist, politically self-aware approach to interpretation studies would unlock the enormous research potential of this area of translation inquiry and highlight the importance of interpreting and interpreters in any assessment of the impact of translation on humanity, past and present.

Interpreting and Orality

The planet is currently estimated to have approximately three thousand languages, but only seventy-eight of the languages in existence today have produced a written literature (Ong 1988:7). The existing languages are believed to be a fragment of the many tens of thousands of languages that have existed throughout human history, of which only 106 have been committed to writing to the extent that the production of written literature was possible (Malherbe 1983:24). The overwhelming fact of human language has been its orality. Walter J. Ong in *Orality and Literacy* describes the momentous changes brought about in our understanding of the world through the invention of the technologies of writing and printing. The changes are all the more powerful for being unnoticed, and Ong argues that "freeing ourselves of chirographic and typographic bias in our understanding of language is probably more difficult than any of us can imagine" (1988:77). He bemoans the fact that philosophy and intellectual history have largely neglected orality studies, but his indictment could be extended to translation studies as well.

The inattention to orality in the discipline has two distinct consequences. First, there have been few accounts of how the emergence of translation in its chirographic and typographic mode affected the activity of translation itself. A notable exception is the pioneering essay by Maria Tymoczko, "Translation in Oral Tradition as a Touchstone for Translation Theory and Practice," in which she discusses the oral translation of fixed literary texts, the oral translation of oral multiforms, and the written translation of oral source texts in circumstances influenced by a tradition of oral aesthetics (1990:46–55). She is deeply critical of the neglect of the oral tradition in discussions around literary translation: "In ignoring and failing to account for interlingual oral literary translation, the terms of our very discourse about literary translation presuppose a framework about literature and the workings of literature that fails to account for the position of literature in most of the world at present and the position of literature through most of human history" (1990:53).

The neglect of orality in interpretation studies is equally disturbing. Comments on differences between translating and interpreting in translation history are largely confined to the observation that speech is ephemeral and that evidence for interpreting must be sought indirectly through written sources. The authors of "Interpreters and the Making of History" in *Translators through History*, edited by Jean Delisle and Judith Woodsworth, note that "The spoken word is evanescent. Our knowledge of the past performance of interpreters tends to be derived from such sources as letters, diaries, memoirs and biographies of interpreters themselves, along with a variety of other documents, many of which were only marginally or incidentally concerned with interpreting" (Bowen et al. 1995:245). The observation, while self-evidently true, tends to miss a more fundamental point about translation and orality. Orally based thought and expression are additive not subordinative, aggregative not analytic, copious, (dynamically) traditionalist, agonistic, participatory, homeostatic, situational, and close to the human lifeworld (Ong 1988:31–77). Any examination of the role of interpreting in translation history, therefore, cannot examine an oral practice through the explicative apparatus of chirographic and typographic translation. It is not simply a question of the words vanishing once spoken. The context of primary orality results in an exchange whose meaning will be strikingly different from a similar exchange in the context of literacy. If we do not recognize the specific psychodynamics of orality, then our analyses of interpreting encounters will repeat assumptions that underlie depictions of unsophisticated and dissembling natives.

The fact that an oral culture may not deal in items such as geometrical figures, abstract characterization, the reasoning processes of formal logic, comprehensive descriptions, and explicitly articulated self-analysis often leads to the biased conclusion by external commentators that non-literate persons are, at best, naive and, at worst, confused and dishonest. Literates have generally failed to recognize the specificity and sophistication of oral thinking, and as of this writing historians of translation have also failed to fully appreciate the importance of orality studies for their subject area. Indeed, it might be argued that the hold of literacy on our analytical worldview means that we tend to exaggerate the importance of textual translation and ignore the far-reaching historical and political effects of interpreting encounters.

The second direct consequence of the marginalization of orality is the relative neglect in interpretation studies of areas where there is high residual orality. The impact of writing and print technology has been such that few areas on the planet have escaped the influence of the literate mind. The penetration of literacy has, however, been uneven, and many areas, from rural Ireland to North Africa to inner-city ghettos in the United States, have cultures with a significant oral base. In a discipline like translation studies that is dominated by the typographic cultures of highly-literate Western elites who speak majority languages, whole areas of translation practice, informed by residual orality in many different regions of the world, may be either misunderstood or simply ignored.

It might be thought that anthropology and ethnography would have addressed the problem ignored by translation studies, specifically, the role of translation in largely oral cultures. As Kate Sturge has pointed out, however, anthropology and ethnography have, on the whole, been strangely indifferent to the activity of translation, even though translation would appear to be central to the concerns of these disciplines. Sturge points out the importance of orality in ethnographic translation practice that

> undertakes a dual translation, from the oral to the written form as well as from one language to another; the reproduction of the performative aspects of an utterance—its physical, temporal and social contextuality—defies the translator's supposed task of reproducing the meaning intact. Difficulties associated with these aspects of language wreak havoc in any translation, but whereas ordinary translation takes as its object a piece of language already somewhat decontextualized and depersonalized, ethnographic translation is faced with "raw words" hovering around the mouths and ears that produced them. (1997:22)

The problems of ethnographic translation scholars are the problems faced by interpreters in many parts of the world. A chief question is how to understand properly illocutionary and perlocutionary acts in interlingual exchange. Moreover, no adequate account of the role of the interpreter in many cultures can be given if the *entre-deux* is not also seen to include mediation (successful or unsuccessful) between the different mindsets of orality and literacy. If interpretation studies as the study of an oral practice were to take orality seriously, it would also contribute greatly to expanding areas of translation studies such as screen translation and the possibilities of multilingual print-speech conversion in Web development. Secondary orality, the orality of the telephone, radio, and television—as distinct from the primary orality of nonliterate cultures—has expanded exponentially in our age. As an area of translation studies that in theory deals with the phenomenon of human speech in language transfer, therefore, interpreting ideally ought to be able to make a major contribution to the understanding of the interaction between translation and secondary orality. By and large, however, this has not happened.

The Geopolitics of Interpretation Studies

Research on interpretation has been largely dominated to date by the investigation of conference interpreting. Daniel Gile's *Regards sur la recherche en interprétation de conférence* (1995) and the accompanying bibliography provide striking evidence of this trend. Franz Pöckhacker in "Unity in Diversity? The Case of Interpreting Studies," offers the results of a recent bibliographical analysis of the literature on interpreting (1998: 169–76). Of the 414 thematically specific items for the period 1989 to 1994, more than two-thirds dealt with conference interpreting. The remaining items dealt with court interpreting (50), bilateral interpreting (32), sign-language interpreting (12), media interpreting (10) and sight translation (8). There has, of course, been important work in the area of legal and community interpreting in recent years, and at least one international conference and newsletter are devoted to the specific interests of interpreters in the community.[2] Research in interpreting is still strikingly under the sway of the conference interpreting paradigm, however. As Mona Baker noted with respect to interpreting in politically sensitive contexts, "Although some recent work has been done on consecutive interpreting (especially as performed in the conference setting) and on liaison interpreting (in community and court settings), research on interpreting is still heavily influenced by the priority which has traditionally been given to simultaneous conference interpreting" (1997:1131).

One reason for the primacy of this paradigm is undoubtedly geopolitical. Gile declares that most conference interpreters, "ont leur domicile professionnel dans les pays européens, surtout en France, en Suisse, en Belgique et dans d'autres pays d'Europe occidentale" (1995:13) ("are based in European countries, particularly in France, Switzerland, Belgium, and other Western European countries" [my translation]). The largest conference interpreting markets are Paris, Brussels, Geneva, and Tokyo, and almost all the research centers mentioned by Gile are to be found in the developed world. Janet Altman, describing the activities of the Association Internationale des Interprètes de Conférence (AIIC), claims that, "for historical reasons, the Association has remained unmistakably Western European in focus: roughly half of its members are based in Brussels, Geneva, London and Paris; there are around six times as many in Paris alone as in the whole of Africa" (1998:17). Altman mentions approvingly the links that are being established between conference and court and sign-language interpreters, and the organization of the profession in central and eastern Europe, but her concluding remarks leave little doubt as to the basic geopolitical focus of AIIC: "The challenge facing the Association will be how to serve the interests of interpreters who have extremely diverse geographical, social and linguistic backgrounds whilst continuing to appeal to its original constituency, namely conference interpreters primarily in the western world" (1998:17).

The professional concerns of the First World thus become the theoretical concerns of humanity, and the theoretical paradigm of interpreting is restricted to reflect the market and institutional realities of wealthier nations. The relative neglect of other forms of interpreting that are much more extensively practiced, such as community/bilateral/dialogue interpreting—which even Gile admits is "la forme d'interprétation la plus générale" ("the most common form of interpretation" [my translation])—is arguably grounded in material inequalities that universalize First World experience (1995:12). The minoritizing effect of this ideological sleight of hand is threefold. First, the breadth of interpreting activity is ignored by concentrating on what is a minority sector in the overall field of interpreting, thus weakening the impact of interpreting theory on translation studies as a discipline. Second, interpreting practice in developing countries that is not covered by the conference interpreting paradigm is largely ignored. Third, minority groups in developed countries (refugees, immigrants, ethnic minorities) can themselves be victims of this theoretical exclusion, as they often only merit "conference" status when it is not they who speak but others (social workers, government officials, academics, the police) who speak for them. In his critique of postmodern approaches to ethnography, P. Steven Sangren argues that the "anthropological analysis of the authority of ethnography must specify the conditions of ethnography's production and reproduction in society, especially academic institutions, not just in texts" (1992:279). Little critical attention has been paid to the conditions of production (and reproduction) of the theory of interpretation, including the siting of interpreting research centers in academic institutions in the developed world.

One further effect of the recurrent emphasis on conference interpreting is the privileging of positivism in research. Gile laments the prevalence of speculative, reflexive approaches to interpreting theory that were not superseded until the mid-1980s. He argues for a systematic, rigorous empiricism, based on facts that will earn for interpretation studies legitimacy in the scientific community. Conference interpreting offers ideal conditions for observing input and output. The problem of course, as Gile is forced to admit, is that analyzing the actual *process* of interpreting is much more difficult, and, given the complexity of the phenomenon, it is not always easy to isolate separate components for analysis (1995:215, 220). The theoretical danger is that such "scientific" approaches will privilege further depoliticized, minimally contextualized experiments, carefully controlled by a researcher who assumes objectivity, and that these experiments will be carried out almost invariably in conference interpreting on the grounds that the booth is the nearest thing we have in interpreting to a cage.

A Cultural Turn: Boundary Crossings and Monsters

As mentioned previously, there is valuable and ideologically sensitive work being done in areas of interpreting other than conference interpreting. This type of research is still significantly underrepresented in interpreting research, however. In addition, for understandable pedagogical and professional reasons, work in the area of community interpreting, for example, has largely been concerned with issues of training, certification, and practical difficulties facing community interpreters in their everyday work. For these reasons, I want to argue here for the development of a "cultural turn" in interpretation studies. The work of Susan Bassnett, André Lefevere, José Lambert, Theo Hermans, and, more recently, Sherry Simon and Lawrence Venuti has radically altered the focus of research in translation, opening up a whole range of questions and issues linked to race, class, gender, and ideology that had previously been peripheral, if not simply ignored, in translation studies. Studies of interpretation in this sense have not moved on and have remained largely unaffected by the exciting theoretical developments elsewhere in translation studies. The time has come for a material history of interpreting that examines all forms of interpreting as they are grounded in the economic, political, and cultural conditions of people's lives.

A possible cultural turn had been anticipated for interpreting by the sociologist R. Bruce W. Anderson in his essay "Perspectives on the Role of the Interpreter" (1976). He argues: "Whether one is interested in the legal interpretation of plurilingual treaties . . . the politics of international crises . . . attitudes of various ethnic groups towards each other in multilingual societies . . . or problems of integration of ethnic and linguistic minorities . . . understanding the role and behaviour of interpreters is likely to prove relevant" (209). In investigating the role of the interpreter in different situations, Anderson suggested exploring the variables of social class, education, gender, age, and situational factors, such as arena of interaction (political, military, academic, religious) and level of tension. He has also noted the importance of the relative prestige of the national or ethnic groups involved in the interpreting transaction and attitudes toward the languages spoken. Despite Anderson's acuteness, his work did not lead to any significant shift in interpretation studies, and the need for material/cultural/manipulation perspectives on interpreting is as urgent now as when he wrote. Such an approach would not only greatly broaden the scope for research on contemporary situations, but it would also provide an impetus for historical work in interpreting to move from the descriptive to the analytical.

The areas that might be explored by a material history of interpreting are legion, but the focus here is on issues related to colonial history and travel writing. Interpreters are, by definition, those that cross linguistic and cultural boundaries; depending on the identity of the interpreter and the nature of the context, interpreters cross boundaries of gender, class, nationality, and ethnicity. The interpreter's situation is one of dialogue, but dialogue as defined by more recent ethnography. James Clifford and George Marcus in *Writing Culture: The Poetics and Politics of Ethnography* (1986) claim that the new ethnographical use of dialogue "locates cultural interpretations in many sorts of reciprocal contexts, and it obliges writers to find diverse ways of negotiating realities as multi-subjective, power-laden, and incongruent. In this view, "culture" is always relational, an inscription of communicative processes that exist, historically, *between* subjects in relation to power" (15, emphasis in original). Mary Louise Pratt, for example, in *Imperial Eyes: Travel Writing and Transculturation* (1992) offers an analysis of Alexander von Humboldt's 1805 drawing of Mount Chimbarazo. She asks the question, "Did the Andean guides and interpreters who took him there convey to him some of their own knowledge of the ecosystem and their reverence for it?" (143). Though much space is devoted to an examination of Humboldt's transcultural problematic, there is little consideration of the problematic transcultural role of the interpreters themselves. To what extent did the interpreters represent indigenous culture? Did their knowledge of foreign languages mean that the interpreters had a highly ambivalent attitude to their own indigenous culture? To what extent did different cultures—as expressed through languages—lead to insuperable problems of translation? These questions are never asked by Pratt.

Interpreters appear not only in exploration narratives from the past but also in travel accounts from the present. Here, they generally function as native informants, and they are accorded the same epistemological innocence. The Turkish landowner, whom the Swiss travel writer Nicolas Bouvier meets in Tabriz in *L'Usage du monde* (1992), and the English-speaking Merino engineer, whom Dervla Murphy meets on the Tana-Tamatave line in *Muddling through Madagascar* (1990), both *interpret* in the linguistic and cultural sense for Bouvier and Murphy. The native informant/interpreter confers a legitimacy and verisimilitude on the narrative as a privileged source of "inside" information, smuggled out past the language barrier. How representative the views of these informants are, their exact social position within their own communities, and the extent to which their familiarity with Western languages sets them apart from their own people are issues rarely addressed in travel literature itself and, even more surprisingly, in the critical literature on travel writing.

The Swedish anthropologist Göran Aijmer points out the political and epistemological problems that beset the use of informants, although (typically) he does not mention the question of language: "Informants' insights into their own society are interesting, but generally the interest lies in the extent to which the informant grasps his own social environment. There are also other issues, such as the way in which an informant's account forms a conscious strategy for self-presentation and the anthropologist's refutation of indigenous explanations, which have an obvious place in anthropological discourse" (1992:296). A conscious strategy for self-presentation can also be a covert strategy for self-preservation. Neither strategy has endeared interpreters to their compatriots, and it is possible to argue that interpreters are fit subjects for a new cultural teratology. Rosa Braidotti in *Nomadic Subjects* defines monsters as "human beings who are born with congenital malformations of their bodily organism. They also represent the in between, the mixed, the ambivalent as implied in the ancient Greek root of the word *monsters, teras,* which means both horrible and wonderful, object of aberration and adoration" (1994:77).

An example of ambivalent responses to the interpreter can be seen in the *Lienzo de Tlaxacala,* an Indian picture history dating from around 1550. The history shows Doña Marina, Cortés's interpreter, looming over the other figures in the illustrations, including Cortés himself. Doña Marina spoke Mayan because she had lived among the Tabascans, and she spoke the language of the Aztecs as she was of Aztec descent. After her capture by the Spaniards, she is said to have learned their language quickly. For some cultural commentators in post-independence Mexico, Doña Marina was monstrous: "mother of a bastard race of *mestizos* and a traitress to her country" (Mirandé and Enríquez 1979:24). For others, her resourcefulness and cultural flexibility have excited admiration, and she has been presented as a "herald of the culturally hybrid societies of the future" (Bowen et al. 1995:262). Interpreters thus become recurring objects of ambivalence, in-between figures, loathed and admired, privileged and despised. Like the monstrous, they inspire awe and alienation.

The central problem of translation in general and interpretation in particular is the problem of control. Anderson says of the interpreter that "his position in the middle has the advantage of power inherent in all positions which control scarce resources" (1976:218). Proximity is both desirable and dreaded. The desire is to manipulate and the dread comes from the fear of being misled, either by the native interpreter or by the nonnative interpreter going native. The difficulty for the imperial agent is dealing with this monstrous doubleness, the potential duplicity of interpreters. William Jones, in his *Grammar of the Persian Language* (1771), stated that for British officials, "It was found highly dangerous to employ the natives as interpreters, upon whose fidelity they could not depend" (qtd. by Niranjana 1992:16). These suspicions were in many instances justified. In a celebrated court case in Ireland in the eighteenth century, the Gaelic poet Seán Ó hUaithnín was put on trial for writing pro-Jacobite poems. He was acquitted because the court interpreter, Mícheál Coimín, another Gaelic poet and neighbor, deliberately mistranslated the poem to make it sound thoroughly inoffensive to the Crown (Morley 1995:76).

The choice for the architects of empire was between what might be termed *heteronomous* and *autonomous* systems of interpreting. A heteronomous system involves recruiting local interpreters and teaching them the imperial language. The interpreters may be recruited either by force or through inducements. An autonomous system is one where colonizers train their own subjects in the language or languages of the colonized. The conflicting merits of both systems are vividly illustrated in a letter of Pedro Vaz de Carminha, dated 1 May 1500, in which we find an account of a Portuguese admiral asking whether two Tupis should be taken by force to act as interpreters/informants. A majority of Portuguese officers are reported as claiming that "it was not necessary to take men by force, since those taken anywhere by force usually say of everything that they are asked about that they have it in their country. If we left two of the exiles there, they would give better, very much better information than those men if we took them; for nobody can understand them, nor would it be a speedy matter for them to learn to speak well enough to be able to tell us nearly so much about that country as the exiles will when your Majesty sends them here" (de Caminha 1947:49). The "exiles" were those Portuguese whose punishment for breaking the law took the form of banishment to live among the indigenous peoples in Portugal's newly discovered colonies.

The Portuguese officers might have added that the return of the native is rarely comforting. Return offers the promise of closure, the synthesis of retrospection, the gathering in after the voyage out. However, the Prodigal Son is a figure of disquiet and Ulysses's arrival in Ithaca is marked by a bloodbath. The Bible and Homer intimate that return usually unsettles, disturbing the settled community. The dilemma for interpreters in colonial contexts is whether they can return as *native*. If they do, the risk, of course, is that they *go native*. In 1830 Captain Fitzroy, later captain of the HMS *Beagle*, abducted a number of Fuegians on his first trip to Tierra del Fuego. His crew gave them nicknames that stuck, Jemmy Button (exchanged for a mother-of-pearl button), York Minister, and Fuegia Basket. Jemmy Button was a huge success in England and became noted for his fastidiousness about cleanliness and dress. He learned English and was presented along with Fuegia Basket to Queen Adelaide. Button's English sojourn did not last indefinitely, and in 1833 he was back in Tierra del Fuego along with York Minister and Fuegia Basket. They had traveled there on the *Beagle* with a young English naturalist, Charles Darwin (Beer 1996:38–40).

One reason for the repatriation of the Fuegians to Tierra del Fuego was the belief that their knowledge of English language and culture would facilitate trade in the area. Years later, W. Parker Snow, in his *A Two Year's Cruise off Tierra del Fuego, the Falkland Islands, Patagonia and the River Plate: A Narrative of Life in the Southern Seas* (1857), gives an account of meeting Jemmy Button, "quite naked, having his hair long and matted at the sides, cropped in front, and his eyes affected by smoke" (Beer 1996:69). Parker Snow goes on to note that Jemmy's tribe was the least reliable—they had learned a double language and behavior.

Not only did Jemmy speak the indigenous language, but he also spoke English, the language of the imperial trader. As a result, the English found that Jemmy's tribe was considerably more adroit in its dealings with them than other tribes and more likely to manipulate than to be manipulated. The returned native had indeed gone native, but because he was not wholly native he was even more dangerous as a native. Here "abduction" in the more usual sense of the word becomes the Peircean "abduction" or retrospective hypothesizing. This is the type of hypothesizing we find in the Victorian detective story, where clues allow Holmes to retrace a certain path back to secure origins. The interpreter is returned to his language and culture of origin, he has retraced the path from his B language to his A language, but the origins have now become uncertain, a potential site for duplicity.

The shift to autonomous modes of interpreting is notable in Champlain's decision to set up the institution of *interprète-résidents* where young French adventurers went and lived among the tribes with whom the French traded and learned the language of the indigenous peoples. Later in the century in 1669, as a result of a decree drawn up by Colbert, the French Court arranged to train French-born children known as "enfants de langue" in Turkish, Arabic, and Persian (St-Pierre 1995:16–17). These trainee interpreters were assigned to French ambassadors and consuls abroad where they learned and perfected their knowledge of different foreign languages. Any material history of interpreting would need to investigate the growth of foreign-language instruction in imperial countries and the move toward autonomous modes of interpreting.

The shift toward language autonomy should not be viewed as solely the concern of empire, however. Developments in tourism in the nineteenth century show similar preoccupations with the pitfalls of language heteronomy. In a nineteenth-century French advertisement for the *Grand Hôtel Royal* in Cairo, one of the services offered by the hotel, clearly indicated in bold type, is "Interprète parlant plusieurs langues" (Behdad 1994:51). The *drogman* is a familiar figure in Orientalist literature, but the presence of the guide/interpreter was not always welcome. Karl Baedecker, indeed, saw the advent of the guidebook as a step on the road to freedom from interpreting. In his preface to the eighth edition of the guide to Germany (1858), Baedecker speaks of releasing the traveler from the "unpleasant, and often wholly invisible, tutelage of hired servants and guides (and in part from the aid of coachmen and hotelkeepers), to assist him in standing on his *own* feet, to render him *independent*, and to place him in a position from which he may receive his own impressions with clear eyes and lively heart" (Mendelson 1985:387–88, emphasis in original). In *The Beaten Track: European Tourism, Literature, and the Ways to "Culture"* 1800–1918, James Buzzard devotes a whole section to the genesis of the guidebook, in particular to the pioneering works of Karl Baedecker and John Murray (1993:65–79). There is no mention whatsoever of the question of language, however. The omission is all the more striking in that one of the main reasons for hiring the guides that are the object of Baedecker's scorn was their knowledge not only of local history but also of the local language. The guidebook *translated* the foreign culture into the mother tongue of the traveler. The traveler no longer had to rely on the oral translation of the guide/interpreter because the guidebook provided the written translation. The Murray and Baedecker guides thus facilitated the transition from heteronomous dependency on the oral interpreter to an autonomous mode of traveling grounded in literacy.

Jemmy Button's shift in allegiance has many other historical parallels, and what they point to is that ethics in interpreting cannot be considered in a universal, ahistorical fashion, isolated from hierarchical relationships of power (Delisle 1987; del Castillo 1926). When Margareta Bowen, David Bowen, Francine Kaufman, and Ingrid Kurz claim in their chapter on interpreting in *Translators through History* that interpreting has a "history of problems," they attribute this history to intimate contact between people who often have strong personalities. The "problems" are defined as "issues of loyalty (interpreters jumping ship or changing sides), along with breaches of etiquette or even ethics" (Bowen et al. 1995:273). To describe these issues as "problems" seems strangely naive in view of the evidence adduced in the chapter, which points to the strongly political nature of many interpreting transactions. The understatement completely occludes questions of ideology and power. In *The Imaginary Canadian*, Anthony Wilden has described the phenomenon of "symmetrization," which he defines as "the ideological and unreal 'flattening out' of a hierarchical relationship as it exists" (1980:77). The boss's door is always open, but the boss remains the boss, and the putative equality is a consoling fiction. The role of interpreters throughout history has been crucially determined by the prevailing hierarchical constitution of power and the position of interpreters in it. In this respect, if you or your people are seriously disadvantaged by the hierarchy, the most ethical position can be to be utterly "unfaithful" in interpreting in the name of another fidelity, a fidelity of resistance. This is not a "problem," but a strategy for survival. Adopting a strategy of "symmetrization" in interpreting history, therefore, can lead to strongly decontextualized readings of historical encounters and inappropriate judgments of motives and practices.

Hermeneutic Subjects

In her discussion of Mungo Park's *Travels in the Interior of Africa* (1860), Mary Louise Pratt describes "arrival scenes" as "particularly potent sites for framing relations of contact and setting the terms of its representation" (1992:78–80). Park's desire for communication with native Africans is consistently frustrated, and he becomes mainly an object of curious scrutiny for the indigenous peoples in these arrival scenes. Pratt at no point mentions language, though it would appear obvious that at first, in the absence of a common language, the Europeans and Africans could do little else but stare at each other. Moreover, Pratt misses the link between the dependence on the visual apprehension of reality and the collapse of language-based systems of communication. In the absence of language, the arrival scene is a tableau, a spectacle where the native Other becomes an object of consumption. It is in this context that the full significance of the interpreting transaction must be understood.

From Descartes in his *Discours de la méthode* (1637) and F. Max Müller in *Lectures on the Science of Language* (1861), to Claude Hagège in *L'Homme de paroles* (1985) and Noam Chomsky in his discussions of discontinuity theory, writers have seen language as defining *homo sapiens*. If language differentiates the animal from the human, then denying the utterances of others the status of language-that-can-be-translated is to reduce them to the condition of animals. Charles Darwin made the following observation about the language of the Fuegians: "The language of these people, according to our notions, scarcely deserves to be called articulate. Captain Cook has compared it to a man clearing his throat, but certainly no European ever cleared his throat with so many hoarse, guttural, and clicking sounds" (1986:17). Edward Tylor, in *Primitive Culture: Researches into the Development of Mythology, Philosophy, Religion, Language, Art and Custom* (1920), noted that the hunting down and killing of indigenous peoples of Tasmania was possible because colonists heard the languages of the aboriginal peoples as grunts and squeals. Deprived of language and therefore of culture, the Tasmanians were dehumanized and treated as prey for imperial hunters.

If a central problem of nineteenth-century anthropology is whether human beings are the positivistic objects of a natural science or the human subjects of a hermeneutic inquiry, then it is arguable that the presence of the interpreter, the emergence of language mediation, is a crucial moment in the shift from the positivistic object to the human subject. The surgeon Wilson on the HMS *Beagle* uses the classic language of positivist objectification to describe the Fuegians: "The Fuegian, like a Cetaceous animal which circulates red blood in a cold medium, has in his covering an admirable non-conductor of heat" (Beer 1996:60). Alongside this observation, however, is a rudimentary vocabulary of Fuegian languages. This juxtaposition is significant because it points to the borderline of translation, the paradigm shift that results from access to language through interpretation. One could argue that the moment of translation marks a shift from an encounter scene as a site of consumption to a site of interaction. Through the newfound ability to communicate via translation, the traveler is no longer an observer but part of what is being observed.

The shift from nonhuman to human status that is implicit in accession to language and, by association, to culture does not mean, of course, that there are no other means of exclusion. The other language can be described as inferior; its speakers as lazy, malevolent, and treacherous. Nonetheless, once understanding is admitted through the possibility of translation, then the way of dealing with or describing the Other must be fundamentally reorganized, if only because liberal elements in the imperial centers will accord full, hermeneutic status to the subjectivity of the colonial Other on the basis of the evidence of translated language. It is precisely because Montaigne wants to challenge the pseudo-objectivity of Eurocentrism that he is intensely frustrated when the interpreting proves inadequate, as he relates in his famous essay on "Des Cannibales": "Je parlay à l'un d'eux fort long temps; mais j'avois un truchement qui me suyvoit si mal, et qui estoit si empesché à recevoir mes imaginations par sa bestise, que je n'en pues tirer guiere de plaisir" (Montaigne 1988: 214; "I talked to one of them for some time; but I had an interpreter who followed my meaning so badly, and was so hindered by stupidity from grasping my ideas, that I could hardly get any satisfaction from him," Montaigne 1978:119).

There are many other substantive areas that might be explored in a material/cultural theory of interpretation. One obvious area is interpreting and gender, which has had many ramifications from the colonial period to the present. Here are questions that might be legitimately explored by philosophy, history, and psychoanalysis, where control of the speaking subject often implies control of the body. The control is rendered problematic, however, by the difficulty in controlling/monitoring the translation flow. It was a practice, for example, for certain Crown informers in the period of the Tudor conquest of Ireland to take Irish-speaking wives so as to enhance the intelligence-gathering activities of these Crown agents. The problem was that the women on occasion would change sides and act as double agents, supplying the Gaelic Irish with valuable information on troop movements (Jackson 1973:21–28). Hence, there was the repeated conflation of notions of personal fidelity and politicolinguistic fidelity. Fidelity to colonizer becomes infidelity to the colonized, and the colonizer's fidelity, of course, is often purely instrumental. Cortés demands political, emotional, and linguistic fidelity from Doña Marina. She must serve the Spanish cause, remain his lover, and give him a true account of what the natives are saying. Cortés's own fidelity is purely strategic, however, and he abandons Doña Marina on his return to Spain in order to marry a woman of appropriate social rank.

Although the gender status of droids is uncertain, their obedience is usually unquestioned. C-3P0 is a dutiful droid until its transfiguration at the end of *The Return of the Jedi*, the third film in the original *Star Wars* trilogy. The droid is deified by the Ewoks on account of its ability to speak their language. C-3P0 is a protocol droid, responsible for etiquette and interpreting, and masters a modest six million forms of communication. The elevation to deity embarrasses C-3P0 on two counts. First, the droid has to inform Hans Solo that Solo is the main course for that evening's banquet, and, second, it confesses that impersonating a deity is against its programming. C-3P0, the rebel's interpreter, offers a heroic if humorous figure for interpretation theory, in the droid's struggle against empire and its skepticism regarding divine omnipotence. But interpreting does not have to be programmed for theoretical powerlessness. The antiquity of interpreting, the continued importance of orality as a feature of everyday life in a multilingual world, the crucial importance of the interpreting transaction in countless situations where questions of power and control are to the fore, show that there is a more urgent need than ever to bring a new materialist perspective to bear on interpretation studies to illuminate our translation past, present, and future.

Notes

1. The author gratefully acknowledges the assistance of Barbara Godard and Mona Baker in identifying sources for some of the material that has been used in the preparation of this essay. The conference "Translation and Power" was organized by the University of Warwick, England, 12–14 July 1997.

2. The First Conference on Interpreting in Legal, Health and Social Service Settings was held in Geneva Park, Canada, 1–4 June 1995. The international newsletter for community interpreters is *The Critical Link / Un Maillon essential.*

ROSEMARY ARROJO

Writing, Interpreting, and the Power Struggle for the Control of Meaning: Scenes from Kafka, Borges, and Kosztolányi

From the perspective of psychoanalytical thought, the writing of fiction and the desire to master reality are inextricably intertwined.[1] Freud claims that as the creative writer "creates a world of fantasy which he takes very seriously—that is, which he invests with large amounts of emotion," his primary goal is "to rearrange the things of his world in a new way which pleases him" (1983:25). If "imaginative writers" are, thus, comparable to "dreamers in broad daylight," and if their "creations" are equated with "daydreams" over which they feel they can have the ultimate control, what such writers finally seek is a feeling of "invulnerability," which reveals "His Majesty the Ego, the hero alike of every daydream and of every story" (25–26). In his philosophy Nietzsche explores the connection between creation and power more fully, far beyond the limits of fiction writing, particularly through his concept of the "will to power," generally described as "the creative and procreative impulse of life." This is perfectly compatible with the philosopher's view of language as being fundamentally rhetorical and, therefore, incapable of revealing essences or intrinsic meanings (see, for example, Schrift 1990:192).[2]

If truths and meanings are not to be discovered or found but, rather, constructed (and, consequently, also deconstructed), any claim to knowledge can be directly associated with what Nietzsche has called "the pathos of truth," or that which "strives for fixity, for static conceptual points of reference around which to organize a systematic body of beliefs," and which, as something that could be static and fixed, would be "capable of being possessed" (Shrift 1990:128). To the extent that they rely on a belief in the possibility of discovering and taking possession of conceptions that would be directly related to essentially indisputable truths, all disciplines and institutions—like philosophy and religion—are the necessary outcome of "a longing for property" (Nietzsche 1979:60). According to Nietzsche, if one achieves any sense of security as a consequence of the illusory possession of temporary truths, it is only at the expense of denying one's creative power of inventing and building concepts: "Only by forgetting [the] primitive world of metaphor, only by the congelation and coagulation of an original mass of similes and precepts pouring forth as a fiery liquid out of the primal faculty of human fancy, only by the invincible faith, that *this* sun, *this* window, *this* table is a truth in itself: in short, only by the fact that man forgets himself as subject, and what is more as an artistically creating subject: only by all this does he live with some repose, safety and consequence" (1973:184).

Because the will to power, masked as the will to truth, is also a will to construct, "one may . . . well admire man, who succeeds in piling up an infinitely complex dome of ideas on a movable foundation, and, as it were, on running water, as a powerful genius of architecture" (Nietzsche 1973:182). Moreover, architecture is "a kind of rhetoric of power" just as "pride, victory over weight and gravity, the will to power, seek to render themselves visible in a building" (Nietzsche 1968:11); thus, the writing of philosophy, science, or fiction could be basically related to the same needs and the same fundamental goals. Nietzsche himself used architectural metaphors (such as the beehive, the Tower of Babel, the medieval fortress, the Egyptian pyramid, the Roman columbarium, the spider's web, the dungeon, and the stronghold, among others) to depict conceptual systems found both in ordinary language and in science as types of construction. Thus, he denounces both the fragility and the power struggles at stake behind the various models of knowledge that human beings have elaborated under the name of truth or science. In her analysis of Nietzsche's metaphor of the beehive, developed in his well-known "On Truth and Falsity in Their Ultramoral Sense" (1973), Sarah Kofman remarks that "the 'beauty' of the edifice is not disinterested but is symptomatic of the initial neediness, the motor for the whole construction, at the same time as it masks it" (1993:62). In such a context, Kofman continues, "just as the bee constructs cells in order to survive and fills them with the honey which it has been to get outside [sic], so science constructs an empty formal architecture and makes the whole world fit inside" (62).

The far-reaching consequences of this kind of reasoning for a general reflection on language and the subject have been often discussed, particularly in the last two decades, in connection with postmodern scholars' notions of textuality, which owe a direct debt to Nietzsche's deconstructive philosophy.[3] In fact, one may say that the import of Nietzsche's thought for contemporary language theories is basically related to his textualization of all there is, which implies a radical redefinition of our relationships with reality, with each other, and even with ourselves, to the point where nothing or nobody could claim to be outside the domain of interpretation. The transformation of reality or even the subject into texts, however, does not by any means entail the possibility of establishing fixed objects. Rather, it implies that, precisely as objects, they are the inevitable result of a comprehensive, incessant process of rewriting that is forever reconstituting them in difference and in change. From such a perspective Nietzsche's notions of textuality point to the conclusion that there is no text in itself apart from the activity of interpretation. Because we cannot separate the text from its reading, the latter is inextricably related to the will to power and, thus, is a way of taking over rather than protecting or merely reproducing someone else's meaning. In Nietzsche's own words: "all subduing and becoming master involves a fresh interpretation, an adaptation through which any previous 'meaning' and 'purpose' are necessarily obscured or even obliterated. . . . The entire history of a 'thing,' an organ, a custom can in this way be a continuous sign-chain of ever new interpretations and adaptations. . . ." (1969:12).

Kafka's Tormented Animal and the Architecture of the Labyrinth as Text

Of all the architectural metaphors employed by Nietzsche, I am particularly interested in the one that relates the labyrinth to textuality and interpretation, and that has been considered both as "a basic Nietzschean image for the structure of the text" and as "an allegory of his conception of textual interpretation" (Schrift 1990:196). It is certainly effective in suggesting the perpetual proliferation of meaning that surrounds and constitutes us in the world as text, in the midst of which we feel utterly lost unless we find an adequate interpretive thread to give us the illusion of knowing which direction to take and how to (temporarily) master reality. To explore such an image further, particularly in connection with the relationships that are usually established behind the scenes where writing and interpreting seem to be conceived by the same will to power, I propose to examine some of its main implications through a reading of a haunting text by Franz Kafka, "The Burrow." Originally entitled "Der Bau" ("The Construction") this story is read here as a poignant illustration of Nietzsche's notions of the text and the world as labyrinth.[4] Such a reading is particularly interested in exploring some relationships between the Nietzschean conception of creation and the creator's desire to build an artifact that could be protected from difference and otherness as represented, for instance, by the potentially shattering interference of an intruder.

As the story opens, we learn from its narrator/builder, presumably an animal that lives underground, that he has "completed the construction of [his] burrow and it seems to be successful" (1971:325). What follows, however, is a detailed, tormented account of the builder's own recurring doubts regarding the actual completion of his work and his painful obsession to create a totally flawless structure, an object that could be absolutely protected from invasion and deconstruction. The basic paradox within which Kafka's narrator finds himself is thus presented from the outset: the allegedly finished construction that should shelter and protect its architect is also a hole, a burrow. Thus, instead of a definite solution, it brings an indecipherable problem; instead of illumination, it brings darkness; instead of security, fear and anxiety. In brief, as Henry Sussman notes, "the construction is already a deconstruction to the same extent that it has been constructed" (1979:149).

The burrow, like a text, has "passages" that have to be constantly reviewed because of the "manifold possibilities" of their uncontrollable "ramifications" (Kafka 1971:329): "I begin with the second passage and let it take me back again to the Castle Keep, and now of course, I have to begin at the second passage once more" (342). Moreover, this textualized burrow is the "outcome rather of intense intellectual than of physical labor" (1971:327). Even the constructor's most important physical effort within the labyrinth, that is, the burrowing motion that constitutes his basic constructing strategy, is a form of compulsive "head work," because it is with his forehead, his "only tool," that the animal pounds the loose, sandy soil "thousands and thousands of times, for whole days and nights," feeling glad "when the blood comes" for that is "a proof that the walls [are] beginning to harden" (328). Thus, figuratively speaking, the construction of the text/labyrinth is the result of painful, hard "head work" aimed at fulfilling its architect's "dream of a completely perfect burrow" (339).

Also like a text, the supposedly finished burrow adamantly resists completion as its builder does not seem to be able to devise a defensive strategy that would render it invulnerable to any other burrowing creature. Such a strategy would require not only the design of a perfectly disguised entrance but also the possibility of finding "a universal principle or an infallible method of descent" (336). Distressed at his own observations, which are "extremely heterogeneous, and both good and bad" (336), however, Kafka's architect is painfully aware of the fact that the definite mastery of his burrow is directly dependent on the definite establishment of his own conclusions: "now I am on fire to discover whether my conclusion is valid. And with good reason, for as long as that is not established I cannot feel safe, even if it were merely a matter of discovering where a grain of sand that had fallen from one of the walls had rolled to" (344).

If the construction of the unconditionally perfect burrow is intimately related to the discovery of definite truths and forms, it also involves the pursuit of absolute silence because it is only in eternal stillness that the constructor could be completely assured of the invulnerability of his construction and, consequently, of his total control over it: "the most beautiful thing about my burrow is the stillness. . . . For hours I can stroll through my passages and hear nothing except the rustling of some little creature, which I immediately reduce to silence between my jaws, or the pattering of soil, which draws my attention to the need for repair" (327). In the construction as text, the plenitude of stillness would guarantee not only the constructor's unequivocal control over his passages but also his ultimate mastery over diachrony and chance. As a consequence the noise that betrays the potentially uncontrollable dissemination of meaning within the burrow, the sign of deconstructive danger, would also be forever kept at bay.

Because the dream of a blissful plenitude occurs when the idea of totality and absolute mastery—including total possession of truth, total control over the proliferation of meaning, and total neutralization of dif-ference—seems conceivable within the labyrinth, it is expected that the constructing animal worries most of all about "the defect of the opening" that marks the end of his "domestic protection" (333). The opening is "that point in the dark moss" in which he is specially vulnerable and which prevents him from living "in peace, warm, well nourished, master, sole master of all [his] manifold passages and rooms" (333). But who is the intruder? Who might threaten the completion and the stillness of the labyrinth? First, as its architect imagines, the enemy, probably "a filthy scoundrel who wishes to be housed where he has not built" (337), would obviously come from outside, through "that point in the dark moss" that makes the burrow potentially exposed. As the constructor himself rec-ognizes, what makes his textual labyrinth particularly vulnerable and, thus, what makes him enraged at the prospect of having to fight any possible invader, is precisely his relentless determination to be the sole master of his creation: "simply by virtue of being owner of this great vulnerable edifice I am obviously defenseless against any serious attack" (355). Yet, in his tireless self-analysis, the burrowing creature is acutely aware that he and the burrow have somehow become one—"the joy of possessing it has spoiled me, the vulnerability of the burrow has made me vulnerable; any wound to it hurts me as if I myself were hit" (337)—and that he cannot clearly separate himself from the deconstructive Other.

As the borders between subject and object are seriously shaken, the architect finds it impossible to distinguish clearly the legitimate owner from the unlawful intruder, or the constructor from the deconstructor; he even considers the possibility that his worst enemy may not really be outside: "outside there nobody troubles about my burrow, everybody has its own affairs" (352). But in passages that betray a truly Kafkaesque wisdom, this awareness is often conveniently forgotten: "the danger is by no means a fanciful one, but very real. It need not be any particular enemy that is provoked to pursue me; it may very well be some chance innocent little beast which follows me out of curiosity, and thus, without knowing it, becomes the leader of all the world against me" (337). And, as the story develops, we are made to witness the builder's obsessive attempts to distinguish himself from the intruding Other whom he imagines as a faithful projection of himself, endowed, for instance, with a "furious lust for work" solely aimed at the definite conquest of the labyrinth (354).

As this "human, all too human" animal cannot succeed in separating construction from deconstruction, even within the limits of his own text whose passages he cannot help changing with every revision and with each round, he seems to be driven ultimately by a will to power that is also an anxious attempt to defer the consciousness of mortality.[5] The definite mastery over the construction that would bring its architect an absolute protection against difference, establishing a clear-cut opposition between inside and outside, proprietor and intruder, writing and interpreting, would also grant him the full control over that which could be an irrefutable origin or essence: the burrow's "Castle Keep," "the inmost chamber of [the animal's] house," the ultimate protection and source of complete satisfaction, where he "sleep[s] the sweet sleep of tranquility, of satisfied desire" (326–27). Though creation is inevitably associated with the animal's relentless will to power aiming at the exclusive possession of truth, the achievement of absolute completion and stillness seems to be conceivable only in eternal sleep, as the constructing being himself, when awake and alive, cannot help but undo and redo his own work.

If the construction of a text/labyrinth is inevitably related to revision and reinterpretation, forever resisting any possibility of completion or perfect closure, we find the creating animal painfully divided between his human condition, which binds him to the provisional and the finite, and his desire to be divine, that is, to be the totalitarian, sole master of truth and fate. As a dazzling illustration of such a division, Kafka's character reflects the pathos of every author and of every interpreter, inevitably torn between the desire to control and to forever imprison meaning, and the human condition, which subjects both writers and interpreters to an endless exercise of meaning production.

A Reader/Detective Meets a Deadly Author Figure in a Borgesian Labyrinth

While Kafka's burrowing animal sheds some light on the impasse of a creator battling against his own humanity, in a story titled "La muerte y la brújula" ("Death and the Compass") Jorge Luis Borges examines certain aspects of the conflict and the competition that Kafka's narrator fears so intensely.[6] In Borges's plot we witness the complex encounter between a cultivated reader and a fierce author figure and labyrinth maker, both relentlessly engaged in a power struggle that entails the virtual elimination of one of them. The reader in question is the detective Erik Lönnrot who, together with his colleague Treviranus, is investigating three alleged murders apparently committed by the same person. Unlike Treviranus, however, Lönnrot is not interested in a plausible, simple solution to this criminal enigma. Instead, he proposes to find an answer in what he takes to be the murderer's written messages and in their connection with the books found in the first victim's hotel room. As an "objective," diligent reader/detective, Lönnrot is driven by the desire not simply to decipher the mind and the writings of the author/assassin but also to anticipate his moves and, thus, finally to outwit and arrest him. The cold, crafty gunman Red Scharlach, on the other hand, represents the powerful author figure who, after learning of the first crime and of Lönnrot's investigations, decides "to weave" a deadly, "firm labyrinth" around the detective who once arrested his brother (1956:160). He plans to construct his textual maze by plotting a second murder and by staging a third one in such a way as to make Lönnrot believe that the three supposed killings are the work of the same man and also are connected with the written message found on a sheet of paper in the first victim's typewriter: "the first letter of the Name has been spelled out" (150).

The text/labyrinth designed by Red Scharlach, whose first name can be read both as an English word and as the Spanish noun *red*, 'net', is first and foremost a trap aimed at snaring and killing Lönnrot. To the extent that the detective's obsessive reading enterprise is also aimed at entrapping the one he imagines to be the author of the crimes, it seems that the goals and the will to power that trigger both Scharlach's and Lönnrot's textual enterprises are basically the same. The assassin and the detective, the author and the reader, share similar motivations and goals as they share the same name: *Red* and Lönn*rot*. Furthermore, to the extent that Scharlach's name seems to echo Scheherazade's, particularly in its Spanish version, 'Schaharazad', we can also relate Borges's peculiar author figure to the exemplary narrator of *The Arabian Nights*. Just as Scheherazade's life is saved by her ability to create a textual labyrinth in which she entraps the sultan who is about to kill her, transforming her potential assassin into a loving husband, Scharlach's fate is certainly reversed by his authorial strength as he manages to lure his intruding reader and worst enemy into a deadly, well-designed maze. Therefore, Scharlach's ability to weave the strong net of his textual trap not only misguides and imprisons the reader Lönnrot but also turns him, usually the relentless pursuer of Scharlach and his fellow gunmen, into the pursued, defenseless victim.

In Borges's story the labyrinth, as the construction of a text that is both a protection and a trap, finds an exemplary image in Triste-le-Roy, the abandoned villa where Scharlach finally catches Lönnrot. Significantly, the villa's architecture mirrors Scharlach's maze, for it abounds "in useless symmetries and in eccentric repetitions" (157). Among such architectural devices and ornaments, "a two-faced Hermes" that "project[s] a monstrous shadow" reminds us of Scharlach and his double Lönnrot (157–58), both appropriately related to the Greek god whose name in fact means "interpreter" and is known for his rhetorical abilities and for his theft from his fellow gods of precisely the objects that somehow identify them: Apollo's bow and quiver, Venus's girdle, Neptune's trident, Vulcan's tools, and Mars's sword.

Lönnrot's careful exploration of Triste-le-Roy's architecture may also be read as a reflection of his relentless efforts to interpret Scharlach's misguiding clues. Just as he tries to undo that which he sees as the assassin's text, Lönnrot is convinced that he knows the preferences of Triste-le-Roy's architect and sets out to master his labyrinth: "Lönnrot explored the house. Through halls and galleries he reached similar courtyards and repeatedly came back to the same courtyard. He climbed dusty flights of stairs and found circular antechambers; he was infinitely multiplied in opposing mirrors; he exhausted himself in opening or partially opening windows which revealed, outside, the same desolate garden from different heights and different angles" (158). The most representative of the repeated motifs that are found in both the assassin's alleged writings and Triste-le-Roy's design is the recurrent play on the numbers three and four, also mirrored in the references to rectangular and quadrangular shapes, pointing to the solution of the puzzle: the deciphering of the Tetragrammaton, or the four-letter name of God, spelled out by the murders staged by Scharlach.

In the end, as the defeated Lönnrot is about to be shot dead inside Scharlach's retreat, his request that the next time he is trapped and killed it should be done in a "straight-line labyrinth" may also suggest that the kind of conflict the two represent is bound to be infinitely repeated in the vain search for that which could end all interpretation and all plotting: the final deciphering and mastery of nothing less than the name of God. From this viewpoint both Scharlach and Lönnrot share with Kafka's burrowing animal the same futile, human desire to achieve divine mastery over meaning, which is ultimately also the quest to control life and death. The remarkable force of this desire seems to allow Lönnrot to patiently accept his impending assassination and even reason with Scharlach about the way he would like to be killed in a future life. Paradoxically, the possibility of having an authorial participation in the planning of his next death is more attractive to Lönnrot than actually fighting for his life. Moreover, if the labyrinth, which for Scharlach mirrors the world from which "it is impossible to escape" (159), could also be a straight line, and thus could also mirror any kind of relationship between subject and object (such as the relationship between any reader's gaze and the text being read), it may be argued that all acts of interpretation ultimately take place inside a labyrinth. That is, they are always already subject to the inevitability of interpretation and thus to the same struggle for the control over meaning that brings Lönnrot and Scharlach to confront each other in Triste-le-Roy.

Finally, as Lönnrot tries to decipher Scharlach's text and as he enters the labyrinth in an attempt to find his author's truth or, rather, the confirmation of his own truth regarding his author's writing, he also provides us with a reflection of ourselves, professional readers of literature. As such we cannot help but impose our own meanings on texts and also on Borges's carefully designed structure in his detective story. Like Lönnrot and unlike Treviranus, we would not settle for a simple, "uninteresting" interpretation and are thus also caught by the narrator's misleading clues as we approach his textual maze. But if we are Lönnrot, Red Scharlach must be Borges, the true "Sad King" and maker of labyrinths, who tries to dictate what must be true inside his construction and who even makes a subtle appearance in his text in order to make it clear whose story "Death and the Compass" really is. As his narrator informs us of Lönnrot's trip to Triste-le-Roy, we learn, for example, about the "brook of muddy waters" that runs in the city of "*my* story" (156, my emphasis).

As the provisional designer and master of his plot, Borges turns Scharlach/Schaharazad into the eternal winner of the ghastly conflict that has brought a skillful author face-to-face with a cultivated reader in a plot in which the latter is eternally doomed to be entrapped and eliminated by the former's powerful textual strategies. Yet, even if Borges expresses the strength of his authorial desire as he sides with Scharlach and tries to establish clear-cut limits between writing and reading, Borges cannot protect his story from our reading, which, precisely because it is a reading, necessarily finds an opening in his text and, thus, necessarily interferes with it, taking our own authorial stance as we weave our own hypotheses and attempt to find the thread that will show the way out of the labyrinth.

The Translator's Incurable Compulsion to Steal: Kosztolányi's Gallus

If, as Nietzsche argues, any attempt at mastering a text, or the world as text, "involves a fresh interpretation, an adaptation through which any previous 'meaning' and 'purpose' are necessarily obscured or even obliterated" (1969:12), the implicit relationship that is usually established between authors and interpreters is not exactly inspired by cooperation or collaboration, as common sense and the essentialist tradition would have it but, rather, is constituted by an underlying competition, by a struggle for the power to determine that which will be (provisionally) accepted as true and definite within a certain context and under certain circumstances. As Kafka's and Borges's stories have shown us, in this textualized, human world, where immortal essences and absolute certainties are not to be found, the indisputable control over a text, its full completion, and the definite establishment of its limits cannot be simplistically determined nor merely related to its author once and for all. If one cannot clearly and forever separate the author from the interpreter, the text from its reading, or even one text from another, and if the will to power as authorial desire is that which moves both writers and readers in their attempts at constructing textual mazes that could protect their meanings and, thus, also imprison and neutralize any potential intruder, is it ever possible for interpreters to be faithful to the authors or to the texts they visit?

Obviously, it is not by chance that this has always been the central issue and the main concern for all those interested in the mechanisms of translation, an activity that provides a paradigmatic scenario for the underlying struggle for the control over meaning that constitutes both writing and interpretation as it involves the actual production of another text: the writing of the translator's reading of someone else's text in another language, time, and cultural environment. As it necessarily constitutes material evidence of the translator's passage through the original and as it offers documented proof of the differences brought about by such a passage, any translation is bound to be an exemplary site for the competitive nature of textual activity. In a tradition that generally views originals as the closed, fixed receptacle of their authors' intentional meanings, the struggle for the power to determine the "truth" of a text is obviously decided in favor of those who are considered as the "rightful" owners of their texts' meanings and who supposedly deserve unconditional respect from anyone who dares to enter their textual "property." In such a tradition, translators are not only denied the rights and privileges of authorship but also must endure a reputation for treachery and ineptitude while being urged to be as invisible and as humble as possible.

In a brief venture into Dezso Kosztolányi's story "The Kleptomaniac Translator," a revealing commentary on the alleged inadequacies of translation, I problematize the widespread contempt for the translator's task that tradition implicitly and explicitly opposes to the usually uncritical, prevailing acceptance of authorial power as the exclusive prerogative of those who write originals.[7] If the author and interpreter cannot enjoy a peaceful encounter inside the labyrinth as text, and if tradition has determined that the author is the only legitimate producer of meaning to be allowed in this special retreat, it is not at all surprising that translators have been traditionally accused of chronically improper behavior.

In Kosztolányi's story, we learn from the narrator, a respected writer, that Gallus, an old acquaintance of his, was a promising, well-educated young man of remarkable qualities and language skills who had even taught English to the Prince of Wales himself. All of his accomplishments, however, were unforgivably tarnished by a "criminal addiction," a compulsion to steal, which defied all his serious efforts to change. Because the only thing Gallus knew how to do was to write and because he could not do so under his own name, the narrator introduces Gallus to a compassionate editor who needs someone to translate an English detective novel entitled *The Mysterious Castle of Earl Vitsislav*, described as the kind of trashy literature respectable writers would not want to read or deal with. At most they would translate it, but with gloves on. The hungry, unemployed translator promptly accepts the task and devotes himself to the job so completely that long before the deadline he is able to deliver his neatly typed manuscript, which is, nonetheless, rejected by the editor.

As the narrator decides to investigate the case and reads Gallus's translation, he is filled with admiration for the translator's "precise and scrupulously meticulous work," which is a much worthier text than the original. As the editor urges the narrator to actually compare Gallus's manuscript with the original, however, the enigma is clarified. Even though there are no mistakes and the translation is "fluent, artistic and, at times, poetic" (1996:9), it becomes clear that the translator has not controlled himself and has simply stolen property from the author's settings and characters. Thus, for example, while in the original a female character is wearing precious jewelry, in the Hungarian version she is not wearing any. A similar fate is reserved for castles, rugs, safes, watches, suitcases, cash, silverware, and even small objects of little value such as toothpicks and handkerchiefs.

In his comments on Gallus's "incurable disease," the narrator seems to synthesize some of the most widespread notions about translation ingrained in essentialist conceptions of language and the subject. From the perspective of those who share a general belief in the possibility of stable meanings safely stored in texts, which should be properly related to their authors' conscious intentions, originals and translations, authors and translators do belong in radically different categories. Within such a context, translators, like Gallus, are viewed as mere copyists or marginal hack writers who, in spite of their talents and skills, are usually expected to do the dirty writing jobs that respectable writers would not do. If, as we learn, such writers would only consider doing translations "with gloves on," without actually touching the texts in question, it is also clear that the conception of translation ethics implicitly accepted by the narrator repeats the traditional one as it entertains the possibility of translating without actually interpreting or rewriting the so-called original. Therefore, what this tradition must repress at all costs is precisely the translator's authorial will to power that, in Kosztolányi's plot, is symptomatically rendered as a form of criminal behavior or, euphemistically, as an "incurable disease."

In Gallus's story the marginality and the oblivion to which the translator is condemned are explicitly presented as a form of exemplary punishment not only for his daring attempt to compete with his mediocre author and for having actually turned the latter's second-rate original into an artistic piece but also, most of all, for having indulged in his addictive authorial pleasure against which he was not able to fight. As his translation betrays a "criminal" appropriation that threatens the "almost unquestionable sacredness of private property" (7), the transformation that the translator's interference brings to the author's "property" is perceived as a form of loss or outrageous impoverishment, even when it is also recognized to be enriching. In the exploration of this conflict between the author's desire to be the exclusive master of textuality and the interpreter's authorial will to power, Kosztolányi's characters and plot remind me of those of Borges and Kafka, and even seem to complement them. Hence, while Kafka's burrowing animal illustrates the creator's obsession to devise a perfectly invulnerable textual labyrinth, and while Borges's Scharlach and Lönnrot actually rehearse the main scenes of the violent struggle for the control over meaning that both separates and brings together authors and interpreters, in "The Kleptomaniac Translator" some of the consequences of such a pervasive conflict are actually made explicit, particularly by the narrator's speculation on the reasons why Gallus had such a peculiar need to take possession of someone else's property.

As the narrator takes stock of all the items "illegally and indecently" taken away by the translator, in an attempt to solve "the true enigma of this detective novel," he concedes that whatever Gallus did steal "existed only on paper, in the realm of [the author's] imagination" (10). Yet, in spite of his interest, the narrator decides not to further understand the reasons for such theft on the grounds that such an investigation would go too far, simply concluding that the translator, as "a slave to his criminal addiction," was not "man enough" and, consequently, "did not deserve the support of honest people" (10). Who or what, one may ask, is the narrator trying to protect in his refusal to further investigate Gallus's "unforgivable" crime? As I play the detective in this textual puzzle, I propose to locate the basis of a plausible answer in another well-known text by Borges, "Las versiones homéricas" ("Versions of Homer"), according to which the problems posed by any translation do shed some unflattering light on the "modest mystery" that surrounds original writing and literature in particular (1980:181).

As it necessarily addresses a "visible text" and not an "invaluable labyrinth of past projects," any translation is bound to deconstruct and decanonize originals, revealing perhaps that "the modest mystery" that surrounds such writing is nothing but "the fear of confessing mental processes which are dangerously ordinary" (181). Arguably, what Gallus's impeccable work stole from "the realm of [the author's] imagination" and could not be fully learned by Kosztolányi's narrator (who is definitely siding with the original and with its author, no matter how inadequate he finds them to be) is not simply the"mystery" of originality, or the widespread notion that originals are inherently superior to their translations, but, first and foremost, the illusion that authorship could in fact grant writers an exclusive mastery over their texts. Thus, Gallus's translation also shows that instead of constituting a form of protection of the original and its author's illusive mastery over meaning, the translator's task may actually represent a threatening interference, particularly when it is recognized to be a flagrant improvement. To the extent that Gallus refuses to be strictly faithful to his mediocre author and ends up exercising his authorial desire (when he is expected instead to be humble and invisible), he, too, seems to be following Hermes, the Greek god, the "interpreter," also known for his rhetorical talents and for having stolen from his fellow gods exactly those objects that give them their very identity.[8] It is from this kind of appropriation that the story's narrator seems to be defending not merely originals and their authors but, ultimately, also his own writing and, we may infer, Kosztolányi's as well.

In revealing the conflict that takes place between original writing and translation, the Hungarian story is efficient in exploring some of the most important implications and consequences of the translator's interfering power. Though Gallus is not by any means innocent and is in fact irrevocably "guilty" of being visible and human, Kosztolányi's narrator, as the typical writer who associates original texts with the "indisputable sacredness of private property," reflects the generally defensive reaction that essentialism displays toward translation, counting on the strategy of blind fidelity as a form of antidote against difference and intervention. As in the stories of Kafka and Borges, Kosztolányi is eloquent in expressing the violence associated with the will to power as the will to control meaning that seems to trigger both writing and interpreting. Whereas Kafka's architect and Borges's Scharlach display explicitly murderous behavior toward their competitors, the kind of "crime" we find in "The Kleptomaniac Translator" is more easily related to the actual world of writers, readers, and translators, as it epitomizes, for instance, the widespread disregard for translation as both a theoretical issue and a legitimate profession. When the narrator gives up investigating the translator's thefts and chooses to abandon Gallus to marginality, he mirrors the kind of treatment translation and translators usually receive both from the general public and from the great majority of academic studies that still revolve around the possibility of establishing some kind of objective control over the translator's visibility and unwelcome interference. The basically asymmetrical relationship that opposes original writing to translation and author to translator is also reflected in the relationship that involves the "honest, compassionate" editor, as well as the allegedly generous narrator who claims to have tried to be the translator's protector, and Gallus himself who becomes a translator because there is nothing else he could possibly do. Emblematically, just as in tradition, Kosztolányi's story treats the translator not as a professional who knows how to achieve respect but as someone who is only entitled to a marginal form of employment obtained through charity.

Finally, like the labyrinth in which Scharlach and Lönnrot will be forever struggling for the impossible, pre-Babelic power to transform words into definite truths, and like the burrow in which Kafka's animal will be forever searching for the absolute closure of his textual construction, Kosztolányi's story seems to be directly related to that essential longing for property that Nietzsche associates with the primary impulse of life. And if, in the world as text, the search for authorial mastery also drives readers and translators, what one is never able to achieve is precisely the definite stability of meaning or the neutralization of difference that could ultimately free us from our own circumstances and end all conflict and all struggle. It is precisely the acceptance of difference and, thus, the acceptance of the interpreter's authorial interference in the processes of reading and translating that, in the wake of Nietzsche's antiessentialist textual theories, has begun to change the general plot that has traditionally captured authors, readers, and translators. In such a context the translator's visibility has ceased to be regarded as an incurable disease or as an unforgivable crime that should be repressed at any cost and has begun to constitute an actual object of study. In this sense, unlike Kosztolányi's narrator, we do not have to be discouraged by the complexities that are involved in the undeniable power of translation. We are beginning to chart the almost unknown ground in which writing and interpretation overlap as we attempt to review the old clichés that have devalued the impact of the translator's task on the shaping of history and culture.

Notes

1. This essay is part of a research project sponsored by the Brazilian Council for the Development of Science and Technology (CNPq). An earlier version was

presented to the Second International Congress sponsored by EST (European Society for Translation Studies), in Granada, September 1998.

2. Schrift (1990) provides a thorough introduction to the association between Nietzsche's philosophy and contemporary notions of language, text, and interpretation.

3. See, for example, Philippe Lacoue-Labarthe's early observation according to which without Nietzsche, "the 'question' of the text would never have erupted, at least in the precise form that it has taken today" (qtd. in Schrift 1990: 194). Nietzsche's notions of text and textuality are certainly recognized as some of the most important foundations of postmodern thought, having exerted an obvious influence over the work of contemporary thinkers such as Jacques Derrida, Roland Barthes, Michel Foucault, and Paul de Man. See, for example, Koelb 1990.

4. My reading is based on the English version of Kafka's story by Willa and Edwin Muir. Part of this reading relies on unpublished material from my doctoral dissertation (Arrojo 1984).

5. With Kafka's remarkably human animal, we might very well associate one of Nietzsche's aphorisms in "Man Alone with Himself" from *Human, All Too Human*: "No matter how far a man may extend himself with his knowledge, no matter how objectively he may come to view himself, in the end it can yield to him nothing but his own biography" (1986:182). I am not by any means implying that Kafka was familiar with or influenced by Nietzsche's thought. Though the examination of such a possibility certainly transcends the goals of the present essay, I refer the reader interested in the issue to Erich Heller's "Introduction" to Nietzsche's *Human, All Too Human* (1986:xv).

6. All references are my translations from the original Spanish.

7. My reading of Kosztolányi's story is based on the Portuguese version by Ladislao Szabo (1996:7–11). All references are my translations from the Portuguese.

8. For another discussion of translation as a form of theft and of the translator as Hermes, see Arrojo 1995b.

ADRIANA S. PAGANO

Translation as Testimony: On Official Histories and Subversive Pedagogies in Cortázar

The poststructuralist dissolution of generic boundaries that has characterized literary theory and cultural studies in the last three decades points to the redefinition of the concept of *theory* and the emergence and consolidation of critical theory as a postmodern genre (Beebee 1994b:11). Characterized by its interdisciplinary nature and its interrogation of the disciplinary discourses with which it interacts, critical theory redesigns the boundaries between traditionally exclusive categories, including fiction and nonfiction. In this sense the Argentine writer and critic Jorge Luis Borges is indisputably connected to the reshaping of the concept of *theory* and its exchange with fictional discourse. His *Ficciones* (1994a), originally published in 1944 and translated into English as *Ficciones* in 1962, inaugurated the practice of theorizing through a seemingly fictional text that actually fictionalizes the theoretical concerns of the writer. Genre fluidity is the keynote of Borges's epistemological proposal, epitomized by the implicit password to his work: just as all theories possess a fictional character, so too do all fictional works contain a theoretical component.

The incorporation of fiction as a medium of theoretical speculation has broadened the horizons of critical and literary theory. As an alternative source of experiencing and recording history, "fiction," the Argentine critic Ricardo Piglia states, "narrates metaphorically the most profound relationships between cultural identity, memory, and tradition"

(1991:66, my translation). In the field of translation studies, the study of fiction as a source of translation theorization was no doubt one of the main contributions to translation theory in the 1990s, a moment the Brazilian critic Else Ribeiro Pires Vieira calls the "fictional turn" in translation studies, defining it as the move in the discipline that signaled "the incorporation of fictional-theoretical parameters" as a source of theorization on translation and other hermeneutical processes (1995:51).

The fictional turn in translation studies is characterized by a twofold movement concerning the triad fiction-theory-translation. On the one hand there is the fictionalization of translation by theorists and novelists who use translation as a "theme for expressing new configurations of cultural space" (Simon 1992:173). For example, writers such as Hélène Cixous and Nicole Brossard use translation within their fictional work in order to reflect on the movement of displacement that characterizes the "in-betweenness" of woman, the translator, and the migrant. Cixous's *Vivre l'orange* and Brossard's *Le Désert mauve* take the form of narratives made up of "originals" subsequently followed by their "translations," in a kind of counterpoint that leads the reader to move continuously from one language to another, from one text to its translation. The interpretative leap that attempts to bridge the gap between a so-called original and its so-called translation is always detoured to an Other place, an Other text, a movement that for Cixous and Brossard characterizes acts of reading, such as translating, interpreting stories, and, ultimately, writing history. Translation is also a theme in the work of the Maghrebine writer Abdelkebir Khatibi. His novel *Amour bilingue*, for example, elaborates on translation as a love relationship whose structure, unlike conventional conceptions of love and translation relationships, is not dyadic but triadic. Translation gives birth to a *bi-langue* whose meanings "lie in the interstices" between words and their associations (Beebee 1994a:71).

On the other hand there is a movement of critics and theorists who approach fiction as a source of translation theorization. Drawing on novels and short stories that thematize translation and translators, these scholars examine the articulation of translation, memory, and history as captured by the fictional piece. The Brazilian critic Rosemary Arrojo (1993), for instance, plunges into the work of Brazilian writer João Guimarães Rosa and, with the aid of psychoanalysis, explores the instability of meanings and the notion of untranslatability present in Guimarães Rosa's fiction; she continues such explorations in her essay in this volume.

From a different theoretical perspective, Else Vieira (1995, 1996, 1998) reads work by Mário de Andrade, João Guimarães Rosa, and Gabriel García Márquez, speculating on the site of translation in Latin American postmodernity and focusing on alternative practices that challenge the notions of invisibility and inequality in the translation process. Drawing on the work of writers and translators in twentieth-century Argentina, Christopher Larkosh theorizes about translation, migration, and sexuality, rereading history from the perspective of the "in-between" places that allow a discussion of marginal cultural identities (1996, 2002; see also his essay in this volume).

Situating myself within this movement of reading fiction as a source for translation theory, here I examine the relationship between fiction, translation, and history in the work of Argentine writer Julio Cortázar. His novels and short stories incorporate translation into their plots and also portray the experience and insights of characters who are themselves translators (cf. Pagano 1996). Cortázar theorizes translation as a *locus* of violence and tension: violence resulting from the imposition of words and meanings to translate reality; tension between the plurality of meanings that, though consciously suppressed, are always there, ready to challenge the most carefully planned transfer of meaning. To Cortázar, himself a practicing translator, any ontological discussion of translation leads inevitably to an ideological consideration of meaning production and, consequently, of issues such as power relationships and censorship within the context of meaning production. In this essay, I focus particularly on his novel *Libro de Manuel (A Manual for Manuel)* and discuss its treatment of translation as a strategy for memory preservation and subversion. The concept of translation as testimony elaborated by Cortázar in this novel is explored with special reference to his own political stance and literary career. In order to contextualize Cortázar's reflections on translation processes, I first briefly canvass some of his other works that thematize translation and translators.

Fictionalized Translations

An analysis of Cortázar's novels and short stories points to the pervasive presence of translation along with specific literary and theoretical concerns. His masterpiece *Rayuela* (translated as *Hopscotch*, 1967b), written in 1963 can be read as an exploration of the resources and limits of writing and, therefore, of reading and interpretation as well. In its preface Cortázar suggests two possible readings for the novel, one following a linear and the other a nonlinear sequence. The conventional reading of the chapters (following their numerical sequence) and the alternative path suggested by the author (hopping back and forth between the chapters) are actually two proposals for translating the plot, each one rendering a different story. The readers for Cortázar become the authors of the novel in that they must decide which way to traverse the text and which story to subsequently re-create in their reading. Cortázar's proposal of multiple plots within the same novel challenges conventional notions such as the linear reading of texts, univocal interpretations, and, most significantly within the discussions of translation, the role of the readers in the re-creation of a text.

The same concerns are also the subject of Cortázar's 1959 short story "Las babas del diablo" (literally, 'The Devil's Drool', translated as "Blow-Up," 1967a), renowned for its filmic adaptation *Blow-Up* by Michelangelo Antonioni. The protagonist, as is also the case in *Hopscotch*, is a Latin American in Paris, more specifically a Franco-Chilean photographer and translator who speculates on the difficulties he encounters in articulating the story he wishes to write. While trying to better reproduce the facts, he experiences difficulties in translating a treatise from Spanish into French, in capturing reality through his camera lens, and even in following the swift movement of the clouds adrift in the sky. Some pictures he takes incidentally of an apparent amorous encounter awaken his curiosity and lead him to enlarge the pictures in order to try to solve the mystery implicit in that scene. The blown-up photographs allow him to reenact the scene in the park, adding to the original impression important details that come to suggest a different story, in this case one not of love but of prostitution. "Las babas del diablo" thus frames one of Cortázar's main concerns in his fictional/theoretical wanderings, specifically, the displacement of meanings involved in all processes of reproduction.

Translation, however, is thematized more explicitly in Cortázar's 1968 novel, *62—Modelo para armar* (*62: A Model Kit*), whose main protagonist is Juan, an Argentine translator and interpreter who works for UNICEF in Paris. The opening scene of the novel describes a translation error made by Juan while mentally transposing into Spanish a nearby customer's order in a Parisian restaurant. The Spanish rendition of "Je voudrais un château saignant" ("I'd like a rare steak") becomes

"Quisiera un castillo sangriento" ("I'd like a bloody castle"), a mistranslation that reveals a curious displacement of signifiers. Through the filter of a Latin American translator in France, the rare steak becomes a castle bathed in blood, an image of violence, of medieval oppression, and subsequently a point of departure for the reconsideration of the colonization of America by the European world. The use of "château" (an abbreviation of the French cut of steak called *Chateaubriand*) further reinforces the context of the mistranslation, explicitly signaling the connection between colonization and writing. The word evokes Chateaubriand, whose "epic" poems were to become "foundational fictions" for many generations of Latin American intellectuals. Thus Chateaubriand, who gave the name to the rare steak, spawns the castle bathed in blood. "Throughout the process of translation," states the Brazilian critic Silviano Santiago, "the imaginary of the Latin American writer is always onstage" (1978: 23, my translation). Santiago points to the cultural and historical bearings on the process of production and transference of meaning. The signifiers in French awaken in the translator unexpected associations of words, triggered by chains of meaning constructed by history and memory.

Cortázar also focuses on the historical conditionings of the subject's interpretative filter in his 1977 short story entitled "Apocalipsis de Solentiname" ("Apocalypse at Solentiname"). Unlike the previous examples, this story takes place in Latin America in the rural village of Solentiname, Nicaragua. The protagonist, a photographer and an intellectual (representing Cortázar himself?), visits Solentiname and takes pictures of the "harmonious and pacific" atmosphere that permeates the place. Solentiname is experienced by the photographer as an idyllic place, a place where people look at things through a pure, primeval gaze, "the clean look of a person who describes what's around him like a song of praise" (1980:121–22). The protagonist is dazzled by the beauty and the purity of Solentiname, an isolated community in Nicaragua, an "island" within Latin America. When the photographs are exposed, however, they reveal pictures of torture and suffering, violence and murder. In the process of developing the pictures, the photographer discovers that beautiful scenes at Solentiname reveal the suppressed tragedy of a Nicaraguan village through images that represent the censored dimension of Latin American history.

The story deals with the tension between an idealized view of Latin America and its sordid reality. Here it is necessary to explain that "Latin

America" is for Cortázar a notion that encapsulates South America (both Spanish America and Brazil) and is supported by a political project of unification and engagement in common struggles against common causes of oppression. Throughout the 1960s and 1970s, Cortázar was a firm supporter of the leftist movements in Latin America and even wrote in favor of several causes in magazine articles and essays. His novels and short stories, however, were usually criticized for not being directly concerned with social and political issues.

Not only his fictions but also Cortázar's life can be read within the context of translation and of theoretical processes in general. An Argentine born in Belgium, Cortázar lived most of his adult life in Paris after going into self-imposed exile in 1951 during the Peronist period (1946–55). Thereafter Cortázar worked as an interpreter and translator for UNESCO, a task he was familiar with since his college years in Buenos Aires, when he would translate in order to earn a living.[1] Multiple cultural contradictions characterized Cortázar's life: he was an Argentine in Paris, living far from the atrocities of the Peron regime and the military regimes that followed, and also a self-styled "Latin American" in Europe, living far from the left-wing revolutionary movements that wished to unite the region and define a common cause of resistance. For these reasons Cortázar's life and literary career have always been subject to both praise and criticism from a political perspective. The tension arising from his being away from Argentina and Latin America, and from the criticism of the lack of explicit social and political denunciation in his fiction, permeates his interviews and essays, many of which deal with the reconciliation of aesthetic concerns with political engagement.

Cortázar himself defines his locus of enunciation as subject to displacement and to what he calls "el sentimiento de no estar del todo" (1976) ("feeling not all there," Cortázar 1986:17). This feeling, according to Cortázar, allows the writer to have a double perspective on the world, a double gaze, as one who is and is not present at the same time. The site of the writer is, hence, in a third position: a space *in between* experience and memory. Interestingly, most of Cortázar's novels and short stories present male characters set in an ambivalent relationship to two places, two languages, and two different historical periods. Juan, the protagonist of *62: A Model Kit*, wanders simultaneously through the cities of Paris and Buenos Aires; *Hopscotch* is itself divided into two sides, Buenos Aires and Paris, which are intermingled according to the selected reading option for the novel; and the photographers and translators in all his fictions hop randomly between languages and images.

In *Libro de Manuel*, however, these ambivalent positions are enacted by two different characters, each of whom represents one facet of the source of tension in Cortázar's life and work: the depoliticized intellectual and the politically engaged revolutionary. The novel thematizes translation by redefining its role within the context of ideological problematics and political engagement. Translation is proposed as a strategy of reading for subverting power relationships governing the process of meaning production. *Libro de Manuel*, written in 1973, narrates the story of a group of Latin Americans in Paris who devise a subversive plan to kidnap a Latin American officer linked to repressive paramilitary agents working in Paris. The group meets at the home of Patricio and Susana, who, alongside their political activities, prepare a scrapbook of press clippings about politically sensitive issues meant to be a manual for their son Manuel when he grows up. The kidnapping takes place, but the police and the secret forces manage to find the kidnappers and eventually kill one of them, thus putting an end to the whole plot of the conspiracy.

The historical context in which the novel was written and published is central for grasping many of the understatements and implicit arguments that characterize the style chosen by Cortázar to portray the secret activities of a subversive group of Latin Americans in Paris. The novel was published in the early 1970s, a decade marked by intense confrontation between the governments of many Latin American countries, including Argentina, Uruguay, Chile, and Brazil, and diverse groups of political activists, some of them leftists who were trying to overturn the regimes. The confrontation was characterized by what we could term "institutionalized violence," because the armed forces and the police operated secretly through paramilitary agents to exterminate the opposition parties and groups. The secret activities of repressive agents and their support by institutionalized forces prevented any open discussions or denunciations of the activities, thus contributing to the institutional silence and manipulation of the facts that characterized official versions of the history of that period. Information could only be obtained through partial and tendentious pieces of news in the press that only those skilled in reading between the lines could manage to translate. Another source of information came to be fiction, that is, novels and short stories that thematized the historical facts and that could only be published openly abroad or clandestinely at home.

Libro de Manuel is an example of a fictional piece that brings in records of historical facts through pieces of news, which are inserted throughout the novel, as well as through a dossier made up of file records of statements by political prisoners and interviews of U.S. agents who participated in the training of Latin American repressive agents. The novel clearly indicates its politicohistorical context by reproducing news such as the escape of the guerrillas who were members of the People's Revolutionary Army, Ejécito Revolucionario del Pueblo (ERP), from a prison house in Córdoba, Argentina; the kidnapping of the West German ambassador in Brazil by leftist groups; talks between Argentina and Britain about the Malvinas/Falkland Islands; the freeing of the Brazilian ambassador in Uruguay, kidnapped by the Tupamaros group, in exchange for a member of Tupamaros who was in prison; the killing by repressive agents in Brazil of Captain Lamarca, the former Brazilian military officer turned revolutionary leader. The novel also inserts news about the youth movements in Europe at the time and reports issued by Amnesty International on human rights issues in the world.

Publishing *Libro de Manuel* posed no political problems for Cortázar because he was living in self-imposed exile in Paris, far from the reach of political repression. It marks a departure in Cortázar's literary career because this is his only novel dealing explicitly with political issues. Critics such as Jorge Ruffinelli (1987) have claimed this was Cortázar's way of coming to terms with the expectations that intellectual circles had imposed on him and of reconciling a politically engaged stance with purely aesthetic concerns. In this sense it is interesting to remember that Cortázar donated his 1974 Médicis prize money for *Libro de Manuel* to the United Chilean Front.

The two extremes of political engagement and depoliticization, frequently used to pass judgment on Cortázar's life and work, are clearly present in *Libro de Manuel*. Two Argentines living in Paris—characters that play contrasting roles in the story—may be taken to epitomize the tension between the two political attitudes with which Cortázar himself was associated throughout his literary career. One of the characters is Marcos, a political activist, and the other is Andrés, a depoliticized intellectual living in Paris.

Andrés is defined by his friends as someone who "is in Paris for no specific purpose, but has his own theory of elective places" (Cortázar 1978: 29).[2] In this sense Andrés is affiliated with a generation of nineteenth-century Argentine intellectuals, for whom Paris, the city of Enlightenment, is one of their *elective affinities*. Unlike Andrés, Marcos does have a reason for being in Paris, and that sole reason is to undermine the repressive para-military forces allied to certain sectors of European governments. Andrés takes no part in the group's subversive actions, whereas Marcos is an active participant and dies as a result of an eventual confrontation with the repressive forces.

The apparent irreconcilability between the two positions is worked out by Cortázar through his proposal of a deferred future action. Plots may succeed or fail; reasons for alleged political interventions may sometimes be obscure or partially supported by ideological commitments. Testimony of recorded facts is put forward as the task of the writer and translator: a manual for Manuel, an education for a future adult and, ultimately, for the reader, which can guarantee a recording of history and an alternative way of translating it. The novel clearly advocates a pedagogy for the future, an initiation into political literacy that Manuel gets through his manual and that the reader obtains through a dossier of political prisoners' statements and interviews with mercenaries, which are included as a kind of a coda to the novel. This pedagogical policy is put into practice through the task of translation that the group members perform in each of their meetings and that the narrator (a partially omniscient one) exercises whenever an item of news is introduced.

¡Traducile al Muchacho!

The press clippings that are set aside for Manuel's manual are subject to close scrutiny and translation for the "uninitiated" members of the group. The task involves not only interlinguistic rendition in Spanish or French, but also, and most important, an interpretation of the facts being reported in the news. The urge to translate, persistently expressed by commands such as "traducile al muchacho" ("translate for the boy"), is thus an urge to reinterpret historical records and to recover, from between the lines, silenced statements and facts.

The translation of the news turns into an annotated translation, the translator providing the missing links in the original text, as in the case of the translation of this statement by a student who reports police abuses: "They make me get into the car and they start up, leaving the others lying on the ground. They keep on beating me along the way, threatening to kill me all the while (with an injection of cyanide or by drowning). After stopping in the courtyard of a building, where they continue clubbing me . . ." (39).[3] From the perspective of what is unsaid, the translator reinterprets what is said regarding all the silenced details concerning the places where abuses were perpetrated and comments: "here I must say that it's not clear whether they were only beating Étienne or whether there were others getting it in the courtyard too" (39).[4]

The translator also frequently comments on the way news is reported: "The Embassy of Switzerland in Montevideo was attacked on Friday by four guerrilla fighters belonging to the Armed Revolutionary Front of the East Bank (FARO), the extremist wing of the extreme left-wing Tupamaros. The reporter puts in so many extremes that you can't see the middle" (80).[5] The translator reflects on the linguistic choices in the original that attempt to conceal, but ultimately reveal, details of the process of construction of the news. While rewriting the information, the translator discovers the subtle play of concealment and censorship that governs the production of the media discourse and that the movement between languages inevitably exposes. A sudden change of verb tense or lexical item, as the excerpt below shows, reveals a tension in the moment of writing the original piece of news, which the foreign language captures and discloses:

> A car stopped across from me. A squad of seven people gets out,
>> This change of tense is always rough in Spanish . . .
> One of them
>> Here too, you can see, from people, which is feminine, he changes to one of them, masculine and with a club. (39)[6]

The lexical connection built in the original in French between *personnes*, 'people', and *l'un d' eux*, 'one of them', which the character Susana translates into Spanish as *personas* and *uno de ellos*, reveals the attempt by the news reporter to avoid exposing the sex of the authors of that criminal act (clearly male, the sex usually associated with repressive agents and the police) by first using a feminine gender noun: *personnes* in French and *personas* in Spanish. This generic and feminine noun, however, does nothing but defer the disclosure of the sex of the repressive agents, as the pronoun chosen to refer back to the generic noun—a masculine one (*eux/ellos*)—in fact reveals the male sex. Both the news reporter and the translator in the novel could have used a feminine subject pronoun to refer back to *personnes/personas*, but it seems that for both—news writer and news rewriter—the masculine pronoun readily comes to mind when producing information on the repression of leftist groups by institutionalized forces. The cohesive link established between the noun *personnes/personas* and the referring pronoun *eux/ellos* counteracts the initial attempt to manipulate language and fully displays the violence committed by a squad of men, clearly policemen armed with clubs. Here it is interesting to notice how the rendition of this passage into English by Gregory Rabassa reveals some problems concerning word gender in translations from languages with explicit gender marking of nouns, such as French and Spanish, into languages with no explicit gender, such as English (Cortázar 1978:39). Rabassa opts for a literal transposition into English, leaving the reader to figure out the connections existing in the source text.

Cortázar seems to suggest that sub-versions, such as those derived from reference pronouns that disclose information, or words that are carefully chosen in order to manipulate and control the news are written into texts and need only be decoded through the process of reading and reencoding. Survival in such circumstances is often dependent on cracking a code as well as communicating through one's own devised cryptograms. Thus, in *Libro de Manuel* characters are continually coding and decoding messages, while secretly hiding and avoiding tapped telephones:

> "Have him send me the melons directly to Little Red Riding Hood's."
>
> The key to those things, Andrés thinks, the melons must be pamphlets or pistols, Little Red Riding Hood is no doubt Gómez, who shaves every two hours. (33)[7]

The author's demand that readers "read between the lines" is actually embodied in the typesetting of the novel. It is worth remembering that Cortázar is renowned for his experimentation with different means of breaking the linearity of language and reading, such as intermingling lines in order to represent simultaneous actions or trying out visual patterns on the written page that might suggest a nonlinear reading. In *Libro de Manuel* a piece of news concerning a revolt of teenage girls in the custody of a Juvenile Hall is translated for a French audience with the following comments:

> " 'An unexpected black-out,' " Susana read in French for Monique and Roland, " 'was the occasion for the start of an infernal battle between the personnel and the juvenile girls who had showed themselves to have been extremely restless for the past few days.' Oscar talks about the full moon, but you'll soon see the official explanation . . ." (108)[8]

The news keeps reverberating in one of the characters' minds while he mentally searches for an alternative explanation for the facts. The simultaneity of thoughts is represented by Cortázar through a different typeface between the main lines of the written page:

> . . . who says that wasn't a full moon that night, actually it was
> an unexpected blackout was the occasion for the start of an infernal battle
> the darkness that gave them the chance to escape. (129)[9]

The characters' alternative readings of the facts are keys to the novel and to the pedagogical proposal set forth by Cortázar. Cortázar's thematization of translation is presented as a methodology for ideological disentanglement: its practice allows the reader to reread "sub-versions of history" while decoding the facts recorded by the news in the press. Translation is also seen as process of political education, a view that establishes a counterpoint to the traditional role translation had in Argentine culture in the nineteenth and greater part of the twentieth century.

Translation as Education

The novel clearly advocates a pedagogy for the future, an initiation into political awareness that Manuel discovers through his manual and that the reader obtains through the news translated by the characters and a dossier of political prisoners' statements in the novel's coda. Throughout the story this pedagogical policy is put into practice via translation, a task continually exercised by the group members. Manuel is to be the recip-

ient of a manual, a collection of texts that will make up his cultural heritage. In fact the manual is compared to the series *El tesoro de la juventud*
(*Classics for the Young*) and to other traditional magazines for children
(e.g., the Argentine magazine *Billiken*) that have typically played a substantial role in the development of cultural literacy and the initiation of
the young. Its pedagogical aim is complemented by the character of its
historical record: the clippings are meant to be reread "against the grain"
and translated in order to render new versions—sub-versions—of the
facts.

This association between translation and education is not new in
Latin American culture. Translation was a traditional part in the education of nineteenth- and twentieth-century intellectuals in Argentina who
were first initiated into reading in foreign languages and later practiced
translation as an exercise. In the essay that follows in this volume, Larkosh
discusses the role of foreign nannies in the life of Argentine intellectuals
and shows that the program of instruction was actually meant to avoid
the need for translation because children were first initiated into foreign
languages before learning to read the national tongue. Taking the Argentine writer and literary patron Victoria Ocampo as an example, Larkosh concludes that the kind of foreign instruction Argentine intellectuals
received allowed "little space for critical discussion of or response to imperial historiography and the more brutal moments in her [Victoria
Ocampo's] own nation's nineteenth-century history" (Larkosh, see page
109 below).

The case analyzed by Larkosh offers an interesting parallel to Cortázar's *A Manual for Manuel*. Victoria Ocampo belonged to one of the
rich, estate-owning families that held considerable economic and political
power and that had strong cultural ties with Europe. These families spent
regular periods of time in Europe and, when at home, hired European
instructors to educate their children. Their affinity with European standards and ideals often created in them a bias against national concerns,
especially in the case of sensitive issues such as the intervention of European countries in Argentina's domestic affairs. The European education
they so eagerly sought for their children ensured the perpetuation and
acceptance of values that were dear to their cultural and political milieu,
preventing any questioning of the status quo.

Victoria Ocampo's education by English and French instructors is an example of foreign ideals and foreign languages put to the service of ensuring a univocal interpretation of history. In Ocampo's instruction there was no space for discussion of the ideological stance of imperial powers toward their colonized territories or to the territories under their influence, as was the case of Argentina in relation to Great Britain. Nor was there room for questioning national policies such as the massive extermination of the native peoples that took place in Argentina in the 1870s. Education as repression can be seen as a thread running through Argentine cultural history from its very beginnings. A hundred years after the native peoples' annihilation, as *A Manual for Manuel* shows, there is still no space allocated for the discussion of the extermination of opponents to the military regimes in Latin America, whose voices are only heard through their testimonies in unofficial records.

The idea of a foreign instructor who initiates children into the use of a foreign code is clearly subverted by Cortázar in *A Manual for Manuel*: the manual is meant to promote translation of the facts, critical readings of history, and, most significantly, a recording of brutal moments bound to be erased from official documents. The dossier of torture and killings included by Cortázar as a coda to the novel further reinforces that aim.

Unlike the teachings of Ocampo's nannies, Cortázar's manual puts foreign languages to the service of translation, here understood as a re-reading of culture and history. Displacement of meaning such as that produced by the process of translation is welcomed as an alternative space for repressed potentialities to come to the fore. Manuel's manual also subverts traditional educational models that usually involve initiating the young into the reading of classical literature and an encyclopedic knowledge of the world. Manuel's manual proposes a *Bildung*-like process in which the young develop sensitivity to concerns pertaining to human rights banned from school textbooks and casually consigned to the spaces between the lines of the popular press. "It's a good introduction to the news item we're going to translate for your edification" (26), announces one of the translators in the novel to one of her "pupils," in this case not little Manuel, but a newly arrived Latin American in Paris. As pointed out throughout the novel, education involves the task of translation, and newspapers are the textbooks in which one can learn "a little contemporary history along the way while they translate" (16).

The Plot of Translation

Another aspect of *A Manual for Manuel* that directly concerns translation is the plot of the story. As we have seen, translation forms part of a conspiracy whose immediate aim is the kidnapping of a member of the repressive forces, but whose ultimate aim is to allow repressed facts and meanings to emerge through the reading of news against the official history. In the novel translation is used as a strategy by a group of subversive Latin Americans secretly operating in Paris who hold translation sessions of the news in the press whenever they meet. For their protection they also communicate through telegrams that need to be decoded and translated. Translation is not only present in all activities of the group but in those of their opponents as well. Both sides conspire against one another through messages written in code and through false names, passwords, and mixed languages. Translation is also part of the perverse play of signifiers subject to the power of official institutions, as illustrated by the interpreter at the police station who translates as briefly as possible "to the special delight" of the officer in charge (297).

Cortázar clearly thematizes translation within the context of tension between opposing parties and the tension of conspiracy. Unequal access to the press and unequal rights to free expression confine the activities of the Latin American group to clandestine actions, which include the production of alternative information—sub-versions of the facts—in order to counteract the violence of words subject to the manipulation of those in control of the production and transmission of the news. But Cortázar's reflection on translation transcends the immediate political context and extends to general issues concerning epistemological processes. In fact the novel itself expresses his concern with the ideological aspects of the production of meaning in general. The institutionalized violence that characterizes the context of the novel is a result of a particular historical moment and also of historical processes that have shaped the experience and memory of Latin American nations from colonial times. In the news and reports of historical facts, Cortázar argues, words exercise violence on meanings that are repressed and confined to the spaces between the lines of written texts. Language is actually one more weapon in a strategy of suppression and manipulation of meaning. As Cortázar shows by means of an episode continually reviewed in the novel, the words used to report the flight of some teenage girls from a juvenile detention center exercise the same violence as that physically inflicted on the girls by their tutors and the police in order to punish their behavior.

To summarize, translation becomes a strategy for subverting texts and allowing silenced versions to come to the fore. Speaking from his politicohistorical stance, the Latin American translator can perform subversions, including the movement from French into Argentine Spanish, whereby a rare steak becomes a castle bathed in blood. Paradoxically, translation also becomes a strategy for the preservation of memory. Testimonies of absent bodies and voices can be incorporated into the official history through the translation of the facts from a different ideological stance. In this sense Cortázar himself as an interpreter and translator for UNESCO was perfectly aware of the role of translation in the construction of national histories. Because the plot of the novel focuses on kidnapping a repressive agent, in *A Manual for Manuel* conspiracy and fiction are fused as the setting in which translation is practiced and discussed. The writing of official histories demands strategies that will subvert alternative versions, which are, as such, thus, bound to be used clandestinely, carefully, and attentively. This seems to be for Cortázar the site of translation in Latin America, where the transference of meanings from one language into another can never operate in an ideological vacuum. Throughout the process of translation, the imaginary of the Latin American writer is always onstage.

The Fictional Turn

Being himself a practicing translator and a writer continually probing into the process of translation, Cortázar is no doubt an exemplary source for translation theorization. Because Cortázar is an exile, a writer banished from his homeland and his mother tongue, his fiction thematizes the displacement of signs that is inherent in translating and rewriting. Exile prompts displacement, which, in turn, opens up language to allow for multiple readings of texts. Most significant for Cortázar, displacement allows for alternative ways in and out of the past, alternative means of instruction and learning. Language transfers operate as catalysts that set off difference. Like Juan, the main character of *62*, who enters a Parisian restaurant and mistranslates an item on the menu, the translator sets meanings in motion, enabling those readily accessible misplaced signs to actually come to the fore, to the scene of the text: thus a steak becomes a bloody castle, a feminine noun discloses male action of repression and violence. If there is something that makes Cortázar an especially rich source for the translation theorist, it is the writer's continual exercise of translation by all his characters who are translators. As stated earlier, translation is perhaps *the* primary recurrent theme of Cortázar's fiction, one that carries with it notions of exile and displacement, particularly interesting because of the intricate connections linking history, language, and translation.

Cortázar's deep concern about the capacity of language to translate reality seems to be constantly linked to his similar concern about history's capacity and willingness to record facts, two operations that, for him, can be carried out more adequately or more sensitively through fiction. In this sense his novels and short stories are manuals for the initiation of the reader into thinking about language and meaning production within the constraints of sociohistorical contexts. Like Manuel's textbook, Cortázar's works instruct the reader about issues such as randomness and the linearity of language, words and multiple meanings, truth and multiple perspectives. Their fictional character apart, Cortázar's works can be read as theoretical-practical manuals of semiotics, psychology, and translation, in which an integrated view is offered. His works, mostly written from the 1950s to the 1970s, anticipate discussions introduced by translation studies theorists in the 1980s, especially by those pursuing an interdisciplinary approach. Cortázar's fiction provides a contextualized analysis of the translation process, reading language in connection with history, discussing cultural identity in connection with the specific loci where meaning is produced.

Of particular interest to the translation researcher is the problematizing of translation offered by fiction writers like Cortázar, for whom any ontological discussion of translation requires an ideological consideration of meaning production that includes such issues as power relationships and censorship. Because it is a task inherently related to language production and control, translation is seen as a site of violence and tension, where words impose themselves and are imposed on others, and where meanings fight to escape suppression and oblivion. In the specific case of Cortázar, a writer engaged with political causes and human rights movements, translation is theorized within the scope of the processes of rewriting and manipulation. For the purposes of translation theory, Cortázar's view of translation as inherently linked to secret plots, secret places, hideouts, and censorship is particularly revealing for a theory of alternative modes of the production of meaning.

A fictional turn in translation studies can be accounted for by Ricardo Piglia's definition of the function of fiction, which was introduced early in this essay and now gains further resonance from this analysis of Cortázar's work. As it "narrates metaphorically the most profound relationships with cultural identity, memory, and tradition," fiction represents a genre that informs translation thinking from a comprehensive perspective, sensitive to relationships and movements difficult to capture through more orthodox analyses that do not consider fictional texts. Moreover, such texts need to be approached without bias as regards their so-called fictional character, especially because the very borderline between fiction and nonfiction has become more and more blurred. Critical theory has demonstrated this blurring through one of its favorite means of theory production, the essay, a hybrid genre widely exercised by Jorge Luis Borges, whose *Ficciones* also present intricate accounts of the translation process.

This analysis of Cortázar demonstrates that the fictional turn can introduce a political dimension into the task of rethinking translation. As it reenacts history, fiction translates facts, recording versions once suppressed or erased from official texts. Cortázar's work is, in this sense, exemplary. Read today, his novel *Libro de Manuel* acquires the status of testimonial writing, another hybrid genre often examined by postmodern theory. Fictional story, manual, academic treatise, and testimony, Cortázar's text remains a record not only of reflections on translation but also of reflections on historical facts that can be found in the files of human rights organizations, in publications such as *Nunca más* (1984), Argentina's report on institutional violence during the military regime. The fictional turn in translation studies, therefore, explores the most profound relationships with cultural identity, memory, and tradition.

Notes

1. Besides his work as a freelance translator in Buenos Aires and Paris, Cortázar translated a variety of authors and texts for Argentine and Spanish publishing houses: Louisa May Alcott's *Little Women*, Henri Bremond's *La Poésie*

pure, G. K. Chesterton's *The Man Who Knew Too Much*, Walter de la Mare's *Memoirs of a Midget*, Daniel Defoe's *Robinson Crusoe*, André Gide's *L'Immoraliste*, Edgar Allan Poe's prose works, and Marguerite Yourcenar's *Mémoirs d'Hadrien*.

2. All page numbers in citations of this novel refer to the 1978 edition of *A Manual for Manuel*, translated by Gregory Rabassa.

3. The original reads "Me hacen subir al auto y arrancan, dejando a los otros dos tirados en el suelo. En el curso del trayecto me dan de latigazos, a la vez que me amenazan con matarme (con una inyección de cianuro, o ahogándome). Después de un alto en el patio de una casa donde me siguen pegando con la cachiporra . . ." (Cortázar 1973:44).

4. The original reads "aquí te diré que no se entiende bien si solamente le pegaban a 'Étienne o si en ese patio había otros que tambíen cobraban . . ." (Cortázar 1973:44).

5. The original reads "La embajada de Suiza en Montevideo fue atacada el viernes por cuatro guerrilleros pertenecientes al Frente Armado Revolucionario Oriental (FARO), ala extremista de la organización de extrema izquierda Tupamaros. El periodista puso tantos extremos que no te deja ver el medio" (Cortázar 1973:82).

6. The original reads

"Un auto se detuvo frente a mí. Baja un comando de siete personas,
    Este cambio de tiempo verbal es siempre un poco duro en español.
Uno de ellos
    Aquí también, vos ves, de personas en femenino se pasa a uno de ellos, machito y con cachiporra" (Cortázar 1973:44).

7. The original reads "Que me mande los melones directamente a lo de Caperucita. Las claves de estos puntos, piensa Andrés, los melones deben ser folletos o automáticas, Caperucita seguro que es Gómez que se afeita a cada dos horas" (Cortázar 1973:38).

8. The original reads "—'Un sorpresivo apagón—les leyó Susana en francés a Monique y a Roland—fue la ocasión para que se librara una infernal batalla entre el personal y las menores que se habían mostrado sumamente nerviosas en esos días.' Oscar habla de la luna llena, pero ya vas a ver la explicación oficial . . ." (Cortázar 1973:109).

9. The original reads

". . . vaya a saber si había luna llena esa noche,
un sorpresivo apagón fue la ocasión para que se librara una infernal batalla
en realidad, fue la oscuridad lo que les dio la chance de huir" (Cortázar 1973:130).

CHRISTOPHER LARKOSH

Translating Woman: Victoria Ocampo and the Empires of Foreign Fascination

Traducir in Spanish means to translate as well as to convert. To recognize the striving for self-presence and self-identity of the concepts of text and meaning that underpin classical translation theory is to understand, to some extent, the widespread impact translations have had. The refusal of translation studies to question these concepts is a refusal to examine the political consequences of translation seriously.

Tejaswini Niranjana, *Siting Translation*

The idea of translation, I suppose, is that which so successfully recaptures the tone and texture of the original that it seems as if the original had not so much been reshaped but reincarnated.

C. Balakrishna Rao, Symposium on Translation, New Delhi, 1962

What do translators look for in translations, not only their own but in those of others, and is it ever possible for these translations to fulfill their expectations, fantasies, or desires? One possible answer may be found in the title of a book that the Argentine Victoria Ocampo (1890–1979) chose to translate from English into Spanish: Mohandas K. Gandhi's *My Life Is My Message*. Gandhi's life/message is one that begins in India, in a source language, Gujarati, inaccessible to the translator; it then passes through English, the common language of author and translator, to be translated finally into Spanish, a language as inaccessible to the author as his native language is to the translator. For a twentieth-century Buenos Aires readership generally unfamiliar with India,[1] this translation provides another view of India, not that of the British colonialist but of a particular colonized subject. Gandhi, when asked what he thought of Western civilization, said that it would be a good idea, underscoring his ambivalent relationship with the English language and modern technology. One can assume, moreover, that the Indian contemporaries of these Spanish-language readers were no better informed of the faraway country that had received Gandhi's translated message than the Argentine readers were of India. The improbable arrival of this message encourages a double—or even multiple—reading of literary translations: not simply as the message of the author, but also as that of the cultural mediators who take on the task of the work's further dissemination. In this way it becomes possible to read translations as documents not only of cultural politics but also of desires often more intimate and difficult to categorize in the broader context of official histories.

At first glance this translation process illustrates how Argentina and India have long shared an imperial language that has made communication possible between them; this should come as no surprise, as their economies were both linked to each other by British economic domination in the latter part of the nineteenth and early twentieth centuries. If India were indeed the jewel in the imperial crown, Argentina was that country which tested the very limits of the former British Empire, one which could be thought of as a borderline case of imperial domination. Although it was not under direct colonial rule, it had an economy linked more closely to the British Empire than perhaps any other nominally independent nation in the world.[2] Argentina thus presents a problem within that field of study that has come to be known as postcolonial theory. Not formally an imperial dominion (i.e., one of the "pink bits" or "red sections" on British maps still revisited in theoretical discussions as the official limit of empire[3]) yet far from being economically independent, Argentina and its shifting cultural orientations challenge notions of cultural analysis in which the cultural identities of colonizer and colonized are easily color-coded, separable, and identifiable.

In this cross-cultural exchange, Gandhi is the former British colonial subject who sends his message out in English in order to reach a global English-speaking readership, and Ocampo is the English-speaking Argentine woman who receives his message and extends its readership into another language once again after his death. This mediated line of communication exemplifies the ways in which messages are often received over distance and translated. The itinerary of the message from imperial metropolis to two disparate points on its world map underscores the common usage of an imperial language, though it is by no means a similar one, as the relationship to this language differs between countries and individuals with varying experiences and positionalities with respect to the imperial culture. In spite of this differing relationship to the intermediary language, a dialogue between Argentina and India on the colonial and postcolonial experience and its relationship to literature and translation is perhaps possible. In this case the line of communication represented by an imperial language is English, but in other circumstances it might be French, Spanish, or those of non-Western empires, such as Turkish, Arabic, the Persian of Hafiz and Saadi, or the Urdu of Iqbal and Ghalib. How might other linguistic registers for a renewed discussion of postcoloniality be imagined through translation, a common language not yet possible but nonetheless prefigured in such attempts at translating "against the grain" of global cultural diffusion? In Ocampo's Gandhi, it is not simply the author's work that is translated but space itself, transforming the geographies of the cultural landscape to allow a heretofore unimaginable proximity between cultures.

When the life/message becomes not only that of an author but also that of a translator, who performs the act of literary translation *strictu sensu* and also participates in a broader project of intercultural dialogue in the context of the global diffusion of literary texts,[4] this message extends beyond the text being translated to include the particular act of translation as well. The message is no longer simply that of the original, for in many cases one of the most interesting messages a reader may find is how the text has been brought to speak in another language, in spite of the difficulties involved in its transmission. In such a life marked by translations, *translation is the message.* This message of translation is one often ignored, but one whose implicit choices can and should be read in literature. If we are to believe Walter Benjamin, the greatest promise of translation is that it will not respect even the most irreversible border crossings. The unfulfillable promise of translation as "afterlife" attempts to challenge death itself by allowing works to "cross over" in what one may call a literary reincarnation, an act that resembles what Gilles Deleuze and Félix Guattari in *Mille plateaux* (*A Thousand Plateaus*) might call a "literary seance," in which the translator, through the text, attempts to communicate with the spirits of the dead: "Speaking in tongues. To write is perhaps to bring this assemblage of the unconscious to the light of day, to select the whispering voices, to gather the tribes and secret idioms from which I extract something I call my Self (Moi). . . . My direct discourse is still the free indirect discourse running through me, coming from other worlds or planets. That is why so many artists have been tempted by the séance table" (1987:84).

In this context, is not Ocampo, as the female creator and director of a translating and publishing machine, a medium in more than one sense of the word? Not only does she displace the centrality of "man" in mediating a literary communications network of global scale, but also, in her taking up of Gandhi as a project for translation, she attempts to incorporate an element of his spiritual and anticolonial mission—an element that, incidentally, could be said to replicate itself here. Thus, is not this project of interpretation and translation also one of interpretation and translation of Ocampo's own work?

Translating Woman

What is the message of this translator when she translates? In analyzing the literary activity of Victoria Ocampo, it is possible to initiate a discussion not only of original and translated literary texts, but also of translation's economic and cultural contexts: in this case, what a translator is capable of when she has achieved the highest degree of professional freedom and institutional power. Born into one of Argentina's oldest and wealthiest elite families, Ocampo's example, like many literary translators before her, provides an alternative model of freedom in that she did not need to assume the unpleasant task of translating works assigned by an editor merely to earn money. Anyone familiar with translation as a career knows that many professional translators are seldom free to choose what they translate because their work is more often than not subject to the desires of publishers and markets. As the founder and director of the Buenos Aires literary journal *SUR* (1931–70), by contrast, Ocampo was able to translate and publish what she chose. Hers was a freedom prefigured in the work of one of the writers she admired most—Virginia Woolf—but, ironically, Ocampo's wealth made the minimum material prerequisites that Woolf considered essential for any woman writer—a room of one's own, 500 pounds a year—seem paltry in comparison. According to Ocampo, writing as a woman can occur only when one has ceased to write solely from a secondary and implicitly inferior position of response to another (1981b:12). Here she attempts what one might call a *writing out of identity*, one that begins with response but that is still distant from the ultimate freedom that she calls "writing as a woman," in which feminine identity is no longer as necessary a point of reference or return. By thus attempting to articulate her identity, the writer has already begun its disarticulation through a critical reexamination of the conventional epistemological limitations of cultural identities, including, but certainly not limited to, those of gender.

In this context of exceptional freedom for a woman, one already attained yet still to be both written out and written out of, the act of translation can also be viewed all the more clearly as a possible, but by no means ensured, act of cultural intervention; "freedom of choice," if only a distant desire, is already a legible part of the translator's message. As she suggests in her 1920 essay "Babel," moreover, the desire for greater freedom in this literary milieu is comparable to that of women and other "immigrants" to literature (1981a:33). Victoria Ocampo's life, as woman, translator, and literary migrant, is also a legible message; it is one lived both between languages and in the feminine, but one so exceptional, in spite of the social and moral pressures of the period, that it exemplifies that freedom and mobility which has, unfortunately, proved to be all too elusive for women, translators, and those colonial subjects who involuntarily pass through bilingual or multilingual spaces as a result of institutional attempts to impose on them a single unifying official register of language.

What is known about Ocampo's life from her autobiography and testimonies comes to form an unavoidable element in the reading of her literary oeuvre. This is, however, only one way of understanding Ocampo's translation of Gandhi's title, as she was aware that what was important to others about herself was not always what she achieved or wrote but, rather, what she represented. This is seen clearly in another early work, *De Francesca a Beatrice* (1926), in which she explores the traditional role of woman in the production of literary texts: that of the muse/lover who provides inspiration with her body. In such cases, the resulting literary work is a product of this sexualized textual intervention. It is ironic that, in spite of her extensive writing, Victoria Ocampo is often known as a representative of a literary world not written down but lived through an extensive network of "literary relationships," ones that often incorporated an intimate or even sexual dimension. Attempts to correct that misconception have become more common (Arambel-

Güiñazú 1993), but perhaps, as Ocampo's translation of Gandhi suggests, there is nothing entirely misguided in reading her life as her message as well.

Ocampo is only one of innumerable points of departure for representing a transcontinental literary world of the late nineteenth and early twentieth centuries; personal contact with the figures of her world was often as important to her as their work, and often an inseparable key to her understanding of it. Her life provides a particularly complex model for literary association, as all the literary figures that her life connects need not necessarily "agree" within a certain ideological or aesthetic rubric in order to communicate with each other, nor must they necessarily be the most historically durable or brilliant of figures, although many are still widely considered to be so. One begins to recognize how the myth and metaphor of literary community, images of literary figures, and other cultural references that circulate along the increasingly global lines of literary communication that Ocampo has only begun to suggest are cultural forces to which one invested in literary activity can never imagine oneself totally immune. Ironically, for many who succeeded her in the Argentine literary arena, Ocampo was spoken of purely in terms of what she represented, as a diva more concerned with performance than literature, as if the two were somehow diametrically opposed. In the work of Ocampo, literary activity—not only "original" writing but also autobiography, literary criticism, and translation—is performance.

Is it possible, then, to retell Argentine literary history from the point of view of the translating woman? If so, what shifts in authorial perspective would such a history imply? Translation challenges the conventions of historiography by proposing a historical perspective that is never univocal, for in translation events often occur *in a different order*, not only chronologically but epistemologically as well. In this context, might a history of literary translation approach not the conventional norms of historiography but, perhaps, those of a translated autobiography or testimony, in which the protagonist never claims to be "great" but allows (perhaps by way of that literary *understatement* considered so typical of both Anglophiles and translators) an exploration of those connected to her and through her? In such a case, Ocampo represents these literary figures and ties them into a narrative, a narrative truly about literature, yet not focused exclusively on "great authors" but also on those such as editors, publishers, and translators who provide authors with their necessary connections.

Enrique Pezzoni (1986), former editor of *SUR* and one of twentieth-century Argentina's best-known translators, suggests that the figure of Victoria Ocampo represents a way of narrating canonical nineteenth-century Argentine literary history—exemplified by figures such as Domingo F. Sarmiento, Lucio V. Mansilla, Eduardo Wilde, and Miguel Cané—one that highlights the continual fascination with the foreign and the will for technological progress according to European models. For Pezzoni she is not only the author of her own writing but also the author of the works of those later writers who wrote out of opposition to what they imagined her to represent, as the main catalyst of a renewed debate on national identity. Such topographical mappings of this network of symbolic images are legible throughout the writings of Victoria Ocampo; in the second volume of her *Autobiography* entitled, appropriately enough, *El imperio insular* (*The Insular Empire*, 1980a), Ocampo talks about a transatlantic crossing in which she is chosen by her compatriots to symbolize them: "During the crossing they threw a party, the kind which are never lacking on board. In the boat were Chileans, Brazilians, Uruguayans, Peruvians. The Argentines agreed (*une fois n'est pas coutume*) that I would represent them. My role and that of the other women wasn't difficult: wrap ourselves in a flag and come into the dining room in this attire. They made me a Phrygian cap and put it on my head. I was announced as the Argentine Republic" (Ocampo 1980a:180, my translation). Here Ocampo dresses up in a red Phrygian cap as Miss Liberty and wraps herself in the flag to symbolize the Argentine Republic itself. If, as Francine Masiello notes, it is here that in the work of Victoria Ocampo "self-representation comes to stand for national culture" (1992: 164), it is an admittedly uncommon moment. Remember that these Argentines are on a luxury liner crossing the Atlantic, and the disclaimer Ocampo attaches to her power to represent her country is uttered in French: "Une fois n'est pas coutume." Her choice of words in another language once again underscores the fact that her status as outsider was often voluntarily self-imposed and even openly preferred. Although she is no doubt referring to the preconception that Argentines rarely come to an agreement about anything, there is another possible reading: that it is only in transit, in this indistinct zone between the national and the foreign, that she can represent her country, or that it is in fact in this transatlantic passage between cultures, languages, and literatures that she has come to represent Argentine culture.

What does it mean for Victoria Ocampo, as translating woman, to represent all of these things at the same time, to be presented repeatedly in Argentine literature as a purely symbolic figure? Literature and translation reveal themselves through this feminine figure not simply as isolated acts of writing but also as part of a far-reaching system of business, politics, and interpersonal relationships. For example, Ocampo's father was an engineer who extended the national network of railways; it is apparent, however, that there is nothing "national" about this network, that it was in fact, in ownership and administration, as British as that of colonial India. (In an anecdote, perhaps an urban myth yet one no less familiar to many natives of Buenos Aires, the downtown train station called Retiro was originally to be built in Bombay, but the architectural plans of it and a smaller station were mixed up in London, resulting in the larger station being built in Buenos Aires.) In this context of a railway network that connects Argentina with India, the very idea of transit, through this series of national and urban spaces, was institutionally implicated from its inception to every corner of Britain's far-flung "Victorian" empire. In this invocation of disparate and multiplying Victorian spaces, one is reminded of that moment in Ocampo's *Testimonies* (1963) when she describes that uncanny feeling she experiences in reading President Sarmiento's dedication to her aunt, also named Victoria, in one of the books in the family library; in one letter, Sarmiento compares his addressee to her imperial majesty herself, the most famous Victoria of all, one who would come to symbolize an age, if not to represent the victory of Empire.

It thus comes as no surprise that, when speaking of Ocampo's father's legacy to his daughter, Blas Matamoro argues that she could also be seen as bringing the same sort of "progress" to the Argentine landscape, embodying another sort of network or empire: "The spaces change, as does the direction of history. If the father is the pioneer who brings the extension of the railroads from the capital to the interior, through the virgin land, the daughter would be a creature of the city, of an insufficiently Europeanized city, which she would help to Europeanize" (1986:17, my translation). If that is the case, one might argue that this latter-day Victorian network, although it emerges in the twentieth

century, might be subject to the same sort of critique as were those original nineteenth-century notions of progress and civilization that emanated
from the projects of European colonial expansion. It is thus possible to
view the literary landscape Victoria Ocampo creates not merely metaphorically but as an actual physical network, a series of communications
that connects radically different spaces and points of literary reference,
both national and foreign. In its extension it grows increasingly more
complicated, and any claim that such a network might make to "progress," in its conventional linear sense, was called ever more into question
as the twentieth century continued.[5]

Back to Class in Argentine Literature:
Victoria Ocampo's Nannies

Ocampo's preparation for a life of translation and international communication begins years before, in the earliest years of her childhood, by
way of the foreign-language education she received at home; hers was a
life apparently multilingual from the very beginning. This reading of the
limits of the translatable foreign, in Argentine culture and beyond, is thus
implicitly also one of class. In the colonial context, such references ac-
centuate the highly differentiated access to privileged registers of literary
languages, which, in the case of turn-of-the-century Argentina, distinguished the ruling oligarchy from the gaucho peasants of the interior and
the majority of newly arrived European immigrants. The childhood education of Argentine authors such as Victoria Ocampo seems to challenge
the notion that their later translations were indeed made from "foreign"
languages: the childhood home of her contemporary Jorge Luis Borges
was a veritable "English library," and, for Ocampo, contact with the English and French languages preceded conscious memory.

It was not her immediate family, however, who took primary responsibility for initiating her into the privileged domains of imperial languages but, rather, a series of imported instructors and servants. In an
essay by Ocampo entitled "El reinado de las institutrices" ("The Reign
of the Governesses"), she describes her experience with the two women
in charge of her education:

> In the years of my childhood, our lives were thus governed by En-
> gland and France. And from an early age I learned to differentiate

between England and France, perhaps in quite an unjust manner toward both countries, as the distinction I established was at first the
simple reaction of a pup. Something instinctual which was born of
the characteristics and particularities of the two women. Miss Ellis
was England; Mlle. was France. I felt great affection for both, save
for the moments when I hated them—above all Mlle.—and wished
on them some prolonged, although not fatal, illness (so as not to
allow my remorse to dampen my good fortune). (1963:48, my
translation)

The relationship with nannies and with countries is a personal relationship, one begun in early childhood, and one that appears to show the
marks of its ambivalence from the start. Although she is quick to correct
her initial childhood impression that these women somehow "represented" their countries of origin in their totality, there is undoubtedly
something of the nation in what these women represent for her. Perhaps
one of things they taught Ocampo was that one day she, too, in her
contact with foreigners, would be expected to be representative of her
country as a whole. There would be no need to hire foreign nannies, after
all, if they did not provide the education that national leaders like Sarmiento considered necessary to the education of every Argentine, that
contact with what could be considered the very nucleus of the Argentine
translatable foreign: England and France.

Ocampo notes that these *institutrices* (a word that, in Spanish and
French, evokes their roles within cultural institutions or as an institution
in and of themselves, to a greater extent than the English words *governess*
or *nanny*) form part of a larger, untold history of women educators. In
this essay, she interpolates her own personal experience within a more
general history of English governesses gleaned from reading a book entitled *A Galaxy of Governesses*—or perhaps it is the general history that
takes second place alongside that of her own experience, one that seems
to exemplify this Anglo-French education. Even in a text written in Spanish, Ocampo finds it unnecessary to provide a translation for the phrase,
"The english [sic] governess has been a great civilizing agent in the past.
. . . The very fact that one is a product of it makes the questioning of
such a phrase all the more difficult" (1963:44). The guiding assumption
of this statement—that English culture is somehow a more suitable environment for educating and civilizing children than the one that they

are born into—is never addressed. As Ocampo notes, there are areas of this education in which no questioning is possible, but the process of induction into this educational institution comes not without a measure of ambivalence. The love/hate relationship she describes brings up, once again, the question of whether it is possible to survive the encounter with education without becoming overcome by resentment or by an unfulfilled need to respond that comes to dominate all of one's later writing and activity.

Victoria Ocampo is aware of these women's complicity in a much larger cultural act: "Like a gigantic fifth column, according to Bea Howe, these *institutrices*, these *nannies* invaded the Continent, America, the world. But it wasn't a fifth column in the bad sense of the word" (1963: 49, my translation). Those critical of the more brutal moments of British and French colonial history (e.g., the 1857–58 Sepoy Revolt or the 1919 Amritsar Massacre in India) may wonder whether there really is such a thing as a fifth column in the *good* sense of the word. Even in this idealized memory of a doubly colonial childhood, education is accompanied by discursive barriers that, as Ocampo admits, allow little space for critical discussion of or response to imperial historiography and the more brutal moments in her own nation's nineteenth-century history (e.g., General Roca's 1879 Conquest of the South, in which Argentina wrested the southern part of its territory from the Indian tribes inhabiting it, decimating them in the process). The only benevolent thing about this colonial education, in fact, might be its duality; by allowing a comparison of two different institutional encounters with colonial authority, neither of the two can claim universality. In her colonial fantasy imagined nostalgically under the rule of familiar foreign-language "phrases," one is reminded of those that the French governess used to discipline the young Victoria Ocampo. In retrospect they might appear quite comical, if only as absurd attempts to, in the French of Foucault, "surveiller et punir":

> —Vous ne savez pas? Il fallait savoir.
>
> —.......
>
> —Eh bien, vous le copierez vingt fois.
>
> —.......
>
> —Il n'y a pas de mais.
>
> —.........
>
> —Vous mériteriez le bonnet d'âne.

—...........

—Vous me conjuguerez le verbe "répondre."

—.............

—Je vous le repète pour la dernière fois.

—..............

—Vous appelez ça savoir?

—.................

—Vous êtes une fiéffée parasseuse.

—...................

—Impossible n'est pas français.

As one can see, in that period when one didn't speak as much
of nationalisms as one does today, they already existed.

The result of which (not Mlle.'s nationalism, but her demands),
I learned everything, for better or for worse, whether I wanted to or
not. (Ocampo 1963:47, my translation, although in this case the act
of "translation" also implies a measure of not translating.)

In the space of this classroom, this lesson cannot be translated into
Spanish (or in the case of this essay, into English) as it would defeat the
purpose of what is being taught, as the point of Mlle. speaking only
French is not only to retain the linguistic upper hand in the constant
discipline of the pupil but also to ensure the most complete assimilation
of the national language in which the lessons are presented—that is, if
language and lesson are not one and the same.[6] Although Ocampo states
that her teacher's statements have been recorded in her, if not engraved
in her ("se me quedó grabado"), the young girl's own responses in this
presumed "dialogue" do not appear; they are recorded as silences, or are
erased in an act of self-censorship. She adds in conclusion:

What we owe to those hours of class, to the often detested company
of these two governesses is perhaps one of the most precious gifts for
those who love books as an important part of life: the privilege of
entering directly, without intermediary, as in our own home, into the
masterpieces of two of the richest literatures.

I wonder, in conclusion, whether the decorated diplomats in
their dazzling uniforms or the luxurious embassies have rendered to
their countries as much as these badly dressed women have: perse-
vering, true to their cause, at times maniacal, at others so self-

sacrificing, anonymous workers who take in their hands the most delicate of human materials, one often rebellious and exasperating, including when their own good qualities deserved greater effort and sacrifice. Quite frankly, I don't think so. (1963:50, my translation)

The main "privilege" of this education in imperial languages is not to facilitate translation but, rather, to avoid the need for it entirely, at least from these two languages. If these literatures are "rich," all of those who made possible unmediated access to them are not; this image of European colonization is of "badly dressed," "anonymous" working women who seem to have more in common with the other women of an immigrant Babel than with any colonial master. After all, these literary languages, as conduits of privilege, will be recurred to long after the French and English governesses who first made them legible are but a distant memory.

A Passage to Tagore: Beyond the Anglo-French Literary Encounter

There is a wealth of cultural knowledge, of course, that this colonial education cannot teach; such knowledge comes from beyond the limits of what can be taught, precisely because it refuses to operate according to that which is at the core of the colonial education, namely, an unquestioning belief in its own cultural superiority. As the encounter between Tagore and Ocampo illustrates, when the moment comes for a message from beyond the limits of the translatable foreign to be received, it has the power to cause an irrevocable crisis in the network of European literary reference and absolute translatability.

In 1924, the thirty-four-year-old Victoria Ocampo was hosting the Bengali poet Rabindranath Tagore in a house in San Isidro, on the banks of the Río de la Plata outside of Buenos Aires. Ten years earlier in Paris she had read his book of poems, *Gitanjali*, in André Gide's translation from English into French, the English text itself a translation from Bengali by the author himself. Her first reading of Tagore occurred in a moment of great emotional crisis related to her affair with Julián Martínez de Hoz, a liaison that she was compelled to keep secret from her parents. The work moved her deeply, provoking a profound spiritual shift; such a powerful reaction cannot be explained by a single reason, but beyond the ideas she found there, anyone familiar with Ocampo's relationship with the French language might also consider pertinent the fact that Tagore first spoke to her in French. The ideas came to her in a language not quite native and not the original, but the language of her intellectual life, that language in which for her "thinking was possible."[7] Ironically, although many in Argentina have come to regard Tagore as a "mediocre" writer (perhaps because of the often mediocre translations into Spanish),[8] he continues to be a significant cultural figure not only in his native Bengal, but throughout the South Asian subcontinent and beyond, and many consider him to be *the* national writer of modern India. In her lectures on Tagore, Ocampo often stressed his importance as a multifaceted literary figure, as renowned for his lasting mark on national institutions (among them, a university, the national anthems of both India and Bangladesh, and the films of Satyajit Ray) as he was for his own writing, music, and painting.[9]

Victoria Ocampo's relationship with language—not only her native language but also other languages, in various degrees of foreignness—illustrates how one comes to make demands on translation. One of the first translations Ocampo ever requested (and one that, as her direction of *SUR* would come to prove, was far from being her last) was carried out when Tagore fell ill during a visit to Buenos Aires, and she arranged for him to stay in the home of a relative on the bank of the Río de la Plata in the affluent suburb of San Isidro. In this relaxed atmosphere Tagore began to write poetry once again, and one afternoon Ocampo asked him to translate for her one of the poems he had just finished writing:

> He bent over the pages spread out before him, and I was able to see, indecipherable, like the marks of birds' feet in the sand, the delicate mysterious lines of the Bengali characters. Tagore took the page and began to translate—literally, he said. What he read, at times haltingly, seemed tremendously enlightening to me. It was as if, by some miracle or accident, I had come in direct contact, at last, with the poetic material (or materia prima) of what was written there without the pair of gloves that the translations always have. The gloves which numb our sense of touch and keep us from picking up words with our bare hands . . .
>
> I asked Tagore if he would write down the English version. He gave it to me the next day, written in precious handwriting. I

read the poem in his presence and could not hide my disappointment. "But so many things that you read yesterday are not here," I reproached him. "Why did you omit them? They were the center, the heart of the poem." He replied that he thought that those things could not interest Westerners. Blood rushed to my cheeks as if I had been slapped. Tagore, of course, told me that he had done it because he was convinced that it was the correct thing to do, without imagining that it could hurt me. I said it with a vehemence that I rarely allowed myself with him (although impetuosity is natural in me) that he was terribly wrong. (Ocampo 1982:77–78, my translation)

Here Ocampo's fascination with the foreign is at least twofold; first, with a Bengali original that is both foreign and incomprehensible, and then with an English translation that holds out the promise not only of mere understanding but even of "enlightenment." It all seems so close, pressing up against the tips of the fingers, against the skin, that most intimate boundary with the foreign, as the meaning hides behind the unfamiliar script of the Bengali language, as if nature were writing a temporary message in the sand that the wind or the river would soon erase, but which for a brief moment is legible. This momentary glimpse of "enlightenment" in the foreign has all the markings of a mystical encounter: the master reads, translating literally, simultaneously, haltingly, and one cannot but wonder if it is the impatience before the awaited message that infuses even the short pause with the sublime. It is perhaps through the pauses of the spoken word of the master that Ocampo is able to imagine direct contact with what is on the other side. This contact is imagined as one of "undressed," physical touch with what is called "materia prima."

The literary encounter in translation, then, is not with the words themselves but, rather, with that which has no words, perhaps that "essential substance" that Walter Benjamin, only a year before, had described in his essay "The Task of the Translator" as "the unfathomable, the mysterious, the 'poetic,' something that the translator can produce only if he is also a poet" (1969:70). When Tagore reads before his listener, however, there is no doubt that the translator is a poet, as transmission of this "essence" occurs with none of the supposed fears of conflict between author, translator, and reader. What is mystical about this experience in translation is that, in witnessing Tagore simultaneously translating his own poem aloud, Victoria Ocampo is able to witness all three essential creative incarnations of the act of translation—the author, the translator, and the reader—present and at work before her simultaneously and in the same person. This singular experience is perhaps responsible for the illusion that the ultimate fantasy of translation is fulfilled: that all barriers between the author and the reader have vanished, that meaning flows freely into the reader, without obstruction by the differences in individual languages. Ocampo recognizes something of a prophet in this poet (see Sengupta 1990), and perhaps that is the moment when he most resembles the translator. Tagore is a prophet when he travels with his message and a poet when he dedicates himself to his art in solitude, but when this prophet/poet conveys the message, is he the author, or merely a messenger, translating the message he receives from a place beyond all language?

This encounter with the "materia prima" is mystical and, perhaps for that very reason, fleeting; when she receives the written translation she requested one day later, it is not surprising to discover that, for Ocampo, so much seems to be missing. This disappointment before translation occurs at one of its most "common places": in the notion that something once again has been "lost in translation." After all, how does she know "it" was there to begin with? In other words, what is the nature of the fantasy of contact, be it with something mystical or simply something from the beyond the familiar limits of Western culture? One might find a less fortunate fictional counterpart for Victoria Ocampo in the episode of the Malabar Caves in E. M. Forster's novel written in the same year, *A Passage to India*. The fantasy of the "real India," which Adela Quested and countless other Anglo-Indians longed to discover in a moment of mystical revelation, reappears not in the Malabar Caves but in a translation on the banks of the Río de la Plata; nonetheless, as this experience recedes from the moment, Victoria Ocampo, like Adela Quested, is also left with no clear sense of what happened in that cross-cultural encounter.

Mahasweta Sengupta argues in "Translation as Manipulation: The Power of Images and Images of Power" that one element lost in translation is "its intricate ambiguity" (1995:169). In the case of Ocampo, this ambiguity might allow a reading of the mystical spirituality that she, like so many Western readers, searched for in Tagore's poetry. In addition, what is "lost in translation" is not only those ideas that she alludes to the day before but also the voice in which they were read, those pauses that allow one to reflect and imagine the poetic meaning that words cannot express in and of themselves. The author is the translator, apparently omitting what to Ocampo was the "center," the "heart" of the poem, but this is exactly what Tagore imagines does not interest the Westerner; he does not translate the "center," the core of the message, but rather the images, the surface impressions that allow Westerners to feel that they have experienced another culture without having to make the necessary shift in cultural perspective that such an understanding would demand. Ocampo knows this shift from her education, as does Tagore: that of learning the language of the Other and its implicit cultural positionality in order to make communication possible. Because the native languages of these two people (Spanish, Bengali) cannot assume the role of common language, however, it is assumed that such a shift in this case is impossible.

What is perhaps most interesting in this scenario is not so much the way Tagore imagines the Westerner (an image informed not only by a familiarity with the preferences of European readers, but also by his own experiences as a colonial subject) but, rather, how Ocampo imagines that Tagore imagines the Westerner. In Ocampo's view, Tagore translates for a Western reader supposedly uninterested in the essential, mystical, inexpressible heart of the master's poetry, if not its sensual surface. This realization exacerbates her fear that she, in spite of her understanding the day before, is seen by Tagore to be this Westerner, one incapable of fully understanding what is in the original. If they really did "share" a common language in English, why was there so much to be desired in their mode of communication? There were many moments in which the two wished they shared a native language. Ocampo wished that Rabindranath Tagore would learn Spanish, he that she would learn Bengali. Or perhaps that she even *be* Bengali: in calling her "Vijaya," the Sanskrit word for victory, Tagore translates "Victoria" herself once again to serve as muse for his later poetry. Perhaps this homegrown or *swadeshi* avatar of Victoria Ocampo, born of translation, was the only way he could "understand" her, for Tagore, like Ocampo, also ran up against his own limits of the translatable foreign in the Other, given only a glimpse of a culture inaccessible in the original, her language, which he considered too difficult to master. This encounter, nonetheless, prefigures countless others that have not yet occurred: not that of colonial subject and colonizer, nor even that of two different colonial subjects from opposite ends of an empire. What is prefigured in this encounter is the desire of two colonial subjects to speak to each other in the native language of the other and to be able to translate directly from one to the other without the need for a common "imperial" language.

In her book *In Your Blossoming Flower Garden* (1988), Ketaki Kushari Dyson explores the literary relationship of Ocampo and Tagore as a prefiguration of a much more extensive one between Latin American and South Asian literary cultures. Dyson's critique of Western scholars of India—that they are concerned solely with either the ancient civilizations or politics and economics—is one that might extend to literary studies: the common assumption is that one studies other languages, literatures, or cultures in order to understand "the past" in the form of a textual corpus already extant or accessible. But what of "the future," that future of communication between cultures and languages that the "Western scholar" has only begun to understand? How much of it continues to be interrupted in a scene that might resemble that of the Bengali master and his Argentine devotee, as, even within the complex, multilingual, and transnational cultural compendium called Latin America, the Spanish and Portuguese languages are increasingly recognized as limited in their ability to claim any universal power of representation or communication. In such a cross-cultural encounter, even the Western polyglot Victoria Ocampo appears strangely monolingual. As Ocampo reveals in her translations of Gandhi, any examination of her own life, precisely through its web of cultural affiliations, contradictions, and limitations, also allows the reading of an increasingly complex message of cultural referentiality.

To Future Writers on the Ends of Empires

This essay has attempted to engage the issue of linguistic difference from a perspective that recognizes the inherent political factors that contribute to and complicate literary notions of foreignness, indicating that any theory of translation is necessarily a theory of alterity, one that tests the limits of perceived notions of self and Other. A theory of translation cannot limit itself to well-known literary "originals," but must also uncover those texts and voices that are suppressed because of the language in which they are written and that, ironically, must be suppressed once again by the act of translation in order to be received. In this context of translation theory, the translator can no longer attempt to disappear as the most effective means of remaining faithful but, rather, must emerge as a subject of literary inquiry as well. The relationship between the positions of author and translator, and the inherently different texts they generate, thus assumes greater importance, documenting the limits of intercultural dialogue within national literary cultures. In spite of linguistic and cultural differences, thinking about translation continues to rely on a series of metaphors: translation as conversion or mentorship; a mourning, reincarnation, or channeling of the dead; cultural appropriation or expropriation; an intimate or telepathic relationship of varying orientation; or a transatlantic migration to Babel or Babylon. Instead of attempting to distance translation theory from these metaphors, a critical revisiting of them may in fact allow a revision of the political optic through which translation has traditionally been conceived and performed. While it is necessary in translation studies to be aware of the images that have frequently served in the history of translation to illuminate the translator's craft, none of these, like the author/translators who propose them, can ever be considered definitive in their scope of reference.

As I continue to trace this network of reference, I find that I too am represented in this act of literary connection and cross-identification that the act of translation sets off. In researching this study, I was struck by a passage written by Juan José Sebreli in which he gives a suggestion for a possible thesis topic for "North Americans":

> Victoria Ocampo, for her part, was able to see the true documental and sociological value of her apparently trivial testimonies when she said: "It would not surprise me if I became one of those posthumous authors that are consulted for a certain type of local phenomena, of something like that of a meteorological order, of how high the mercury of Argentine thermometers went in the year 1920 or 1953 (this consultation would be made in the year 1999)." One might well say the same thing about this book by Goldar [*Buenos Aires: Vita cotidiana en la década del '50*], which will be consulted by North American scholarship recipients in the twenty-first or twenty-second century who come to rediscover the ruins of a culture which will have disappeared a long time before. (1992:8, my translation)

The arrival on the scene of this literary study, perhaps by some future writer at the end of the twentieth-first century, is prefigured by Ketaki

Kushari Dyson in her discussion of the uncommon global cultural connection of Ocampo and Tagore to a "new generation of teachers," "bold
spirits" (and one is never sure in this context whether those spirits will
be living or dead, reincarnated or channeled), "an Argentine exile in the
U.S.A.," or "perhaps [a figure] from some other Latin American country" (1988:352). This unknown future scholar is always awaited, and one
is never sure in researching, reading, teaching, translating, or writing
whether one is truly answering the call or only sending out another call
for that even younger scholar, one who will surpass the limits of knowledge that delimit present perspectives. The awaited manuscript may turn
out to be written in a future language that at present one is only partially
able to understand.

And in writing, I find myself adding myself to this list, assuming
this most self-effacing task, albeit in perhaps the most arrogant way, that
of chronicling a history of self-effacement that veils an all-but-forgotten
empire of fascination with the foreign, answering a call that, for all I
know, was not even meant for me, that is, if any project ever truly has
its ideal reader's name or face etched into it *a priori*. Instead, one might
consider how this call might raise the possibility of learning from *the
fictions of translation* and the possibilities for cross-identification (whether
across race, ethnicity, language, culture, gender, or sexuality). Translation—in Argentina and beyond—has been characterized as a primary
mechanism in negotiating intercultural relations and delineating the limits
of national cultures. In the context of Argentine national literature, this
network of translations and transculturations suggests a completely different nation, one in which its preconceived limits are perforated in order
to prepare for the interruption of its imaginary lineage. In this "Victorian" optic, Argentina is a Babelian nation rewritten in the feminine, in
which there is no single official language and no fixed boundaries. It is
connected, nonetheless, to the determinants of class privilege and colonial
power in much the same way that we still are, for as we pass through an
ever-expanding field of cultural activity, we come to recognize how many
of our current projects of writing, reading, and translation, regardless of
language, never quite move beyond the controlling limits of hegemonic
imagery and symbolism. Through these projects of cultural mediation,
we implicate ourselves in this network of literary reference, one endlessly
translated and reincarnated at the limits of the native and the foreign, the
living and the dead.

Notes

1. Argentine readers would have been familiar with portrayals of India in English literature. Borges's readings of Kipling are perhaps the example that most immediately comes to mind. In his well-known essay, "El escritor argentino y la tradición" ("The Argentine Writer and Tradition," 1932), Borges names Kipling's *Kim* (1901) as a main influence for the "nationalist" gaucho novel *Don Segundo Sombra* (1926) by Ricardo Güiraldes, which is centered around the apprenticeship of a European boy with a "native" sage: "the nationalists appear to venerate the capacities of the Argentine mind, but want to limit the poetic exercise of this mind to a few poor local themes, as if Argentines could only talk of riverbanks and *estancias* and not the universe" (1932:271, my translation). In this discussion of national literature, nationalist Argentina and colonial India intersect at a double scene of Europe's apprenticeship: one with the gaucho, the other in a milieu that has come to be known in India and elsewhere as "subaltern." Both Indian subaltern theorist Ranajit Guha in his *Economic Aspects of Peasant Insurgency in Rural India* (1983) and Argentine literary theorist Josefina Ludmer in *El género gauchesco: Un tratado sobre le patria* (1988) depart from Gramsci's conception of the subaltern to predicate their theoretical inquiries of Otherness and marginality in national culture; what interests me here is how a lettered representation of voice might extend beyond the limits of the national into the foreign through the act of translation, one disseminated, as Borges suggests, to question the primacy of nation or *patria* as the main source of literary identity.

2. For a history of the dominance of Argentina's economic relations with the British Empire in the early twentieth century, see David Rock, *Argentina 1516–1987: From Spanish Colonization to Alfonsín* (1987), particularly his discussion of the terms of imperial preference through which other agricultural producers firmly within the British Empire, especially Australia and Canada, attempted to lock Argentina out of the British market for farm goods. See also John King's article, " 'A Curiously Colonial Performance': The Ec-centric Vision of V. S. Naipaul and J. L. Borges," in which he notes the British Ambassador, Sir Malcolm Robertson, as saying in 1929 that Argentina must be regarded as an essential part of the British Empire (1983:229). This British vision of Argentina, by no means representative, nonetheless provides an example of the ways in which it is possible to read nations outside of their institutionally prescribed contexts (Argentina in the context of "Latin America" or "the West") in order to draw other uncommon transnational networks of literary experience: the relationship between Argentina and India.

3. Homi K. Bhabha makes reference to the Conradian color coding of the limits of empire in his essays "The Postcolonial and the Postmodern" and "Signs Taken for Wonders" in *The Location of Culture* (1994). In the latter essay Bhabha identifies the "sudden fortuitous discovery of the English book" as the scene that "triumphantly inaugurates a literature of empire," to explore its uses within and

beyond the limits of empire (102). In this case, however, the "English book" that is discovered and reinterpreted is that of Gandhi: one that evidently also has the power, be it in the original or in translation, to initiate or perpetuate a literary empire of foreign fascination.

4. It is not necessary to read, or even be able to read, Gandhi's work to get this message. In the essay by Shahid Amin, "Gandhi as Mahatma" (1988), he discusses popular interpretations of the Mahatma's message, giving an argument to allow popular responses to Gandhi to be read, not merely as the masses' mis-interpretations of his teachings or their blind obedience to them, but as the spontaneous acts of historical protagonists struggling for their own freedom from colonialism. Another example of the intersection of Gandhi, British imperialism, and Argentina can be found in the article by Salman Rushdie entitled "Outside the Whale," in which he discusses the spate of British films produced in the aftermath of the Falkland/Malvinas war—David Attenborough's *Gandhi*, David Lean's film version of E. M. Forster's *A Passage to India*, and the televising of Paul Scott's *Raj Quartet* as *The Jewel in the Crown*—as "the artistic counterpart to the rise of conservative ideologies in Britain" (1984:129). Here the image of Gandhi serves not to combat but, actually, to perpetuate a romantic view of British imperialism, one which Rushdie calls in its Indian context "Raj revisionism," but which fights its final battle, not against India, but Argentina, over a distant imperial remnant in the South Atlantic.

5. One of the most comprehensive examples of telling histories through a mapping out of world communication networks (publishing, telegraph, the railways, the post office, news agencies, the telephone, radio, cinema, television, telecommunications satellites, and computer networks) can be found in the book by Armand Mattelart entitled *Communication monde* (*Mapping World Communication: War, Progress, Culture*; 1994). As translation undoubtedly plays a large role in the functioning of these world communications networks, one would do well here to add it to this list of rapidly developing mechanisms of global communication: "Cut to the end of the nineteenth century, when communication was consecrated as the 'agent of civilization.' Its universality was that of the Victorian Empire. From railway networks, the electric telegraph, and underwater cable as well as the new Suez interoceanic route and steam navigation was stitched together an image of the world as a vast 'organism,' all of whose parts were in solidarity. Networks covering the globe became the symbol of an interdependent world where domestic economies had given way to a new international division of labor. . . . Cut now to the end of the twentieth century: communication becomes the paradigm of the new global society in an economy based on non-material flows" (1994:vii–viii). Mattelart reminds us how the name Victoria is synonymous with the notion of a nineteenth-century global empire that extends, albeit in newer and often invisible forms, into these present-day communications.

6. In the aforementioned chapter of *A Thousand Plateaus*, Deleuze and

Guattari have characterized all education under the rubric of such "order-words": "The compulsory education machine does not communicate information; it imposes upon the child semiotic coordinates possessing all of the dual foundations of grammar (masculine-feminine, singular-plural, noun-verb, subject of the statement-subject of enunciation, etc.). The elementary unit of language is the order-word [*mot d'ordre*]. . . . Language is not to be believed but to be obeyed, and to compel obedience." (1987:76).

7. Molloy observes, "Torn between a native language which she was taught to consider inadequate (Spanish words were not 'words with which one thinks') and the second language, French, in whose comforting cadences and prestigious rhetoric she seemed to perform best, [Victoria Ocampo] would start out in literature by posturing as a 'French' writer" (1991:72).

8. Piglia argues, "I do not share the opinion whereby we owe to *SUR* a knowledge and the diffusion of the best foreign literature. . . . From Count von Keyserling to Rabindranath Tagore, from Drieu la Rochelle to Roger Caillois, one saw in these overblown mediocrities the masters who were to bring our culture up to date" (1986:48–49, my translation). Mahasweta Sengupta's work on Tagore's translations of his own poetry (1990, 1995) provides insight into the possible reasons for the often misinformed and unfair evaluations of Tagore's work in the West, even if he himself bears at least some of the responsibility by, as Ocampo states, "omitting the heart of the poem" in his autotranslations.

9. See *SUR* 259, July–August 1959, the issue dedicated to Indian literature and culture, which includes texts by Gandhi, Nehru, and Tagore; translations into Spanish of Iqbal's Urdu poetry; and essays on Indian art, dance, and music.

SHERRY SIMON

Germaine de Staël and Gayatri Spivak: Culture Brokers

Across the distance of two centuries, the careers and ambitions of Germaine de Staël and Gayatri Spivak, two prominent intellectuals, show remarkable similarities. As "culture brokers" mediating between different intellectual traditions and reporting back to powerful nations, both devote considerable attention to the impact of translation. The most salient point of difference between them, for our purposes, is that de Staël wrote at the time of the emergence of the modern European nation-state, whereas Spivak testifies to the troubled status of the nation-state in the era of globalization.

Germaine de Staël (1766–1817) and Gayatri Spivak (1942–) both ground their critical projects in a transcultural context. Both wield(ed) considerable influence as high-profile mediators, collapsing intellectual and political agendas. A great traveler and cosmopolitan, de Staël wrote numerous and influential books about the cultures of England, Germany, and Italy. Through the figure of the Bengali writer Mahasweta Devi, Spivak articulates a politics and a pedagogy of translation between "India" and the First World. De Staël's understanding of cultural difference became the guiding paradigm for the discipline of comparative literature; Spivak situates her critical project of translation within Anglo-American cultural studies. In each case the meaning of *culture* and *translation* is aligned with different conceptions of the national frame.

Madame de Staël's work is coeval with that of thinkers who were setting in place the paradigms of national culture as we know it today. Spivak's finds itself linked with modes of criticism that try to "think beyond the nation," to "identify the current crisis of the nation and in identifying it provide part of the apparatus of recognition for postnational social forms" (Appadurai 1996:158). Setting the ideas of these two thinkers side by side allows us to assess the importance of "the nation" for the practice and conceptualization of translation. What becomes most apparent from this confrontation is the extent to which moving conceptual borders throws the practice of translation into crisis and obliges a rethinking of the mission and mandate of cultural linkages.

Historical Shifts

Before discussing the work of these two women, it seems appropriate to survey briefly the historical relationship between translation and the nation in the West, pointing schematically to three major forms of articulation. One of the premises of this essay—and the grounds for the comparison it proposes—is that translation in the West has historically been given the mission to mediate between nations. Yet the forms of those national cultures do not remain stable. Cultural transfer and transmission are enacted within specific cultural configurations. Shifts in the way we think about the nation and national culture will inevitably affect our ideas about the mission and modalities of translation. The high points in thinking about translation in the West have been the Renaissance, late eighteenth-century romanticism, and the last decades of the twentieth century. These are not the only moments that have seen an intense interest in translation (French classicism, for instance, was deeply involved with the translation/imitation of the classics), but these periods propose in very broad terms a new relationship between language and national culture.

It is perhaps not necessary to develop a lengthy argument around the first moment, the Renaissance. There is ample consensus that this was a period of linguistic fragmentation in Europe, accompanied by a frenzy of translation through which national languages acquired their legitimacy. The association among the European artistic Renaissance, the emergence of print capitalism, the codification of linguistic and literary norms, and the co-opting of translation toward these ends is well documented. We know that only at the beginning of the Renaissance was our current understanding of the idea of translation integrated into European vocabularies through the term *traducere*. Earlier Latin and medieval Romance languages had all employed numerous terms to describe various aspects of language transfer, according to the kind of text and the status of the languages involved. By introducting the concept of *traducere*, Renaissance discourse affirmed an understanding of translation as encompassing *all* kinds of linguistic transfer and, therefore, constituting a single model of language exchange. While the Middle Ages had very fluid notions of the boundary of the text, of language, and of nation, the Renaissance worked to fix those boundaries, providing the shape of the terms that were to make translation, in the modern sense of total transfer, possible (Berman 1988; Simon 1989). The gradual demotion of Latin as a sacred transnational language, as the single "truth-language" (Anderson 1991: 14), signaled the move away from the "global community of Christendom" (15) toward the territorialization of specific language communities (19). Benedict Anderson stresses the fact that there was no essential *fatality* that provoked the "assembling" of the varied vernaculars of the Middle Ages into national languages. Anderson argues, "Nothing served to 'assemble' related vernaculars more than capitalism which, within the limits imposed by grammars and syntaxes, created mechanically reproduced print-languages capable of dissemination through the market" (44). These print-languages laid the bases for national consciousness, creating "monoglot mass reading publics" (43).

　　The appearance of the term *traducere*, and then *traduction* in all the Romance languages around 1500, announced the advent of new intellectual frontiers. The protocol for translation became clear as areas of propriety and individuality were recognized: textual/linguistic/national. By enriching the national language, by performing what is widely recognized as a patriotic function, the translator acted in the service of the newly constituted European national language, creating a new space for vernacular literature within the emerging literary canon. Translation exercised a *vertical* function, carrying the prestige of ancient languages and cultures down through time into the fledgling national languages. Classicism completed the work of the Renaissance by making imitation of the Ancients a guiding principle of all writing, thereby collapsing the boundaries between translation and creation (Bury 1995; Charles 1985).

　　The period around 1800 saw a reconfiguration of the link between translation and nation with the writings of Madame de Staël and the

German romantics. The model of "cultural commerce" that emerged at this time, articulated by Goethe, Madame de Staël, and also Friedrich Schleiermacher and Novalis (Friedrich von Hardenberg), was linked to a *horizontal* axis of exchange among national literatures, closely related to the notion of *Bildung*, culture as a movement of self-realization. National literatures were seen as needing one another, needing to interact and learn from each other, in order to grow. Nations that were afflicted with weak, static literatures could be reinvigorated by a dose of energy from more lively national literatures. The idea that translation contributes to the creation of strong national languages and cultures became a received idea during the nineteenth and twentieth centuries, and became the implicit grounds for many practices of translation (see Brisset 1996; Cronin 1996, Delisle and Woodsworth 1995). Translation contributed to the legitimation of national languages in a dynamic of emergence.

The third phase refers broadly to the "nation in crisis" at the end of the twentieth century (Appadurai 1996). A large body of thought, including postcolonial theory, theories of globalization and diasporas, and concepts about the fragmentation of identities, points to the fact that the nation is no longer the primary indicator of cultural identity. Economically, politically, culturally, the nation is swept into large networks that undermine its authority. What are the modes and finalities of translation, then, at the time of the "postnation" (Appadurai 1996:168), when national forms of exchange compete with cultural and economic formations "above" and "below" the nation?

De Staël and the Literary Marketplace

Germaine de Staël did not publish any extensive or full-length works of translation. Yet her writings, especially *De l'Allemagne*, contain much translated work in the form of summaries and quotations. Moreover the group of writers and thinkers who assembled at Coppet, Madame de Staël's home in Switzerland, devoted much of their time to discussing and practicing translation (Bann 1977). Her political ideals of liberalism provided a firm foundation for her thinking about translation. Literatures, Madame de Staël believed, were as "perfectible" as other elements of human existence. They were highly dependent on the social and historical condition of national culture. Only free and vigorous national cultures could produce the most successful literatures. She reclaimed the medieval notion of *translatio*, the idea that vital energy travels from one people to another, and claimed that the best elements of seventeenth-century French classicism moved to Germany. In 1802 she wrote that the human spirit, which seemed to travel from one country to another previously, now resided in Germany (Isbell 1994:388). She echoed this thought in her 1816 article "De l'esprit des traductions," ("The Spirit of Translation"): "The most eminent service one can render to literature is to transport the masterpieces of the human spirit from one language into another" (de Staël 1821; in Lefevere 1992:17).

Literature, like other forms of life, had to constantly renew itself through confrontation, dialogue, and exchange. Madame de Staël was highly critical of the sense of cultural superiority of the French. She wanted to disturb their self-sufficiency by introducing the strongest elements of foreign cultures such as German culture. Romanticism, especially as expressed by the melancholy writing of the north, by the English and the Germans, was to serve as the source of that renewal for the classical literatures of the south, that is France and Italy. The means of this renewal would be translation. Karyna Szmurlo analyzes her strategy this way:

> A pragmatist of movement, she formulates an entire ethics of confrontation as a driving and constructive force. . . . Physical laws reappear in moral life, where the unending action-reaction of internal power against outside circumstances, and of external circumstances against this power is the measure of man's true grandeur. The same horizontal/vertical movement gains in dynamics in the conception of cosmopolitanism, for according to this definition, emancipation is possible within the multinational context through an interdependence of diversities which are best illustrated in the practices of the Group of Coppet. A fluctuating conglomerate of emigrants, an apparently exclusive and isolated group, actively fought oppressive government and influenced all of Europe. (1991:3)

In her letter to the Italians on "The Spirit of Translations," one of the last texts she wrote, Madame de Staël formulates most clearly her ideas of the way translation can be the motor of literary and political change. She suggests that the Italians should use translation as a means of renewing their sclerotic classical traditions. This text was received, as one might expect, with a great deal of controversy and created such hostility to the French that Madame de Staël was accused of working for the Austrians, who were then occupying Milan.[1] Calling upon the Italians to translate German and English literature was to point to the economic, political, and cultural inferiority of Italy. It was also to invite what was referred to as late as 1921 by the historian Paul Hazard, in a signal article in the first volume of the French *Revue de littérature comparée*, as an invasion, a voyage of conquest, in which the hirsute barbarians of the north advanced on the calm and measured peoples of the south. What is most arresting about Hazard's article is the violence of the language used to describe the contact between north and south. This was an invasion, he repeats, a voyage of conquest (30). The confrontation, however, turned into "a lengthy transaction" (56) dominated by translators who exchanged the coarseness and primitive savagery of the northerners for something more palatable to the Latin taste.

Hazard shows himself to be a true disciple of Madame de Staël when he concludes that "the foreign literatures did not realize their full effect (which is nothing other than a return to creative originality) until political life was revived" (66). He continues:

> Therefore the foreign example contributes finally to the renaissance of a true national spirit; it gives it a new self-consciousness, concurrently with indigenous forces which work, at the same time, toward the same end. The invasion of a foreign spirit can seem threatening during the first moments of its emergence. It provokes fashions of excess, and childish imitations. But in reality this is a transitional crisis. With hindsight, one can see that the danger was not so great and that the indigenous forces have reacted vigorously against the invasion. . . . As if some fate protected the specific character of national genius and made sure that everything retained by them served in the end their greatest need. (1921:66)

The influence of English and German literature in Italy was, for Madame de Staël, an illustration of the dialectical process through which translation helps nations to become more fully themselves. Only by using translation as creation, not as imitation, can literary cultures transform the energies of other national literatures into something specifically their own. Madame de Staël valued translation for its role in *transmitting* a cultural heritage and also for its ability to *stimulate* new forms of cultural creation. The first is dependent on the medieval model of *translatio studii*, and the second relies on the German notion of *Bildung*.

Translations are necessary, according to Madame de Staël, for a number of reasons: not only because we can never learn all languages but also because translations bring pleasure in themselves, introducing new colors, unusual formulations, and strange beauty. Translation is not imitation but a form of revitalization. For translation to be successful, however, it must not be carried out "in the French manner," that is, as an instrument of what Antoine Berman has called "hypertextualization" (1984). Translation is not to valorize the host literature by validating existing rhetorical strategies, which was the tradition of "les belles infidèles" initiated during the French classical age by Nicolas Perrot d'Ablancourt and his followers. On the contrary, translation should challenge the norms, the "regularities," of the receiving culture (Berman 1984).

The whole article is pitched in national terms, as was in fact the entire literary enterprise of Madame de Staël. She was forever elaborating on national stereotypes, while at the same time she argued for and exemplified the literary cosmopolitanism of her age. Indeed, Madame de Staël's strong and influential portraits of national character set her up for some strong criticism in the twentieth century (see Carré 1947). Nevertheless, her creed was liberalism, which at the time was associated with romanticism and against classicism. To be liberal and a romantic was to be modern. She was arguing for the promotion of free trade in the realm of the arts, and she defined translation as an essential element of "the commerce of ideas" among nations. Goethe later extended the metaphor of commerce, first introduced by Madame de Staël, when speaking of the German language as a "marketplace" where all the nations of the world offer their wares (Berman 1984:93). The translator is then a mediator whose task, according to Goethe, is to promote a spiritual exchange—a general commerce, moving toward what we would today call global communication. The commercial image of free trade among nations is taken up by Goethe and made part of his definition of *Weltliteratur*, 'world literature'.

This notion is, however, from the start, beset by political ambiguities. How is one to reconcile the notion of a world literature with a single national language? This ambiguity is apparent when Goethe, Schleiermacher, Novalis, and others suggest that the German language may be the language best suited to serve as the medium for a new world literature. Knowing that German translation theory was a response to French cultural hegemony underlines the rivalry and tension nourishing this debate. A passage from Schleiermacher's essay on translation is revealing:

> An inner necessity, in which a peculiar calling of our people expresses itself clearly enough, has driven us to translating *en masse*; we cannot go back and we must go on. . . . And coincidentally our nation may be destined, because of its respect for what is foreign and its mediating nature, to carry all the treasures of foreign arts and scholarship, together with its own, in its language, to unite them into a great historical whole, so to speak, which would be preserved in the centre and heart of Europe, so that with the help of our language, whatever beauty the most different times have brought forth can be enjoyed by all people, as purely and perfectly as is possible for a foreigner. This appears indeed to be the real historical aim of translation in general, as we are used to it now. (qtd. in Lefevere 1977:88)

Similar passages from Novalis, according to Siegbert Salomon Prawer, show that this idea was pervasive. Writing to A. W. Schlegel in 1797, Novalis held that to be German meant to be at once cosmopolitan and extremely original, and that for German culture "translations signified enlargement," and translation was more difficult than writing new poetic works, "a rarer gift" (Prawer 1973:86).

Lawrence Venuti suggests that even Schleiermacher, who seems to be promoting a foreignizing mode of translation, "does not so much introduce the foreign into German culture as use the foreign to confirm and develop a sameness, a process of fashioning an ideal cultural self on the basis of an other, a cultural narcissism, which is endowed, moreover, with historical necessity" (Venuti 1991:139). Antoine Berman is more measured in identifying the ambiguities of this counterdefensive cultural maneuver as it is expressed by Goethe's notion of *Weltliteratur*. Berman suggests that Goethe's thought oscillated between two poles: promoting a generalized movement of intertranslation, and privileging the German language and culture as medium of world literature (Berman 1984:92). Goethe's notion of *Weltliteratur* came out of a long and varied experience of translation. He translated, often at second hand, from eighteen languages, including Gaelic, Arabic, Chinese, Hebrew, Persian, and Finnish. As George Steiner explains, there are philosophical and political underpinnings to this notion, which are linked to Goethe's quest for "primordial unities," like the "*Urpflanze*, the vegetable form from which all other species would evolve." *Weltliteratur*, according to Steiner, sought to articulate a sensibility that belonged to "universal civilities" and "international spirits" characteristic of the age, including the study of other languages and literatures (1996:145–47).

The vocabulary of translation, then, moves between hospitality and hegemony, the hug of welcome and the embrace of control. This dialectic is present in Madame de Staël's own work as a cultural mediator. While it is agreed that her work introduced the French to the realities of other national cultures, critics also stress the "*prisme déformant*," 'distorting prism', through which she showed these cultures. In *L'Angleterre dans l'oeuvre de Madame de Staël* (1954), Robert Escarpit emphasizes the deformations in the image of England that Madame de Staël projected onto France. At the same time many critics have vilified de Staël for the "too pleasant" view of Germany she persuaded the French to share. Some have even held her responsible for the Germanophilia that prevented the French from understanding the dark designs of the Nazis in the years leading up to World War II (Carré 1947). John Claiborne Isbell (1994) has demonstrated in detail how Madame de Staël's translations (in fact, translated summaries) of German drama consistently simplified and distorted the plots of these plays, while José Lambert (1975) has suggested that Madame de Staël's own translations were little better than those of the French tradition she critiques.

The most decisive and long-lasting contribution of Madame de Staël, however, is the vocabulary of nationhood, which was institutionalized within literary studies from the end of the nineteenth century onward under the auspices of the discipline of comparative literature. Madame de Staël's appeal to translation as a positive contribution to the advancement of literature and her own exacerbation of the national sentiment forming at this time set the terms for much of the discussion of translation in the next century. In *De l'Allemagne*, for example, she writes:

Les nations doivent se servir de guide les unes aux autres, et toutes auraient tort de se priver des lumières qu'elles peuvent mutuellement se prêter. Il y a quelque chose de très singulier dans la différence d'un peuple à un autre: le climat, l'aspect de la nature, la langue, le gouvernement, enfin surtout les événements de l'histoire, puissance plus extraordinaire encore que toutes les autres, contribuent à ces diversités . . . (3.31)

Nations should serve as guides, one for the other. They would be wrong to deprive themselves of this reciprocal illumination. Between peoples there are singular differences: in climate, landscape, language, government, and the events of history, which are the most powerful in creating diversity . . . (my translation)

These ideas are central to the development of the terms that will be used by the new discipline of comparative literature, as it takes form from the 1840s onward. This discipline, as Susan Bassnett comments, "first appeared in an age of national struggles, when new boundaries were being erected and the whole question of national culture and national identity was under discussion throughout Europe and the expanding United States of America" (1993:8–9). In fact the institutionalization of the discipline around the turn of the century was set against the "immediate backdrop of Franco-German tensions . . . between the end of the Franco-Prussian War and the outbreak of the First World War" (Steiner 1996:147). According to Bassnett, " 'comparative' [literature] was set against 'national', and . . . whilst the study of 'national' literatures risked accusations of partisanship, the study of 'comparative' literature carried with it a sense of transcendence of the narrowly nationalistic" (1993:21). Translation was meant to be studied within comparative literature as a vector of universalism, as part of a scholarly project "that would transcend cultural boundaries and unite the human race through the civilizing power of great literature" (Bassnett 1993:7). Yet, this ideal fell short of its goals. In fact, comparative literature actively confirmed the pertinence and strength of the national frame. Both French and German practices of comparative literature were characterized by a profound nationalist chauvinism. Translations become part of an elaborate reception theory, which in fact demonstrated the potential for each national literature to absorb outside influences in much the way Madame de Staël had proposed. Significantly Susan Bassnett argues that this heritage of comparative literature has become too burdensome. She suggests that translation studies should become the new disciplinary framework through which literary exchange is studied.

Disturbing Economies of Exchange

A contemporary theorist who echoes but transforms the claims of Madame de Staël is Gayatri Spivak, one of the rare theorists who has given attention to translation in the context of contemporary cultural studies and who has brought translation theory into dialogue with a general theory of culture and cultural relations. With experience in translating Derrida as well as texts by Mahasweta Devi and other Bengali writers, Spivak speaks of translation from a practical as well as a theoretical point of view. She presents these ideas principally in "The Politics of Translation" (1993b), an article whose articulation of gender, culture, and translation merits detailed examination. I have begun this exploration elsewhere (Simon 1996). Here, however, I simply extract the broad lines that directly intersect with the terms introduced by Madame de Staël.[2]

To look at Gayatri Spivak's work as a critic and translator is to approach an economy of exchange in which translation interacts with culture studies (rather than comparative literature), where translations are no longer understood as promoting national aims. It is not my aim here to analyze Spivak's translations from the Bengali (cf. Mukherjee 1991) but, rather, to discuss the terms through which Spivak defines the mission and the values of translation. What is most striking, in contrast with Madame de Staël's reflections on the cultural meanings of literary exchange, is that the nation is now seen as a potentially confusing and even dangerous category within which to frame literary exchange. Spivak does not want Anglo-American readers to be comforted in a recognition of mutual identities but instead wants to jolt the reader into consciousness of the many distances and differences among peoples. In Spivak's front matter to her translations of Mahasweta Devi, Spivak wants to do away with the myth of pure difference (Spivak 1995:xxiv) and replace it with the idea that the translator mediates between two seamless identities. Quoting Derrida, she urges that one should reconsider all the pairs of opposites, not in order to see the opposition eliminated, say, between India and the United States, but "to see what indicates that each of the terms *must* appear as the *différance* of the other, as the other different and deferred in the economy of the same" (Spivak 1995:xxiv). In this respect Devi is a particularly appropriate author to translate and comment on, because, according to Spivak, she seeks in her work to "undo" the name "India" by dealing specifically with the reality of the tribals in India, who have always been marginal to Indian national myths (Spivak 1993a:79). Spivak claims that "the word 'India' is sometimes a lid on an immense and equally unacknowledged subaltern heterogeneity. Mahasweta [Devi] releases that heterogeneity, restoring some of its historical and geographical nomenclature" (1993a:79). Spivak argues repeatedly that Devi is not to be classified with "just Indian women writers." Spivak holds that "objects of knowledge . . . should not have national names" (1993a:188–89). Her political point is that the "nation" imprisons India within the logic of colonialism and promotes the neocolonial agenda, what Partha Chatterjee calls "the hegemonic project of nationalist modernity" (1993:13). For Chatterjee, nationalism is a "project of mediation" (1993:72), a narrative that was written through the grids and categories provided by the West, a narrative imposed by "capital," against "community" (1993:239). To question the category of the nation, like that of the Third World, is to ward off the formation of new Orientalisms and reframe the terms of international justice.

What Spivak seeks to translate, then, is not, like de Staël, the reality of the nation. On the contrary, it is "the space of displacement" traced out by Mahasweta Devi, the space of "decolonization," which is not caught within the dialectic of the reversal between empire and nation. The overall thrust of Spivak's reading of Devi's story "Douloti the Beautiful" is to show how the sophisticated vocabularies of metropolitan critique are at home there, even though Mahasweta Devi's "material is not written with an international audience in mind" (Spivak 1993a:77). Spivak seeks to extend the space of "decolonization" to the very terms of her reading, following Chatterjee's warning that the postcolonial world not be confined to the role of "perpetual consumers of modernity" (Chatterjee 1993:5). This is not to say that either Devi or Spivak takes for granted the postnational status of global capitalism in a postnational framework. One of the principal devices used by Mahasweta Devi to this end is her disparate, multileveled diction, "moving from the tribal to the Sanskritic register by way of easy obscenity and political analysis" (Spivak 1993a:77).

Spivak's translations render this linguistic heterogeneity scrupulously, producing a jarring and defamiliarizing English text. In so doing, she follows Madame de Staël's injunction not to translate "in the French manner," as well as her own advice to translators. The translator, she says, should "yield" to the text and highlight its distinctive rhetoricity. This risk of "violence to the translating medium" is necessary in order to carry across the texture of the original (Spivak 1993b:180). What Spivak cannot do by way of translation, she does in her commentary, for example, emphasizing the way in which one of the last sentences of "Douloti" is "scandalous in the planned clash between content and form" (Spivak 1993a:94). In discussing the last sentence of the story, "Douloti is all over India," Spivak suggests a further level of translation: "the traffic in wealth . . . is all over the globe" (Spivak 1993a:95). In this sentence, Spivak suggests, we can move "from the local through the national to the neocolonial globe" (1993a:95). Spivak's analysis suggests that in order to translate this story, it is necessary to take into account a complex range of frames, from the signifiers of local language, to the national frame of production, to the transnational frame of global exploitation.

In such an economy of "différance," there cannot be a silent mediator; Spivak is rather a participant, a foregrounded link in the interplay between East and West, India and the United States, incarnating the points where they intersect, overlap, and impinge upon one another. Because of the peculiar situation of English in the world today, Spivak is translating into one language but for two publics: into the language of her migrancy, but also into the vehicular language of her "native" land. The English-language translation of the Bengali writer Mahasweta Devi will be read by both Anglo-American audiences *and* English-language Indian readers, confusing the single-directionality and the "foreignness" usually associated with translation.

The doubleness of this audience suggests a difficulty for the translator. Which variety of English should she choose as the "target-language" idiom? Will it be Indian English, increasingly recognized as a language "at home" in the subcontinent, or will it be a more North American version? Responding to the criticism that the language she has chosen is in fact more American than Indian, Spivak argues that Mahasweta's work should not be reified as a national cultural artifact, accessible only to Indians or to expatriates (Spivak 1995:xxiii–xxiv). She refuses to provide the local flavor that would make Devi exotic and distant for her

North American readers. Spivak's translation is faithful, then, to the identity of the translator: a migrant who is neither Indian nor North American, an "expatriate critic" speaking principally to the "multiculturalist US reader" (Spivak 1995:xxiii).

The fact that Spivak's name and writing envelop the translated text in what Spivak calls an "instructive embrace" (the translated text preceded and followed by preface, footnotes, and critical afterword, as well as the spine of *Imaginary Maps* listing as authors Devi *and* Spivak) also signals that the translator has exceeded her conventional task. Besides being a transmitter she remains a critic, insisting on the *cognitive* and *critical* functions of the translated text. Translation does not bring a text across so that it can be simply accepted in its otherness, its difference (thereby comforting identities all around) but, rather, sets out to disturb and challenge the reader. In effect it says: read this so that you will no longer know exactly how to define the cultural Other. Spivak insists on the pedagogical role of translations: "Since the general tendency in reading and teaching so-called 'Third World' literature is toward an uninstructed cultural relativism, I have always written companion essays with each of my translations, attempting to intervene and transform this tendency . . . to bear witness to the specificity of language, theme, and history as well as to supplement hegemonic notions of a hybrid global culture with this experience of an impossible global justice" (1995:197). Indeed, much of Spivak's writing on translation is addressed to the general ignorance and naïveté of the Western cultural studies student, whose relationship to Third World writing is grounded only in a generous desire for solidarity. Good will is not enough, she argues, on the part of those who belong to a hegemonic culture and cannot perceive the multiple differences that make up the reality of the Third World. The role of translation must not be a simple accessibility (Spivak 1993b:191). To foreground the critical role of translations is to insist that translators pay attention to the rhetoric and the textuality of Third World women writers. If not, Spivak argues, a generalized movement of translation of Third World literature into English will only have a new kind of Orientalizing effect, homogenizing these exotic products, transforming hospitality into hegemony.

Spivak elaborates on this dialectic at a variety of levels, describing in what way translation, at best, *alters* the terms of exchange rather than confirming preexisting poles of difference. Translation is not about the transfer of "bodies of meaning" (Spivak 1993b:179). It is about the complex workings of "gendered agency" in language; it is about disturbing the boundaries between texts and cultures, between the translator and her own "others." Spivak describes the working out of these relations in the process of translation, namely the attitude of "surrender," which is her principal methodological guide, and the seduction of the Other, which is her motive for translation. Spivak begins her article in fact by speaking of the "friendship" which is at the basis of translation, the desire to "work at someone else's title," to use translation as a way to "get around the confines of one's 'identity' . . . as one works with a language that belongs to many others" (Spivak 1993b:179). Translation is "a simple miming of the responsibility to the trace of the other in the self" (1993b:179). There is a degree of intimacy required by translation, but this closeness is not fusion. Throughout her text, Spivak emphasizes the continual shifts in positioning between translator and text, between original and translated text. This continual repositioning of difference is closer to the "erotic" than to the "ethical" impulse, an engagement with the surfaces of difference rather than with the fundamental sameness of the ethical: "To surrender in translation is more erotic than ethical. In that situation the good-willing attitude 'she is just like me' is not very helpful. . . . In order to earn that right of friendship or surrender of identity, of knowing that the rhetoric of the text indicates the limits of language for you as long as you are with the text, you have to be in a different relationship with the language, not even only with the specific text" (Spivak 1993b:183).

Understanding another language, another text, and another cultural reality falls between the transfer of substance and the withholding of translation (Spivak 1993b:195). Spivak evokes the figure of the RAT (Reader-as-Translator) to suture this cleavage, showing how the postcolonial reader is always reading from the outside, writing herself into the text. "Other languages" comes to mean the Caribbean language of Wilson Harris or the prose of Toni Morrison, as well as the tongue of scholarship. Translating in the large sense, reading as translation, is what the postcolonial does. The postcolonial "outside/insider" becomes the emblematic figure of the contemporary translator.

Spivak's theory and method of translation emerge out of a poststructuralist theory of language and a postcolonial framework of literary exchange. As such, they are saturated with the doxa of difference "which functions in contemporary thought as an unassailable value in itself"

(Felski 1997:1). Spivak is not after "fidelity" or "equivalence" as much as she is concerned with the "erotic" impulse at the base of translation, the desire that carries the translator outside of her own identity and into the text of another. The translator's appreciation for the difference of the other text, her fixation on the surface textures of its difference, ensures the success of translation. There is no pretense to making the secondary text the "same" as the first. Spivak's insistence on the multiple layers of differences that create the distance of the text signals her participation in a discourse of postcolonial feminism that "is marked by an ongoing tension between the particular and the universal, between the 'thick description' of specific cultural practices and the 'macrosystemic analysis of transnational structures of inequality' " (Felski 1997:12).

Though they give different finalities to the operation of translation, de Staël and Spivak share several important insights. Both see translation as an activity that has broad cultural implications, producing effects that must be analyzed at a national and a global level. They understand translation as being shaped by historical patterns of global exchange, but they also see the ways in which translations can be used to disturb and reorder these relations. For both, translation is an activity of critique and intervention. By promoting certain literary values, by interacting within their new milieu, translations have cultural effects. They enact relationships between partners of unequal status, cultural entities occupying different rungs in the global hierarchy. As such, they are vectors of power.

Both Spivak and de Staël want to use translations in order to initiate new cultural dynamics. De Staël's project is to translate the vigor of northern romanticism into the over-rigid literatures of the south, to inject newness into a sterile literature, and to promote translation as a form of exchange that will create stronger national literatures. Spivak's project is to bring Indian women writers like Mahasweta Devi to Western readers, but she wants to do it in such a way that the Western reader will be "translated out" of her complacent relationship to the exotic Third World. To do this Spivak must mark out and disturb the "nation" as the frame that has come to regulate the passage of cultural goods. She wants the translated text to defy naturalized forms of belonging and to identify itself as a hybrid product.

Where de Staël and Spivak differ, then, is in their definition of the bound entities that are the poles of the translational exchange. While de

Staël seeks to bolster the idea of the nation (within what Homi Bhabha calls the "natural(ized), unifying discourse of 'nation,' 'peoples,' or authentic 'folk' tradition, those embedded myths of culture's particularity" [1992:438]), Spivak seeks to deconstruct its factitious unity and homogeneity. De Staël testifies to an era of curiosity and delight in discovering cultural difference; Spivak points to the limits of cultural relativism, the vacuous celebration of diversity. She speaks from a world in which "diasporic spheres . . . confound theories that depend on the continued salience of the nation-state as the key arbiter of important social changes" (Appadurai 1996:4).

This double perspective on translation persists to some extent today. We live simultaneously with an understanding of translation as a mode of nation-building, as a means of creating ever stronger and more unified national cultures, and with an understanding of exchange as complicated by the instabilities of cultural identity, of the historical weakening of the nation-state, and of the importance of a multitude of cultural influences. The first perspective sees cultural exchange as a movement seeking to come to rest in greater and more solid cultural and national truths. The second sees movement and contingency as central to the creation of culture itself. This second perspective, more adequate to the mobile identities of the present age, sees the movement of symbols across diverse cultural spheres (including the movement across artistic forms) as permanently unsettling. Translation can no longer feed the ethnographic impulse, the desire to account for and contain the Other. The reconstructive and reconstitutive power of translation gives way to its power to trouble and dislocate. Translation, then, is a movement similar to the negotiation of postcolonial positioning, which seeks to reverse and displace the apparatus of value-coding. The postcolonial seeks to participate in and to deconstruct the terms of common discourse. This dual activity is much like translation, which involves reinscription and relocation, a bringing together of disparate things. The process is consonant with the idea of culture as an enunciative rather than an epistemological category, in Bhabha's terms (Bhabha 1994). Our skies may be common, but our horizons are divided, as the subtitle of the anthology *The Post-Colonial Question: Common Skies, Divided Horizons* (1996) by Iain Chambers and Lidia Curti claims: fragments of the incommensurate, the untranslatable, and the unhealable litter our common territories. For Homi Bhabha "there is no 'in itself' and 'for itself' within cultures because they are always subject to intrinsic forms of translation" (1994:10).

These critical perspectives draw attention to the frontiers that have for so long sustained our understanding of cultural realities and that ground much of our thinking about translation. We are used to thinking about translation as a process that mediates between distinct and preexistent entities, as one text, written in one language and emerging out of one national culture, is transformed into a second text, written in a second language and conforming to a second national culture. Historically, translation theory and practice in the West have had a privileged link with the nation and with national cultures. But as a process of hybridization, a bringing together of two previously separated things, translation constantly plays with borders, threatening or confirming them.

As influential mediators both de Staël and Spivak remind us that dynamics of power are both within and beyond translation. Translators articulate—and enact—changing cultural and literary relations. Their work, however, is framed by the overarching forces that direct cultural traffic across the world. It is this double sensitivity that draws the work of Germaine de Staël and Gayatri Spivak together. The size of their worlds is radically different (for de Staël, "the world" was Europe), but they come together as powerful figures of mediation, as women and translators who take over the space of passage, leaving, for a time, the strong imprint of their presence.

Notes

1. In January 1816, Madame de Staël published in the first issue of a Milanese review an article translated as "Sulla maniera et l'utilità delle traduzioni." T. M. Pratt indicates that "this article constituted the first authoritative support in the peninsula for the 'romantic' literatures of the North at the expense of the 'classical' literatures of the South and they made the literary controversy that had already shaken France a national issue for the Italian people. [It] inaugurated a fiercely-fought and at times bitter polemic and as such must be held directly responsible for the genesis of those treatises which have become know as the Italian manifestos on Romanticism" (1985:452).

2. Spivak's translations of stories by Mahasweta Devi are found in *Imaginary Maps* (1995), but also in *In Other Worlds* (1988b). In addition to "The Politics of Translation" (in *Outside in the Teaching Machine*, 1993b), Spivak's

commentaries on translation are found in the preface and postface to *Imaginary Maps* and marginally in "A Literary Representation of the Subaltern: A Woman's Text from the Third World" (*In Other Worlds*, 1988b). I have made extensive comments on "The Politics of Translation" in the final chapter of *Gender in Translation: Cultural Identity and the Politics of Transmission* (Simon 1996).

CAMINO GUTIÉRREZ LANZA

Spanish Film Translation and Cultural Patronage: The Filtering and Manipulation of Imported Material during Franco's Dictatorship

One of the most significant periods for the study of socio-political manipulation of discourse in the recent history of Spain is the era of the Franco dictatorship (1939–75). Film translation took place in a context in which all foreign information had to be adapted to the cultural requirements of the Franco regime by means of a series of norms that aimed at "reducing the complexity and contingency of the impulses coming from the environment" (Hermans 1991:160). In such a situation where threatening values must be replaced, translational norms, or "required relationships between source text and target text" (Delabastita 1991:142), aim at maintaining the ideological uniformity of the target culture.[1] This generally involves simplification and adaptation of imported material. Censorship reinforces those norms by eliminating or replacing subversive material, thereby fulfilling certain intended ideological goals. Such a manipulation of imported cultural information favors the transmission of dominant values. In the case of cinema, a process of "naturalization" allows the dominant ideology to become ingrained in everyday discourse, to become "rationalized as 'common-sense' assumptions about the way things are and the way things should be" (Simpson 1993:6).

In Franco's Spain information control was officially exerted through continual publication in the daily periodical *Boletín oficial del estado* (*Official State Bulletin;* hereafter *BOE*) of ministerial guidelines regarding the censorship of public spectacles and the mass media. At the same time, decision making by the Roman Catholic church exerted a powerful influence on the censorship process, an influence that has been well documented by Juan Antonio Martínez Bretón in his book entitled *Influencia de la Iglesia Católica en la cinematografía española (1951–1962)*, a compendium of valuable and reliable information related to the issues discussed here. With the data from the *BOE* and Martínez Bretón as the main sources, in this study I examine how the vast number of films coming from abroad were chosen to be shown in Spain, what strategies were employed by the civil and religious authorities to adapt the foreign material to the target ideology, and, finally, despite all attempts to censor film, what role film translation played in the crumbling of the Franco regime.

During the Spanish Civil War (1936–39), in part because of the anticlericalism of the Republicans, it was natural for the Catholic church to ally itself with Franco's political ambitions. Franco himself exploited the religious orientation of the Cruzada Nacional (National Crusade) against the communist enemy, a movement that was officially recognized and even praised by Pius XII on a radio broadcast to the Spanish nation on 16 April 1939. According to the *Catecismo patriótico español* (*The Patriotic Spanish Catechism*), which was declared an official textbook by ministerial guidelines of 1 March 1939, the authority of the head of state was supported by both God and the Catholic church, and the religious unity of the nation was seen as essential for achieving the political unity of Spain. The renewal of intellectual and moral values that shaped the ideological structure of the Franco period was therefore based on Catholic religious instruction.

So-called *nacionalcatolicismo* ('national Catholicism') started to develop officially with the declaration of the *Fuero de los Españoles* (the Franco "Bill of Rights" of the Spanish people, published in *BOE* 18 July 1945).[2] The sixth article established Roman Catholicism as the official religion of the Spanish state,[3] and one year later Franco overtly declared before the members of the constituent assembly that the perfect state was a Catholic state. The signing of the *Concordato* (*Concordat*) with the Vatican in 1953 confirmed this ideological link between the political realm and traditional moral values, as represented by the highest figure in the Catholic church.[4] Even though Spain had officially been declared

Catholic, however, this fiat alone could not properly guarantee the preservation of moral standards in the cinema industry and other cultural domains. Right until the very end of the dictatorship in November 1975, there remained a need for the regular publication (via *BOE*) of updated appropriate legislation aimed at legally promoting the legitimate moral, political, and social principles of the totalitarian state, and at penalizing any instances of the abuse of such principles.

The carefully planned and institutionalized processes of film distribution and the workings of the censorship apparatus are not difficult to reconstruct from legal documents issued at the time. The evidence clearly indicates that the interests of both church and state followed parallel trajectories even before the end of the Civil War and that the decisive intervention of the ecclesiastic representatives was constantly welcomed by the civil authorities. The influence that public spectacles in general and the cinema in particular exerted on the life, habits, and education of the Spanish population is frequently stressed in the surviving records. For example, in 1937 (*BOE* 27 March) the provisional General Government for the first time issued a detailed set of guidelines that emphasized the need for strict, precise, and centralized control of the cinema to make it conform to the patriotic norms of cultural morality. For this purpose, two censorship boards were founded, one in Seville and the other in Corunna. They were in charge of the revision and censorship of all Spanish and/or foreign productions that were to be shown in Spanish territory. In an attempt to unify and standardize the operations of both institutions, a different guideline (*BOE* 3 May 1937) included a series of blank forms to be filled in by the members of the censorship boards, whose names and offices were carefully given in detail. The updating and maintenance of the records constituted a complex process, but it was carefully carried out by the corresponding censorship board members following direct orders from the government.

The next measure to govern film was the constitution by law in 1938 of a series of official bodies, among which the Comisión Nacional de Censura Cinematográfica (National Commission of Film Censorship) and the Junta Superior de Censura Cinematográfica (Superior Board of Film Censorship) are the most representative. The organization of those bodies and their spheres of influence took place on 23 November 1942. The Junta Superior was in charge of overseeing the work done by the

Comisión Nacional, which consisted of the so-called Presidente and five other members whose offices and domains of responsibility were as follows:

1. A representative of the military, who supervised military issues and matters of national defense.
2. A representative of the ecclesiastic authority, who supervised moral and religious issues.
3. A representative of the Ministry of National Education, who was responsible for educational and cultural issues.
4. A representative of the Ministry of Industry and Commerce, who was in charge of economic issues.
5. A representative of the Department of Cinematography, who was both a script reader and censor, and who was responsible for technical and political issues, as well as national education. (*BOE* 26 November 1942)

According to their own domains, members were responsible for watching over the integrity of the content of a film and for producing a written report giving their final verdict, either banning or authorizing the film. In the latter case, the report was to specify which cuts or other alterations were to be made. In what follows, I focus on the modification of the content of foreign films. Although other instances of authoritative control occurred, including the screening of propaganda material, such as posters and photographs, and the rating of films in terms of audience age, they exceed the scope of this essay.

During the Spanish Civil War and the early years of the Franco period, the representatives of the military on the censorship boards were preeminent not only as the members in charge of signing the documents that either authorized or banned the exhibition of films, but also as the keepers of traditional values that would preserve the image of Franco, the provisional government, and the military depicted in those films. The ministerial guideline of 28 June 1946 (*BOE* 19 July 1946), however, indicates a change of direction: the preeminent power of the church representatives on the censorship boards was strongly emphasized by the ruling that neither the Comisión Nacional nor the Junta Superior could hold a session without their presence. Moreover, whenever they found a moral justification, they had the right to ban the exhibition of the film in question. This ruling confirms the privileged position of the church with respect to other social groups and the new orientation of the state toward the philosophy of *nacionalcatolicismo*. According to the same guidelines, the joint efforts of both the Comisión Nacional and the Junta Superior were finally merged through the creation of a single body, the Junta Superior de Orientación Cinematográfica (Superior Board of Film Standards). In spite of constant requests for guidelines, however, the political authorities avoided the publication of a set of rules or specific criteria as to what contents were to be banned by the civil boards of censorship until 1963.[5]

In a further attempt to protect the moral integrity of national and imported films, following the directions given by Pius XI in his Encyclical Letter *Vigilanti Cura* (1936),[6] two ecclesiastical bodies, the Comisión Episcopal de Ortodoxia y Moralidad (Bishops' Commission on Orthodoxy and Morality) together with the Dirección General de Acción Católica (Supervisory Board on Catholic Action) approved on 17 February 1950 the *Instrucciones y normas para la censura moral de espectáculos (Instructions and Standards Regarding Moral Censorship of Public Performances).*[7] This was the first Spanish written code of censorship norms, especially designed by the ecclesiastical authorities to provide a unified moral guide for public spectacles aimed at both critics and spectators by means of the following classification:[8] (1) todos, incluso niños (all audiences, including children); (2) jóvenes (young viewers 14–21 years of age); (3) mayores (adults 21 years and older); (3R) mayores, con reparos (adults 21 years and older, with reservations regarding moral grounds); and (4) gravemente peligrosa (seriously dangerous). Broadly speaking these labels correspond to the following criteria:

1. Grade 1 (morally correct): Films that do not cause the viewers to panic or contain any form of violence; some honest love scenes can be accepted.
2. Grade 2 (morally correct): Films that do not depict divorce, laziness, drunkenness, theft, suicide, and, in general, any immoral characters, passion, sensuality, free love, adultery, immodest clothing, family troubles, or criminality; violence can only be treated discreetly.
3. Grade 3 (morally acceptable): Films that do not depict any carnal appetites, sensuality, or disorderly love affairs, sexual perversion,

prostitution, rape, corruption, extremely immodest clothing, or anything else that goes against the state and its fundamental institutions. Other vices such as divorce, free love, drunkenness, laziness, or drug use can only be shown on the condition that they are decorously treated.

4. Grade 3R (antidogmatic and immoral): Films in which the above subjects appear too often or in too explicit a manner.

5. Grade 4 (antidogmatic and immoral): Films in which the above subjects are treated in such a way as to show violence and crude attitudes, lack of moderation, or blatant feelings of anticlericalism or antipatriotism.

Grades 1 through 3 merely constituted acceptance of the moral quality of the spectacle, not necessarily its approval or recommendation, while grades 3R and 4 would have resulted in the banning of the film by civil standards. In this respect, the Comisión Episcopal declared in 1958 (see below) that, whenever a film was officially authorized for adults by civil standards but still raised menacing, harmful objections, it was the church's moral obligation to give adults prior notice of the dangers by classifying it as a grade 3R or 4 film, depending on the degree of danger indicated in the *Instrucciones y normas para la censura moral de espectáculos*. The Comisión Episcopal also declared that the Spanish church had decided not to introduce an even more severe type of moral classification (grade 5) because those films that would have been affected were normally banned by the civil authorities.

Although these moral ratings established by church representatives in 1950 were merely advisory and were not intended to be used by civil censorship boards, Catholic critics and journalists were obliged to include the moral grades of films in their reviews and listings, and it was the spectators' own moral duty to be properly informed before seeing the shows. Those films that deserved a classification of 4, however, could never be technically or artistically praised in case such a judgment was thought to be an indirect recommendation to the public.

By the 1950s the cultural repression on the part of the state was administered by the traditionalist Minister for Information and Tourism, Gabriel Arias Salgado (1951–62).[9] The surprising appointment in 1951 of José María García Escudero as Director General de Cinematografía, the post in charge of the policies on film, opened up a brief period of relaxation. His concept of censorship included an intelligent amalgamation of religious thought and open-mindedness, and he proposed the public distribution of a fixed censorship code, which, for the first time would publicly specify the basic standards according to which civil censorship boards then operated. With regard to the censorship of translated scripts, he was of the remarkable opinion that if the manipulation of dubbed dialogue resulted in a noticeable lack of coherence between images and content, it was not at all desirable.[10] He had no time to put those ideas into practice, however. His flexible character and his willingness to promote certain films that included social criticism led to his early resignation in 1952. With the appointment of the new director, Joaquín Argamasilla, a series of measures was undertaken in order to improve the functioning of institutionalized censorship. The Junta Superior de Orientación Cinematográfica (Superior Board for Film Standards) was substituted for the Junta de Clasificación y Censura (Board of Classification and Censorship) on 21 March 1952 (*BOE* 31 March 1952). It consisted of two different bodies: the Rama de Censura (Censorship Branch), which evaluated ethical, moral, political, and social matters, and the Rama de Clasificación (Classification Branch), which classified films according to their technical, artistic, and economical properties.

The Decline of Traditional Moral Values: The Case of *Ariane*

While the reinforcement of traditional national values was being imposed in Spain, the commercial pressure of American productions in practical terms virtually colonized the Spanish screens and commanded the interest of the generations after the Civil War, who turned the cinema into the most popular form of entertainment. The moral standards portrayed in U.S. films were rapidly diverging from the Spanish principles of obsessive sexual puritanism, and by 1950 both the European and American film industries were evolving toward an ever-increasing explicitness and violation of earlier norms of decency.[11]

As a result in many cases the obligatory dubbing of all foreign films, originally introduced to facilitate the understanding of the dialogue by Spanish viewers, became the main controlling instrument in the hands of the censors.[12] Frequently, thanks to the manipulation of dialogue, which sometimes reached astonishing limits of mental deviousness as will be seen later, and also to precise lip synchrony, viewers would little suspect that the films they watched had once been full of prohibited references. At other times the lack of coherence was all too evident.[13] For example, in *Arco del triunfo (Arch of Triumph*, Lewis Milestone, 1948) Ingrid Bergman is asked whether she is married to the man in the scene, who in the film is her lover, and her negative head gesture is accompanied by the dubbed affirmative answer "sí" in the Spanish version. The same principles of censorship are used to conceal the adulterous relationship between Clark Gable and Grace Kelly in *Mogambo* (*Mogambo*, John Ford, 1953; released in Spain on 15 October 1954); her husband, Donald Sinden, becomes her brother in the Spanish version of the film. The moral hypocrisy of the regime was thus capable of accepting the insinuation of incest, which the censors regarded as most uncommon, but blatantly rejected adultery, which in fact was a very frequent social practice. Censorship at times turned desperate words of love into a prayer (*Las nieves del Kilimanjaro* [*Snows of Kilimanjaro*, Henry King, 1952], released in Spain on 25 September 1953), and a husband into a father (*El ídolo de barro* [*Champion*, Mark Robson, 1949], released on 27 January 1955). The censors even killed an innocent husband in order to remove another adulterous relationship from the screen in *Las lluvias de Ranchipur (The Rains of Ranchipur*, Jean Negulesco, 1955; released on 22 April 1962).

Contradictions in foreign film censorship in Spain are also revealed by changes made in the American film *The Hunchback of Notre Dame* (William Dieterle, 1939),[14] based on the famous novel by Victor Hugo, which in 1940 became part of the list of banned books in Spain. One of the most noticeable aspects of the film is the presence of Claude Frollo, a lascivious priest whose jealousy and evil thoughts drive him to the most sinful desires and even to murder in an attempt to gain the favors of the beautiful gypsy Esmeralda. The cuts and modifications of the dialogue in the Spanish version, *El Jorobado de Nuestra Señora de París*, demonstrate the authorities' attempt to control the potential pernicious effects that the film might have on the audience. Nonetheless, although the censors were aware of the fact that the highly controversial moral issues portrayed in the film had not been fully concealed, they finally decided to approve the distribution of this film on 10 November 1944, probably because the film's box office success was too substantial to reject.

Further proof not only of the contradictions in the censors' verdicts but also of the unexpected permissiveness of the church representatives can be found in the following case study of the translation and censorship of the 130-minute-long American film *Love in the Afternoon* (Billy Wilder 1957). It was assigned the "only for adults" rating and the 4 moral grade when it was finally shown in Spain under the more innocuous title of *Ariane*. This film had to undergo a long and painful process of purification before it was first released in Madrid on 14 October 1957 at the theatre Lope de Vega, to a good reception by the public.[15] The first time that *Ariane* was submitted for censorship by the Junta de Clasificación y Censura (19 July 1957), the distributors did not include any prior voluntary cuts or modifications[16] and, as might have been predicted, the film was banned by the majority of the members of the Junta because it violated the sanctity of the institutions of marriage and the family by presenting an explicit adulterous relationship between Ariane and a rich American man. The distributors responded by making three cuts, two of which removed a couple of kisses, the kind of physical contact that has always proved to be a major concern for film censors because it "stimulates the lower and baser instincts of the public."[17] The second revision by the Junta (26 July 1957), however, introduced six further cuts (two more kisses and a love scene, among others) and some forty modifications within the translated dialogue on the grounds that the grave danger of the film as a whole could thus be averted.

The most significant changes introduced on the second occasion are the following. First, the censors eliminated any overt demonstration of physical contact or scenes of passion on the part of young couples, any references to promiscuous relationships, and any disrespectful comments against the clergy. Second, censors modified the translated dialogue in order to conceal a number of harmful elements, including Ariane's adulterous relationships with men. Of forty changes in the dialogue, twenty-five were of this type, three of which specifically tried to hide the fact that Ariane has a lot of male friends. The terms *amigos* (for *friends*) and *hombres* (for *men*) were often replaced by more neutral terms like *asuntos* ('matters'), *historial* ('background'), and *amor* ('loved one'), and in four different instances the original translation was completely amended to omit such references. The constant replacement of *hombres*, 'men' (which in such a context could only refer to Ariane's lovers), by *novios*, 'boyfriends' (which implies a kind of stable, pure, and socially acceptable relationship between two people who love each other chastely), is the most remarkable modification of this type.

Moreover, several changes were also made to conceal any references to the locations or the physical conditions under which the illegitimate encounters take place, namely, the time of the day (e.g., the evenings) or the meeting point (e.g., the Ritz Hotel); comments referring to parts of the body with sexual connotations were also obscured. In addition censors eliminated comments regarding the moral behavior and fidelity of young ladies, allusions to the foreign source culture (e.g., "kilos" replaced "pounds"), and violations of preferred social habits (e.g., a reference to a drunken Dutchman is eliminated twice).

Most members of the Junta (Don Mariano Daranas, Don Rafael de Casenave, Don Francisco Ortiz Muñoz, and, most surprisingly, both church representatives, Reverendo Padre Manuel Villares and Reverendo Padre Andrés Avelino Esteban) were of the opinion that, although Ariane's visits with a man in his hotel room were a bad influence on young ladies' habits, the new version of the film could be classified as officially valid for adults only. In spite of all the changes that had been made, however, three of the members of the Rama de Censura (Don Pío García Escudero, Don Patricio González de Canales, and Don José Luís García de Velasco) took the view that the new version only mitigated the most obvious love scenes but did not impede the overall harmful effects of the film. Two of the reports are especially significant: both Canales and Velasco focused their criticism on the fact that the promiscuous lifestyle of the protagonist did not disappear by simply introducing the word *novios* instead of *hombres* in the translated dialogue. Both reports clearly state that the innocent nature of the modification even constitutes an insult to the intelligence and good judgment of the censors, who, in the name of Catholic moral standards, might childishly assume that the same woman could be capable of having no less than nineteen purely Christian relationships (all of them obviously aimed at marriage) with a like number of men, or that her visits with a man in a hotel room would be characteristic of a respectable young lady.

The striking discrepancies in the reactions of the censors resulted in a third inspection of the film on 13 September 1957. This final examination reveals the slight shift of the church representative Esteban, who admitted the general immoral tone but thought that the new cuts ordered by the Junta (which in reality were not very substantial) were enough to justify its approval. Canales pointedly referred to the immoral nature of every aspect of the film, sarcastically underlining the fact that adultery is the most decent part of it, but finally accepted the ecclesiastical verdict. It was only Velasco who again recommended the banning of the film in an attempt to forestall future reactions of the public against such a vacuous act of censorship, but his remarks were totally ignored and the film was finally approved for distribution.

If the preservation of the moral standards of films had been the only basis of the verdicts, it seems that both *El Jorobado de Nuestra Señora de París* and *Ariane*, with or without cuts or other alterations, would have been banned by the censors. The eventual authorization of both films seems to support the view that even though the defense of morality was one of the main motivations for government consent, concessions were made to political and economic interests (Gutiérrez Lanza 1999b). Confirmation can be found in the pages of the religious weekly periodical *SIPE* (*Servicio informativo de publicaciones y espectáculos*; Information Service for Publications and Performances) where the battle against foreign immorality was uncompromisingly fought. In this publication the authorities were accused of promoting a savage kind of mercantilism by making a few cuts where necessary but, nonetheless, customarily authorizing the distribution of indecent films, which eventually would only cause the eradication of traditional national values. The seemingly strong foundations of the official Junta Superior were thus called into question on the grounds that it was incapable of assessing the potential damage that the vast number of American films could cause in the long run.

The Relaxation of Censorship and the Final Death Throes of the Regime

It is true that the dictatorial moralistic principles of the *nacionalcatolicismo* were still held as officially valid in the late 1950s, but by then it was also quite clear that the spectacular "corrective" measures of public morality and religiosity that had been in force since the end of the Civil War had not really taken root among the common people.[18] There existed a strong social awareness that all that was publicly sacred was privately profaned. According to Alonso Tejada,

> . . . los poderosos intereses económicos que dependían del turismo
> fueron causa suficiente para que nuestras autoridades cerraran los ojos
> ante las revolucionarias innovaciones en la indumentaria femenina y

> en el comportamiento que los extranjeros traían consigo. . . . Cayeron
> los tabúes sexuales y los principios de la moral tradicional fueron ar-
> rumbados sin resistencia al rincón de los recuerdos. (1977:156)

> . . . the powerful economic interests that depended on tourism were
> enough reason for the authorities to close their eyes to the revolu-
> tionary innovations in female clothing and in the behavior of for-
> eigners. . . . Sexual taboos fell and traditional moral principles were
> pushed aside. (my translation)

The painful realization that twenty years of repression had not been
enough to eradicate even the most obvious examples of social concupis-
cence and indecency, together with concessions made by the Spanish
government for reasons of political and economic opportunism, provoked
a healthy humble reaction on the part of the advocates of public decency.
Most censors showed a certain degree of reluctant indulgence.

On the international level, as Leonard Quart and Albert Auster argue, "as a result of relaxing societal sexual standards and court rulings
overturning rigid obscenity laws, the sexual taboos long governing Hollywood began to fall by the wayside"; in turn, this permitted "a widening
of the range of permissible film topics and gave American films the possibility of depicting a realism in human relationships that they had previously so sorely lacked" (1984:76). As a clear sign of the political and
economic opportunism highlighted previously, the absurdly rigorous attitude of Arias Salgado gave way to a need for a new spirit of cultural
opening in Spain. It became necessary to avoid the international ridicule
that the banning of various prestigious films was likely to provoke. The
new Minister for Information and Tourism, Manuel Fraga Iribarne
(1962–69), initiated a period of moderate tolerance that, though cause
for widespread optimism, in the long run turned out to be quite limited.
His first significant measure was the reappointment of José María García
Escudero as the new Director General de Cinematografía y Teatro. When
he returned to the political arena, Escudero permitted the more explicit
portrayal of sexual taboos and other forbidden subjects, but this tolerance
was predicated on the condition that those topics did not constitute the
fundamental principles on which the artistic and commercial value of the
films in question was based.

As a consequence of the increasing explicitness of foreign cinema,
the liberalization of moral rules, and García Escudero's cultural opening,

ecclesiastic influence in the cinema industry suffered a gradual decline. Martínez Bretón observes,

> ... la información cinematográfica filtrada por el mensaje de la Iglesia es desbordada por la publicada desde otras fuentes del pensamiento, ajustadas al análisis del fenómeno cinematográfico desde coordenadas preferentemente estéticas, narrativas, realistas, mundanas, etc., pero omitiendo la trascendencia religiosa imprimida con anterioridad. (1988:154)

> ... cinematic information filtered through Catholic discourse was overtaken by other currents of published thought and adjusted to analysis of cinematic phenomena by means of primarily aesthetic, narrative, realistic, and secular, etc. points of view, omitting the previously established religious significance. (my translation)

The authority of the representative of the Catholic church to ban the exhibition of certain films through the official channels of censorship was finally abolished by ministerial law on 20 February 1964 (*BOE* 14 March 1964) and the responsibility for censorship transferred to the Minister for Information and Tourism.

Meanwhile, the long-awaited official code of censorship governing civil censorship boards was finally published in 1963 at the beginning of García Escudero's second tenure, and it was approved on 9 February 1963 and made public in the *BOE* on 8 March 1963.[19] The Christian basis of this code is still apparent: for example, it banned suicide (Norm 8.1), divorce, adultery, illicit sexual relationships, prostitution, and attacks against marriage and the institution of the family (Norm 8.4), as well as the justification of abortion and birth-control methods (Norm 8.5). The code promoted the respect for conjugal love (Norm 11) and prohibited any attacks against the Catholic church, the fundamental principles of the state, or the head of state (Norm 17).

Although the publication of these ministerial guidelines silenced the general demand for a code of censorship that made explicit and objective which contents were and were not permissible, the guidelines provoked a number of different reactions and comments. This can be seen in the publication of a 194-page volume of articles, interviews, editorials, and opinion polls, entitled *La censura de cine en España*, edited by Pascual Cebollada in 1963. For many the situation remained more or less the

same: the code was too general, too ambiguous, and too open to interpretation; thus it did not help script writers and translators anticipate the
censors' final verdict. Moreover, the most intolerant critics maintained
that extensive foreign cultural material was representative of Protestant
cultures, whose society allowed both divorce and adultery, and whose
cinema was flooded with marriages heading for disaster and other depictions of sin. In their opinion, instead of effectively banning dangerous
films, the liberal atmosphere and the ambiguity of the code merely represented lip service to moral standards that the general public was not
going to follow voluntarily. By contrast, enemies of censorship did not
believe that the atmosphere was sufficiently liberal and still argued for
more tolerant attitudes.

Another influential measure that was taken under García Escudero's
leadership was the establishment of a higher age limit for adult audiences
by the ministerial guideline of 2 March 1963 (*BOE* 9 March 1963),
which set the adult age for many foreign films at eighteen instead of
sixteen. Controversial topics such as the ones banned by Norm 8.4 were
now permitted as long as images or dialogue did not explicitly raise the
subjects mentioned in the code. In the event they did, the common practice was to introduce a few cuts or modifications of dialogue in order to
make the target text acceptable in the recipient culture. In this respect
comparative analysis of the original and translated scripts of five films
dubbed from English into Spanish at the time indicates that autocensorship was the control mechanism most widely used by Spanish translators
as a strategy to make the dubbed versions acceptable (Gutiérrez Lanza
1999b.[20]

In order to respond to the greater tolerance for eroticism in films
coming from abroad, a private guideline of 12 January 1967 (*BOE* 20
January 1967) created special theaters of no more that five hundred seats
(Salas de Arte y Ensayo) in cities with a population over fifty thousand.
They were destined to show foreign films in the original or in subtitled
versions, as well as Spanish films of special interest. This experiment allowed for films such as *Repulsion* (Polanski, 1965) to be seen by Spanish
audiences,[21] but the interest of the public gradually decreased because
those films were still being visibly mutilated by the censors.

The main drawback of this modest cultural opening, apart from the
fact that it was a mere imitation of foreign habits, was that it was based
on the same old legal, administrative, and political mechanisms that had

been in force for decades. In the words of Alonso Tejada ". . . la liberación sexual debía empezar por las ideas, por la educación. Pero tal cosa exigía una transformación profunda de las estructuras culturales y legislativas del régimen. Y éstas por desgracia seguían siendo las mismas de los años cuarenta" (1977:156–57; " . . . sexual liberation should start from ideas, from education. However, such a thing demanded a profound transformation of the cultural and legislative structures of the regime. Unfortunately, the structures were still the same as those in the Fifties" [my translation]). As a result, there was a general feeling of widespread insecurity among artists and intellectuals on the grounds that nonconformism could be legally repressed by the prevailing apparatus at any time.

Liberal policies were not well received by the most conservative sectors of society, which had seen liberalism strengthened by the substitution of Fraga Iribarne for the more reactionary Minister for Information and Tourism, Alfredo Sánchez Bella, in 1962. The pendulum swung back again later as a result of the reaffirmation of the most traditional standards of decency in the final years of Franco's dictatorship, causing the Salas de Arte y Ensayo to disappear in 1971 and foreign films to suffer again from the rigidity of the censors. The liberal sectors of society did not abandon their more tolerant views, convinced that the transformation of society while Franco was still alive was an impossible dream (Alonso Tejada 1977:241).

The fundamental means of controlling translated films during the Franco regime was the power exerted by the censors either to ban or to authorize the distribution of a film, together with the enforcement of certain cuts and modifications of the dialogue that, according to a set of initially unpublished and later noticeably ambiguous criteria, would turn a dangerous film into an innocuous or even a highly recommended one for the Spanish audience. If we take into account that "having the power to determine things like which word meanings or which linguistic and communicative norms are legitimate or 'correct' or 'appropriate' is an important aspect of social and ideological struggle" (Fairclough 1989:88–89), it can be said that the virtual monopoly of decisions achieved by the Juntas and the church on purely political or moral grounds constituted a form of control with broad consequences. Censorship works under the illusion that "the more mechanical the functioning of an ideological assumption in the construction of coherent interpretations, the less likely it is to become a focus of conscious awareness, and hence the more secure its ideological status—which means also the more effectively it is reproduced by being drawn upon in discourse" (Fairclough 1989:85–86). Because in the censorship of film under Franco, the control of information went beyond meddling with a specific script or tampering with content, operating through the process of wide-scale selection of foreign films as well, a manner of control was exerted that broadly channeled film content toward the requirements of the dominant ideology. There was the intent to give the illusion of intercultural transfer, while at the same time blocking it by means of a carefully planned censorship apparatus and mechanisms, which, especially at the beginning of the dictatorship, used film translation as a means of concealing threatening elements in the fight against foreign immorality.

Such was the intention of the censors. A whole society, however, cannot afford to take the risk of depending on the group in power to supply it with its own cultural needs or even to preserve those things of value that are tradition, heritage, or, as it happened in the case of Spain, the behavior patterns of a whole nation. With respect to social habits, art, and culture, from the mid-1950s onward, certain prevailing moral values had to be gradually pushed aside in the pursuit of economic goals, mainly due to the imperatives of international marketing and internal social pressure. The self-contradictory aspects of the censors' verdicts, the unexpected permissiveness of the church representatives (found in the case studies of the Spanish translation and censorship of the American films *The Hunchback of Notre Dame* and *Love in the Afternoon*), and the noticeable relaxation of civil censorship in the 1960s (Gutiérrez Lanza 1999b) show that film translation could no longer be understood as an impermeable barrier against foreign information, but as an act of intercultural communication and information transfer that was capable of challenging the prevailing status quo by introducing new elements into the target system.[22] Therefore, the case of film translation under Franco represents, to use Mary Snell-Hornby's words, "an act of communication across cultural barriers, the main criteria being determined by the recipient of the translation and its specific function" (1988:47). The degree of liberalization that Spanish society had reached in the final years of Franco's dictatorship, partly thanks to the imitation of foreign habits portrayed in films, turned the final reinforcement of the most traditional standards of decency into a useless and desperate last-ditch attempt to restore the initial power of the censorship apparatus.

Notes

1. For a detailed account of so-called initial, preliminary, and operational norms at work in every act of translation, see Toury 1980 and 1995.

2. Alonso Tejada states that the term *nacionalcatolicismo* refers to the "omnipresencia del clero en los organismos y actividades del Estado, compensado por la intervención de las autoridades civiles en los asuntos de la Iglesia" (1977:18; "omnipresence of the clergy in the bodies and activities of the State, counterbalanced by the intervention of the civil authorities in the affairs of the Church" [my translation]). For an account of the effect of this doctrine on the education of postwar generations through textbooks, comics, radio, and cinema, see Sopeña Monsalve 1994.

3. Artículo 6 reads "la profesión y práctica de la Religión Católica, que es la del Estado Español, gozará de la protección oficial. Nadie será molestado por sus creencias ni por el ejercicio privado de su culto. No se permitirán otras ceremonias ni manifestaciones externas que las de la Religión Católica" (Maura Gamazo 1988:172; "the belief and practice of the Catholic Religion, which is the official religion of the Spanish State, will enjoy official protection. No one will be persecuted for their beliefs or for the private exercise of their religion. Ceremonies and public demonstrations other than those of the Catholic Religion will not be permitted" [my translation]).

4. This agreement between the Vatican and the Spanish government was signed in 1953, and it related to matters of mutual interest such as the declaration of Catholicism as the only official religion in Spain. As Martín Artajo said when he got off the plane from Rome, the *Concordato* was "la consagración formal y escrita del régimen de perfecta colaboración entre la Iglesia y el Estado instaurado por el Movimiento Nacional acaudillado por el generalísmo Franco" (qtd. in Martínez Bretón 1988:48; "the formal and written dedication of perfect collaboration between church and state instituted by the Nationalist Movement led by Generalisimo Franco" [my translation]).

5. These criteria are believed to have existed even during the Civil War, as they are referred to as "instrucciones privadas" ('private guidelines') in *BOE* 3 May 1937, but to date no written account of such guidelines has surfaced.

6. *Vigilanti Cura* highlighted the dangerous potential and pernicious effects of the cinema and pointed out the strong need for a unified moral classification of films.

7. The Comisión Episcopal de Ortodoxia y Moralidad was the bishops' commission in charge of the promotion of honesty in films, the classification of

films by moral standards, and the public circulation of moral classifications within Spanish territory. The group Acción Católica de Propagandistas (ACNP), which was also connected to the Spanish episcopate, was one of the main organizations representing the so-called *catolicismo político*, 'political Catholicism', one of the ideological pillars of *nacionalcatolicismo* in the early 1950s.

8. Adapted from Martínez Bretón 1988:38–40.

9. His moral doctrine has been described by Alonso Tejada in the following terms: "embriagado por el misticismo políticoreligioso del momento, Arias Salgado creyó que su misión primordial al frente del Ministerio consistía en meter en vereda a todos los españoles y conducirlos—por grado o por fuerza—al cielo. . . . España debía, pues, mantenerse como reserva espiritual y de castidad de Occidente" (1977:96; infatuated with the politico-religious mysticism of the time, Arias Salgado believed that his main mission at the Ministry was to control Spaniards and guide them—willing or not—toward heaven. . . . Spain should then remain the West's reserve of spirituality and chastity [my translation]).

10. In his own words, "el bienintencionado empleo del doblaje como auxiliar de la moral, cuando la imagen dice lo que no dicen las palabras, podría llegar a ser en ciertos casos, un remedio peor que la enfermedad" (Martínez Bretón 1988:55; the well-intentioned use of dubbing as a moral auxiliary, when the image says what the words do not, could, in certain cases, make the cure worse than the disease [my translation]).

11. In 1929 Hays and a group of other major Hollywood producers drew up a list of thirty-six specific guidelines for producers, but the fact that these guidelines were not strictly enforced aroused severe criticism from religious organizations. *The Production Code* was drafted in 1930 in an attempt to explain the general moral principles by which Hollywood motion picture producers should be guided. However, the 1930 code was ignored as often as it was observed, which prompted the Catholic bishops of the United States to form the Legion of Decency in 1934. It remained in effect until the 1950s, when it began to be constantly challenged by increasingly popular controversial topics that tested its flexibility. It was finally abandoned in 1968 for a more flexible rating system (see Black 1994; Belton 1996:136–37).

12. The ministerial guideline of 23 April 1941 required the dubbing of all foreign productions by Spanish professionals within the national territory of Spain.

13. The following examples have been pointed out by Gubern (qtd. in Alonso Tejada 1977:143–44).

14. For a comprehensive study see Gutiérrez Lanza 1999b.

15. The fact that *Love in the Afternoon* is 130 minutes long (according to the International Movie Database; *IMDb*, http://uk.imdb.com/, 1990–2000) and the dubbed version is only 120 minutes long (according to the annual summary of cinema releases of 1957, published by the Spanish periodical *Cine Asesor*) demonstrates the substantial cuts that this film had to suffer in order to be shown in Spain.

16. See the letter that J. Gallart, Director of C.B. Films, S.A., sent on 17 July 1957 from their office in Madrid to the Director General de Cinematografía y Teatro. A copy of this letter is kept at the Ministerio de Educación y Cultura, Madrid, in *Ariane*: Expediente de Censura 16411 (*Ariane*: Cinema Censorship File Number 16411). My research on *Ariane* is based on the documents kept in this file.

17. My translation from the final report of the meeting of the Junta de Clasificacíon de Censura held on 19 July 1957 (*Ariane* 1957).

18. For a comprehensive study see Alonso Tejada 1977.

19. In order to give the maximum visibility to the contents of the code of censorship, it was also published in the periodical *Revista internacional del cine* under the title "La nueva reglamentación legal del cine en España," along with a number of other ministerial guidelines, as well as under the title "Normas de censura" in the periodical *Film ideal* (1963:117.1).

20. The five films are *Piel de serpiente (The Fugitive Kind*, Sidney Lumet, 1959), *Días sin vida (Beloved Infidel*, Henry King, 1959), *Pesadilla bajo el sol (Nightmare in the Sun*, Marc Lawrence, 1963), *Repulsión (Repulsion*, Roman Polanski, 1965), and *Desde la terraza (From the Terrace*, Marc Robson, 1960).

21. For a preliminary textual analysis of the release of *Repulsion* in Spain, see Gutiérrez Lanza 1999b.

22. The permeability of cultures has been addressed by Even-Zohar 1990.

LIN KENAN

Translation as a Catalyst for Social Change in China

In recent years there has been an increased interest in the history of translation among Western translation studies scholars.[1] Lawrence Venuti, for example, has delved deeply into the history of English translation in order to find a way to increase the translator's visibility. He concludes that the root cause of the pitiful plight of translators and their invisibility could be attributed to the so-called fluency tendency, which was the norm in English translation for most of the twentieth century. In his anthology *Translation/History/Culture: A Sourcebook*, André Lefevere traces the two-thousand-year-long history of pronouncements about translation in the West, starting with Cicero in 106 B.C.E. He attempts to show that translation has never been merely a matter of linguistics and should not be studied as such but, rather, that it is a component of culture. Noticeably missing in this intensive effort to "make the past serve the present" is an analysis of translation in China. Owing to its geographical distance, to its conceptual divergence, and, perhaps, to Western political prejudice, China is still inadequately known to the West, to say nothing of its history of translation.

To remedy this situation, in this essay—written in English for wider access—I introduce Western readers to the time-honored history of translation in China and to well-known Chinese translators from different historical periods. In the process I also reexamine various historical facts from a new perspective, applying some concepts current in translation studies in the West to the Chinese context, emphasizing the macroscopic aspects of power relations in economics, politics, philosophy, and culture as they relate to the history of translation in China.

A Brief History of Translation in China

Written translation in China began during the East Han dynasty (25–220 C.E.), some two thousand years ago, with the translation of Buddhist scriptures, but scholars speculate that oral translation could have begun as early as the Xia dynasty (ca. 2100–1600 B.C.E.) or the Shang dynasty (ca. 1600–1100 B.C.E.), thus pushing the beginning of translation in China back another two thousand years (Ma 1984:1). Ever since the first written evidence, translation has played an important role in promoting social change in China. Such change is seen in five major waves of translation: the translation of Buddhist texts (148–1037 C.E.); the translation of Western science and technology at the end of the Ming dynasty (1368–1644); the translation of Western humanities and social sciences at the end of the Qing dynasty (1644–1911); the translation of Russian materials in the middle of the twentieth century; and, finally, the massive translation endeavor being undertaken at present. Most of the functions of translation, including the spread of religion, the dissemination of knowledge, the transmission of culture, and the promotion of a national literature—discussed by Jean Delisle and Judith Woodsworth in *Translators through History* (1995)—are manifest in the history of translation in China.

Buddhist translation marks the beginning of documented translation and constitutes, as well, the first major wave of translation in China. Lasting some thousand years, from 148 to 1037 C.E., it was by far the longest of all the translation booms in Chinese history. Chinese translators and monks from what is now India cooperated in rendering thousands of Sanskrit Buddhist scriptures into Chinese. Team translation was apparent from the beginning of this translation movement, for Buddhist translation of the period usually proceeded in four steps. First, a foreign monk recited from the scriptures. As he was doing so, a native speaker of the target language translated orally what was heard into Chinese. Then someone else transcribed it into written script before it was polished and finalized by a stylist. The tradition of team translation has been passed down through the generations ever since and has characterized translation in China throughout the historical record. As recently as the last decade, team translation was practiced in rendering works as disparate as United Nations documents and James Joyce's *Ulysses* into Chinese, and in translating into English the Chinese masterpiece *Hongloumeng* (*The Story of the Stone* or *A Dream of Red Mansions*) and the works of Mao. It is not difficult to trace the origin of modern team translation to the practices of translating Buddhist scripture in ancient times.

The first formulations of translation theory in China also made their appearance during the period when Buddhist translation was dominant (Ma 1984:31). In the initial phase of Buddhist translation, translator Dao An (314–85) formulated the theory of *wu shi ben*, 'five cases of infidelity', and *san bu yi*, 'three difficulties of translation' (Ma 1984:31).[2] He argued against the practice of altering the word order of the original text and against the tendency to oversimplify the source text. Later another translator, Yan Zhong (557–610), put forward the theory of *ba bei*, 'the eight requirements for qualified translators' (Ma 1984:47),[3] in which he urged translators to remain faithful to the tenets of Buddhism and to have a good command of both the source language and the target language. During the Tang dynasty (618–907), when Buddhist translation reached its peak, one of the great translators of Buddhism, Xuan Zang, contended that a translation must be faithful to the original, even as it must be easy to understand. In Xuan's views we seem to see a distant harbinger of the famous theory of translation promulgated by Yan Fu (1854–1921) of *xin* ('faithfulness' or 'fidelity'), *da* ('lucidity' or 'readability'), and *ya* ('elegance' or 'refinement').[4]

Buddhism has exerted a perennial influence in China, continuing to the present. The most conspicuous physical sign of this influence can be seen in the numerous Buddhist temples scattered all over the country, especially in scenic spots, including major tourist attractions. In China four mountains have even been dedicated to Buddhism—namely the peaks Wutai located in central China's Shanxi Province, E'mei in western China's Sichuan Province, Jiuhua in eastern China's Anhui Province, and Putuo on an island in the coastal province of Zhejiang—together referred to as the Four Famous Buddhist Mountains. Much more important, though less conspicuous, is the deeply rooted impact of Buddhism on the collective consciousness of the Chinese people. Because Buddhism was introduced into China through translation, the comingling of and conflict between the exotic Buddhism and the native Confucianism and

Taoism have set the foundation of Chinese thought. By comparison, the translation of other religious scriptures into Chinese came at a much later date and played a much less significant role. Christianity came to China during the Tang dynasty (618–906), and Bible translation in China started with the work of the Italian priest John of Monte Corvina, who arrived in China in 1294 and died there in 1328. He translated the Bible into Mongolian, the official language of the Yuan dynasty (1271–1368) (Ma 1984:156). The first translation of the Qur'an into Chinese came even later with the work of Ma Fuchu (1794–1874), and the first complete translation of the Islamic scriptures was published in 1927 in Beiping in a translation by Li Tiezheng (Ma 1984:174–75).

Coinciding with changes in European science and technology that culminated in the Industrial Revolution, China saw the second wave of translation in the seventeenth century, at the end of the Ming dynasty (1368–1644) and the beginning of the Qing dynasty (1644–1911). This translation movement was characterized by the introduction of Western scientific and technological advancements; in the formulation of Delisle and Woodsworth, it was an example of the "dissemination of knowledge" through translation (1995:viii). Xu Guangqi (1562–1633), a native of Shanghai and a court official of the Ming dynasty, is credited with initiating this translation boom. As a patriotic scientist and the chief organizer of the translation movement, he made a great contribution to fostering the development of science and technology in China. This surge of translation again involved an international effort. In addition to native Chinese translators, many missionaries from various Western countries actively involved themselves in the translation endeavor. Among more than seventy well-known expatriate translators, the most prolific were the Italian Matteo Ricci (1552–1610), the German Jean Adam Schall von Bell (1619–66), the Italian Jacobus Rho (1593–1638), and the Belgian Ferdinand Verbiest (1623–88) (Ma 1984:182–83). Despite fragmentary statistics, they themselves are credited with rendering seventy-five books into Chinese. The subject matter covered in their translations ranges from atlases, astronomy, biology, mathematics, mining, and metallurgy, to the arts of war. Why did missionaries become involved in translating science and technology? I return to this interesting question later and offer a new explanation in the light of current theory in Western translation studies, comparing as well the Ming translation boom with that of the Qing in terms of the psychology of the receptor community as the relative status of the cultures involved in translation underwent subtle changes across time.

The third major wave of translation in Chinese history came after the Opium Wars of the 1840s, when China was invaded by Great Britain and later by other colonial powers. The Qing dynasty was corrupted and greatly weakened by the wars and, as a result, a bourgeois revolution was in the making. From the bitter experiences associated with the repeated defeats in the wars with foreign powers, the Chinese people came to realize that if their nation were to be strong, they had to learn the sophisticated science and technology of the West and, more important, advanced ideologies and modes of government. It took some time before this conclusion was reached, however. I discuss this topic in greater detail below.

During this translation movement Chinese translators became actively engaged in rendering foreign works pertaining to the humanities and social sciences into Chinese. Thus, this translation movement ideologically paved the way for the 1911 revolution that eventually overthrew the last feudal dynasty of China. Amid this upsurge of translation, two prominent translators emerged who were to exert an indelible mark on later translators throughout the following century. One was Yan Fu (1853–1921), who was devoted to translating Western literature pertaining to the humanities and social sciences. His translations, including *Evolution and Ethics and Other Essays* by Thomas Henry Huxley, *On Liberty* and *A System of Logic* by John Stuart Mill, *The Principles of Sociology* by Herbert Spencer, *An Inquiry into the Nature and Causes of the Wealth of Nations* by Adam Smith, *L'Esprit des lois* (*The Spirit of Laws*) by Montesquieu, *A Short History of English Law* by Edward Jenks, and *Elementary Lessons in Logic* by William Stanley Jevons, greatly shaped the 1911 revolution (Ma 1984:26).[5] Through Yan Fu's translations, for the first time the Chinese people had an opportunity to come into direct contact with such new and stimulating concepts as evolution, free trade, the principles of sociology, and the forms of government in the West in which power was shared by the legislative, executive, and judicial branches.

Perhaps the greatest contribution Yan Fu made to translation in China was the formulation of his classic tripartite standard for excellence in translation, namely *xin, da*, and *ya*, or faithfulness, lucidity, and elegance, as previously mentioned. Still today, almost a century after his death, there are people such as translators Shen Suru (Shen 1998:272) and Zhou Xuliang (Shen 1978:76) who claim that Yan Fu's criteria are the best ever formulated for translation anywhere in the world, a fact that demonstrates the influence and tenacity of his theory. Recently there has been speculation in China that Yan might have drawn on the English translator, Alexander Fraser Tytler, who also had three principles of translation,[6] in formulating *xin, da,* and *ya.* But Yan Fu's statements, as well as scholarly research, suggest in fact that his theory was based on concepts contained in Confucian doctrines, including the *Yi Jing* or *The Book of Changes.* The origin of his theory can also be traced back to the principles of translation maintained by the Buddhist translators of the East Han dynasty, thereby indicating that Yan's criteria of translation are deeply rooted in traditional Chinese literary theory.

Another prominent translator of this movement was Lin Shu (1852–1924). Although he did not know a single word of any foreign language, with the help of informants who were well versed in the foreign languages involved, Lin "translated" 183 foreign novels into Chinese, totaling twelve million Chinese characters (Ma 1984:303). This astounding achievement established him as a pioneer in introducing foreign literature to China. As one of the first Chinese translators to produce foreign novels, Lin Shu was extremely influential. Many well-known Chinese writers such as Mao Dun and Qian Zhongshu embarked on the road of literature after reading Lin's translated novels. Lin's translations aroused in such writers a great interest in foreign literature and enticed them to learn foreign languages; they eventually became not only great writers but also translators.

Through his translations Lin also changed the patterns of narrative writing in Chinese. Before Lin Shu, all Chinese literary narratives invariably began each chapter with a couplet revealing the contents of the chapter in question. For example, chapter 6 of *Outlaws of the Marsh* starts with the heading "The Tattooed Priest, and how he pulled up a weeping willow / The Leopard Headed unwillingly enters the Hall of White Tigers." In *A Dream of Red Mansions,* chapter 40 begins with the title "Lady Jia holds two feasts on one day in the Prospect Garden / And Faithful makes four calls on the domino in the Painted Chamber." It was Lin Shu who changed all this by introducing the foreign custom of chapter headings. Now most Chinese novels begin a chapter simply with a number, just as their foreign counterparts do.

Lin Shu influenced the way that the titles of literary works were translated as well. Noticing the differences between the titles of literary works in the West and in China, Lin attempted to make Western titles more attractive to his Chinese audience by translating them in the Chinese way. Thus, Charles Dickens's *Oliver Twist* became *An Orphan in the Foggy Capital* and Shakespeare's *Hamlet* was renamed *The Story of a Prince Seeking Revenge*. Lin's practice of altering the original title of a work to cater to his target-language readers has been followed by modern translators as well. Titles of films have also undergone similar shifts when they were dubbed into Chinese. As a result, *Dante's Peak* was given the more elevated title of *Mountains Crumble and the Earth Cracks* for Chinese cinema-goers, and *Speed* became *A Speed That Decides Life and Death.*[7]

Lin Shu's contribution was not, of course, confined to literary innovation. As Immanuel C. Y. Hsú points out in *The Rise of Modern China*, "through Lin, Western literature was introduced into China, and through his translation the Chinese gained invaluable insights into Western customs, social problems, literary currents, ethical concepts, familial relations, and the glittering world of literature itself" (1995:425). If we say that Yan Fu was the first person to introduce the operating mechanisms of Western society to the Chinese public, then Lin Shu took the lead in introducing Western society itself. The translations of both served as an eye-opener in China and played a key role in the ideological preparation for the 1911 bourgeois revolution.

Beginning in the 1950s there was a short-lived translation boom in China focused on translating Russian works, which may be described as the fourth wave of translation in Chinese history. This was a "patronized" translation boom, in the sense that it was generated by ideology and the principle of class struggle, as opposed to being governed by the supply and demand of a free market. At that time the world was divided into two opposing camps, the socialist camp headed by the Soviet Union and the capitalist camp led by the United States. China belonged to the socialist camp, and it naturally follows that translators were encouraged or only permitted to translate literary works of the socialist countries, especially those of the Soviet Union. The choice for translators was limited regarding what to translate and sometimes even how to translate. From our current perspective, extreme manipulations of source texts ensued, with political criteria, for example the class struggle, determining the representations in translations. Following these criteria, translators tended to choose literary works from the Soviet Union or from other socialist countries. When works of pre-Soviet Russian writers or American or British writers were chosen to be translated into Chinese, they had to depict class struggle in one way or another. Thus, texts to be translated had to fit into a certain political framework, seriously limiting the translators' range of choice. At that time the Soviet Union was the so-called big brother of the Chinese, and China tried to emulate everything Soviet. Moreover, throughout most of the 1950s, China was dependent on the Soviet Union for support, materially and technologically, as it had just emerged from the Sino-Japanese War followed by the Civil War and the Korean War. China sent promising young students to receive higher education in the Soviet Union. As a result the Soviet Union exerted a strong influence on China in a comprehensive way. At that time, all Chinese people, from middle-school students to those in their fifties and sixties, were learning the Russian language, thus preparing themselves for the Russian translation boom. Because political considerations were given priority, other functions of literature such as aesthetics and entertainment were given little consideration. Translation, like other forms of literary writing, was supposed to serve the primary purpose of educating the people ideologically, imbuing them with patriotic and communist ideals. This dominance of Soviet influence on translation in China is best reflected in translation statistics from that time.

Statistical figures may be dry and uninteresting to some, but they do tell a story. In *A Catalogue of Foreign Classical Literary Works in Translation, 1949–1979* (*1949–79 Fanyi chuban waiguo gudian wenxue zhuzuo mulu*) published in 1986, Russian writers published during the period covered by the catalogue take up seventy-seven pages in the book, more than the combined space for English and American writers combined (forty-three pages of English authors and a mere eighteen pages of American authors). These Russian literary works were all produced before the Russian Revolution of 1917. The imbalance in Chinese translation was all the more manifest in the translation of modern and contemporary Soviet literary works in comparison with those of other countries. A second book entitled *Foreign Literary Works Translated and Published between 1949 and 1979: List and Précis* (*1949–1979 Fanyi chuban waiguo wenxue zhuzuo mulu he zhaiyao*), published in 1980, is a thick volume containing 1,412 pages. The section Modern and Contemporary Soviet Writers, listing those translated who wrote after 1917, is 668 pages long.

In sharp contrast, the number of American authors writing in classical, modern, and contemporary times occupies a paltry fifty-seven pages, and the English writers a mere seventy pages. But these figures alone do not tell the whole story: there are also issues pertaining to content that are worth noting. I return to this special period of translation in greater detail in the next section.

At present China is experiencing a fifth wave of translation, initiated in the late 1970s when China launched its ambitious reform and began opening up to the outside world. The current upsurge has some major characteristics that distinguish it from the four previous translation movements. It is the most comprehensive and by far the least restricted translation upsurge. It is so widespread, in fact, that it embraces almost every aspect of social life. Books of all kinds are being translated into Chinese: literature, economics, philosophy, linguistics, and popular materials as well. It can be said without exaggeration that the current movement is a combination of the previous four in terms of scale and intensity—this is apparent alone in the sheer number of books being translated. It is simply unimaginable that during the last decades China could have become what it is today without translation.

China has plans to realize four modernizations—in agriculture, industry, science and technology, and national defense—that will enable China to reach the level of the world's intermediately advanced countries by the middle of the twenty-first century. In order to realize this ambitious goal, China has had to learn the world's latest achievements in these various areas. A huge amount of translation has been involved in this project. Take the field of computer science, for example. Almost every bookstore in China today has a special counter or shelf of computer books in translation, where one can easily find the Chinese version of the operation manuals for Internet access, Windows 98, Excel, and MS-DOS.

Business and trade also are fields where translation is indispensable. As joint ventures spring up across the length and breadth of the country, and as the importance and volume of business keep rising, translation activity increases to keep pace. Laws and regulations governing the operation of the joint ventures have to be translated for administrators from both sides to abide by; instruction manuals in foreign languages have to be made accessible for Chinese workers so that they can run the imported machines properly; and trade agreements have to be negotiated and signed with the help of translators. No wonder graduates with diplomas in foreign languages have an advantage in the labor market. As it has accelerated its drive toward reform, China has desperately needed advanced managerial expertise from other countries. Chinese officials have introduced housing reform from Singapore, set up stock exchanges in Shanghai and Shenzhen, instituted market economy where money-losing enterprises go bankrupt, and retrained workers who have been laid off. Translation makes all of this possible.

In view of these circumstances, it should be no surprise that the autobiography of Lee Iaccoca, the former CEO of Chrysler, was translated into Chinese three times in a single year. Meanwhile all aspects of Western thought have been introduced through translation, from Carl Jung to Sigmund Freud, from Eugene Nida to Peter Newmark. Thanks to translation, Chinese scholars and general readers alike now have immediate access to what is happening in the West in areas of the humanities, social sciences, natural sciences, and technology. People are able to exchange ideas with their Western counterparts without difficulties. China is also experiencing a boom in the translation of literature, art, and the media. Class struggle is no longer the principal criterion by which literary work is categorized, nor is it the sole basis for what can and cannot be translated. Canonical masterpieces are being translated in a systematic way. Thus, for example, the Chinese Academy of Social Sciences is compiling a list of canonical works to be translated and is inviting the nation's well-established translators to render them into Chinese, while publishers in Beijing and Shanghai are undertaking the publication of these translations. In the meantime, unsolicited translators of bestsellers sell their products to numerous literary magazines scattered across the country, among which perhaps the best known is *Yilin*, or *Translations*, a periodical that specializes exclusively in publishing top-ranked bestsellers in translation. Chinese translators have also reached the last frontiers of translation. Some extremely difficult but highly valued masterpieces have at last been rendered in Chinese: James Joyce's *Ulysses* and Marcel Proust's *À la recherche du temps perdu* stand as examples. The translation of *Ulysses* into Chinese was regarded as such an important event that the President of Ireland is said to have sent a personal letter of congratulations to one of the translators, Jin Di, and a copy of Jin's translation was put on display in the James Joyce Centre in Dublin.

A New Perspective on the History of Translation in China

In sharp contrast to the vigor of these five translation movements, which have contributed enormously to social change in China, is the neglect of the historical and theoretical study of translation as a cultural phenomenon. There are many reasons to account for this imbalance between translation practice and translation theory, the most significant of which are perhaps the empirical nature of translation studies and the dominance of Yan Fu's principles of translation in China. Even after the opening of China in 1978, when China started to pick up speed in introducing Western theories in order to enrich and diversify translation studies, Yan's principles of *xin, da,* and *ya* still offered invisible interference with this effort, supporting a marked prejudice against theories that did not conform to the criteria. Gradually, however, Chinese scholars have awakened to the limitations of Yan Fu's framework, attempting to broaden perspectives, even moving beyond the binary opposition of literal/free and the linguistic approaches that were introduced from the West in the late 1970s.

As more and more scholars have begun to show an interest in the history of translation, a number of important works in the field have appeared in Chinese. Their titles (in English translation) include *A Collection of Papers on Translation* (*Fanyi yanjiu lunwen ji,* 1984) produced by the Publishing House of Foreign Languages Teaching and Research, *A Brief History of Translation in China up to the May Fourth Movement of 1919* (1984) by Ma Zuyi, *A History of Translated Literature in China* (1989) by Chen Yugang, and *A History of Translation Theory in China* (1992) by Chen Fukang. The contributions by these pioneers in the history of translation in China cannot be overestimated. At the same time a close examination of these works reveals that such studies in China continue to give excessive attention to listing facts and probing linguistic matters, to the neglect of the cultural and contextual considerations that have given rise to translation in China in the first place. There are issues that still remain to be investigated. As Lefevere points out, "Translation needs to be studied in connection with power and patronage, ideology and poetics, with emphasis on the various attempts to shore up or undermine an existing ideology or an existing poetics" (1992a:10). Moreover, he observes that translation studies must bring together "work in a wide variety of fields, including linguistics, literary study, anthropology,

psychology and economics" (1992a:xi). If Lefevere's points are taken seriously, the whole mindset of traditional Chinese approaches to translation history and translation theory must be rethought.

Contrary to a tenet of Chinese approaches that attributes the genesis of translation to the quality and influence of the original text in the
source culture, current approaches to translation studies in the West stress
that translation often takes place to fill in a gap in the target culture.
Gideon Toury emphasizes this point in *Descriptive Translation Studies
and Beyond* (1995). He observes, for example, "Semiotically . . . translation is as good as *initiated* by the target culture. In other words, the
starting point is always one of a certain deficiency in the latter. . . . [T]he
more persuasive rationale is not the mere existence of something in another culture/language, but rather the observation that something is
'missing' in the target culture which should have been there and which,
luckily, already exists elsewhere" (27). Later Toury elaborates this point
in his discussion of a translation of Hamlet's "to be or not to be" mono-
logue, saying "in this particular case, an aspiration to approximate the target text to the original does not seem to have affected the translator's
subsequent decisions. Rather, his concern was more and more with the
position of his own text in a particular niche of the *recipient* culture"
(Toury 1995:73). The Hong Kong scholar Eva Hung, applying such
arguments to China, notes that Dickens's most appreciated novel in Chinese translation was *A Tale of Two Cities*, though it is considered one of
his less central works in the West (1996:29).

Another productive view held by Western scholars of translation
studies is that translation as a form of rewriting, always involves a process of
manipulation. As Román Álvarez and M. Carmen-África Vidal note,
"Translation always implies an unstable balance between the power one
culture can exert over another" (1996:4). What follows, as Lefevere indicates, is that " 'fidelity' in translation can . . . be shown to be not just,
or even not primarily a matter of matching on the linguistic level. Rather
it involves a complex network of decisions to be made by translators on
the level of ideology, poetics, and Universe of Discourse" (1992a:35).
The achievements of such approaches to translation studies open up new
perspectives for looking at the history of translation in China, offering
numerous alternatives to traditional ways this history has been viewed.
With these sorts of considerations in mind, let us now return to an analysis of the five waves of translation in China that we have identified.

Translation has been, beyond any doubt, a catalyst for social change in China. The demands and needs for translation arose when existing conditions were inadequate or even absent to accomplish a certain purpose. A vacuum appeared and translation stepped in to fill the gap. Generally speaking, popular demand for translation is always "right." These demands and needs have to negotiate the power of those in charge, however. As a result, some needs are satisfied, some ignored, and others ruthlessly suppressed. Broadly one can see translation as a response to the needs and demands of society in the Chinese record: Buddhist translation can be seen as satisfying spiritual needs; the technological translation of the seventeenth century and recent years has propelled material advancement; and translation of the social sciences and humanities has helped ideological evolution and revolution at periods when China has been in great social transition.

The long period when Buddhist scriptures were translated into Chinese must be seen in its cultural context. Buddhist translation was made possible in the first instance because the Silk Route was already in existence, linking China with India and providing the material prerequisite for cultural exchange. At the time Chinese culture was "open," and the emperors of the period welcomed and even encouraged the translation of Buddhist scriptures. Ma Zuyi has suggested that the emperor's motivation was to use this "spiritual opium" to consolidate his imperial rule in China, which may be an oversimplification (1984:13). The emperor's attitude toward Indian culture also reflected the prevailing social context of the time. The Silk Route was opened up with royal approval with a view to coming into direct contact with foreign countries. Along this Silk Route as well as along the so-called marine Silk Route that connected China with Southeast Asian countries, China introduced overseas cultures and agriculture in addition to Buddhism. For example, the Chinese two-stringed violin is apparently of foreign origin. It is still referred to as *huqin*, literally 'tribal people's fiddle', even today. At the same time, China sent silk, clothes, and language to other countries in return. The Japanese kimono and the Chinese characters in the Japanese and Korean languages clearly reflect China's openness during that period. The potential asymmetry of translation is illustrated by this Chinese example, for during the time that Buddhism was being introduced into China, Emperor Tai Zong of the Tang dynasty tried in turn to introduce the Chinese philosophical work *Yi Jing*, or *The Book of Changes*, into India but was unsuccessful in the attempt. That is because Indian culture at that time, according to Yu Feng of Harvard University, was an enclosed culture, rejecting things foreign.[8]

An important aspect of this first period of translation in Chinese history is that the texts to be translated were Buddhist scriptures and, as such, sacred texts. Like other sacred texts—from the Bible to Mao's works—Buddhist scriptures were held in high esteem and regarded as inviolable. To respect this inviolability, translators were almost always required to adopt a literal mode of translation; in the case of the Buddhist translations into Chinese, sometimes even transliteration was widely applied. Some Buddhist catch phrases, such as *Namoemituofo* ('May the Buddha bless us'), still linger on the lips of many today, subtly reminding us how Buddhist texts were first translated.

The dominance of sacred texts in China's translation record for almost one thousand years during this first period of translation is clearly related to the preference in China for "fidelity," leading to Yan Fu's principle of *xin* in the twentieth century and the current focus in translation studies in China on questions pertaining to "literal" and "free." Translation methods and standards were established over a period of centuries in China with reference to sacred texts, making it difficult to shift to other criteria as other text types were taken up in translation. Moreover, due to the long reign of feudalism over the past two thousand years, we in China are accustomed to having one supreme voice dictating standards from above. Translation is no exception in this regard. Because over the years *xin da ya* established their reign in the translation community, it is often considered irreverent if someone comes up with a new theory that contradicts the established criteria. That may be a more deeply rooted reason for why *xin da ya* could have ruled China for the past century and why some, like Shen Suru, hope that these criteria will continue to prevail.

As we have seen, the late Ming dynasty (seventeenth century) and the late Qing dynasty (nineteenth century) each witnessed a boom of translation. Scholars armed with the latest Western translation theories have attempted to compare these periods. One such scholar is Xiong Yuezhi from Hong Kong, who has compared these two translation movements in terms of the psychology of reception, a psychology associated with the balance of power between the source culture and the target culture, during the two periods. Attempting to understand how this balance of power influenced translation patterns, in 1996 Xiong Yuezhi suggested that during the Ming dynasty, China was flourishing and strong, while the source cultures—particularly Spain and Portugal, from which the bulk of the translators came—were defeated nations. Thus the cultural status of the source and target cultures was relatively even, with the target culture having even perhaps greater prestige in certain respects. As a result, according to Xiong, translation was conducted on more or less an equal footing, both psychologically and physically, during the Ming period of translation.

Xiong suggests that during the late Qing period, by contrast, the balance of power was tipped in favor of the Western countries, due to the Opium Wars launched by Great Britain, in which China was defeated and reduced to a semicolonial and semifeudal country. Missionaries who came to China during this period, therefore, looked upon China from a more Eurocentric viewpoint, arrogating to themselves greater cultural prestige, thus widening the psychological distance between China and Western countries. The shorter psychological distance during the Ming period made it easier to spread Western culture, whereas in the late Qing period when the psychological distance was greater, the situation was different (Xiong 1996:13). Xiong Yuezhi here indicates that in assessing the balance of power between a source culture and a receptor culture, the psychological aspect is also important in determining why it is easier at some times to accept a foreign culture in translation than at other times in the history of the same receptor culture. Most of the Qing missionaries came from the so-called Eight Allied Powers, including Great Britain and France, which invaded China in 1900. They brought with them Eurocentrism and reversed the balance of power in the sphere of translation. It should be noted here that China is not an isolated case in this regard. The nineteenth century was the height of European imperialism. The change of mutual status in the wake of the European imperialist invasion of many Asian and African countries greatly changed the position of translation in these countries as well, affecting translators' choices, their ways of translating, and the disparity between the incoming and outgoing translations.

We have seen that numerous Western translators worked in China during the late Ming period, and that many of the translators were missionaries who translated large numbers of Western scientific and technological treatises into Chinese during the period. In view of the fact that these Western missionaries came to China initially to preach Christianity, one might reasonably ask why such missionaries would choose to translate so many scientific and technological books into Chinese? As might be expected, there is debate on this question. Ma Zuyi, continuing his ideological line of argument with respect to the translation of Buddhist scriptures into Chinese, argues that these missionaries translated texts irrelevant to their religious mission in order to win favor from the Chinese emperors and common folk as well; thus translating science and technology was motivated solely, if indirectly, by the purpose of spreading religion (1984:183).

Perspectives from translation studies considered previously suggest an alternate possibility. Both advanced science and technology were "missing" in the target culture. Thus the missionaries translated in these fields in order to fill the gaps, when they became aware of such gaps. Perhaps it is safer to say that the motivation of the missionaries plus the objective lack of advanced technology in the target culture led to the boom in science translation. Calendar translation offers an example. The two calendars in use during the seventeenth century in China were both four hundred years old, and many inaccuracies had been found in them. When a cultural vacuum appears, a need for translation is generated, calling for translation or other means to fill it. In this view cultural disparities led to missionaries assuming the job of translating the Western calendar and other scientific literature, including mathematics and technical fields such as metallurgy, into Chinese. If they had not done so, someone else would have. Moreover, missionaries accrued cultural prestige by being able to fill cultural gaps by means of introducing advanced technology to a relatively underdeveloped country. At the same time it should be recognized that synchronism in the calendar system was essential for the celebration of Christian worship in China.

Translation during the late Qing dynasty offers a contrast to the translations during the late Ming period, further illuminating questions of power in translation, particularly as they relate to the way that demands and needs influence the selection of texts to be translated. During the last days of the Qing dynasty, the need to learn from foreign countries was widely felt and recognized in China. But it took some time for the Chinese people to realize what was most important to learn. This is reflected in the texts that were chosen for translation over a period of several decades. Before the Opium Wars and immediately thereafter, texts from the humanities and the social sciences constituted a meager proportion of all the texts being translated. Immanuel C. Y. Hsú asserts that "of the 795 titles translated by Protestant missionaries between 1810 and 1867 . . . only 6 percent [were] in the humanities and sciences" (1995: 420). Most of the translations, a full 80 percent, were translations of the Bible and religious tracts. The choices were made, for the most part, by non-Chinese missionaries, whose priorities are clear in the selection of texts, a fact indicating that the countries they came from were in an ascendant position in the balance of power during that period.

Later, as the initiative to choose texts for translation shifted to Chinese translators, the proportions of subject matter shifted. Text selection came to reflect the belief that knowledge of military expertise and industrial techniques was more important than the Bible and the Christian religion. During the period 1861–95, the percentage of applied science registered a 30 percent increase among works translated. Only after the Sino-Japanese War of 1894–95, when the Royal Qing Navy suffered a major setback at the hands of the Japanese, did men of foresight in China finally come to realize that China must broaden its understanding of the West. Japan's strength was seen as being correlated with the fact that Japan was a generation ahead of China in opening to the West. Following the Meiji Restoration, Japan had begun a massive program of introducing Western ideas by means of translation, among others. Political institutions, economic systems, and social structures, as well as philosophical thought, came to be seen in China as more essential and more fundamental to social change than science and technology alone. As a result a great number of Western works related to the humanities and social sciences, many of them coming via Japanese translations of Western materials, were rendered into Chinese, forming the substance of the third wave of translation in Chinese history. In turn the translation of such works played an important role in the bourgeois revolution of 1911. It is important to see that the patterns of translation here are more than merely "cultural exchange," the position that Hsú takes in *The Rise of Modern China*: "Yan Fu lived to become a monument in the annals of Sino-Western cultural exchange" (1995:424). The translation patterns, in fact, indicate that translation during this period, including the translations of

Yan Fu, were more politically oriented than culturally oriented. Thus, this wave of translation, like the other four, can be analyzed in terms of power relations as such, which were extremely complex at the time and included China's relationship with Japan.

As we have seen, Yan Fu's criteria of *xin*, *da*, and *ya* are still, on the whole, widely accepted; here a qualification must be added. In past years *ya* has at times incurred harsh criticism. Some scholars have misinterpreted *ya* to mean 'elegance' and ask "What if the original is not elegant?" Others, who know that *ya* refers to a special style of classical Chinese called *erya*, criticize Yan Fu for not using the vernacular language, which has become the norm since the May Fourth Movement of 1919. The fact is that Yan Fu translated before the May Fourth Movement, and his use of classical Chinese was determined by prevailing conditions at the time. As mentioned earlier, Chinese readers of the period were reluctant to accept Western ideas because of the greater psychological distance caused by the changed relative status of China and the West. Yan translated Western literature from the humanities and social sciences for potential readers who were essentially the feudal intelligentsia, people accustomed to classical Chinese, especially *erya*. In other words *erya* was the linguistic norm among the educated gentry at the time. Translators such as Yan had to comply with the linguistic and literary norms if they were to attain their aims of inculcating Western ideas and achieving social change. As is well recognized, the potential readership of Yan Fu's translations tended to be conservative and resistant to new ideas. They were well educated and accustomed to elegant, terse, and fluent classical Chinese. The *erya* form of classical Chinese was the norm of the upper class; as such it was held in high esteem and catered to the taste of these people. If Yan Fu had written in the vernacular, as some of his critics claim he should have done, his readers would have refused to read his translations in the first place, let alone accept the bourgeois, democratic ideas contained therein. Under these circumstances Yan Fu had to conform to the linguistic norms of his time; he wrapped up the advanced ideas of his source texts in a linguistic garb that made his readers feel comfortable. It can be seen from this example that translation must be studied in the broad context of prevailing political and social conditions. It is often impossible to separate translation from its environment so as to focus on linguistic matters alone.

Lin Shu is also a controversial figure in the history of translation in China. Judging by present-day norms, many would deprive him of the status of translator altogether. Jin Di, for one, classifies Lin's translation as *yi xie* ('translation' plus 'creative writing'), believing that Lin Shu's translations are "better classified as adaptations or free-hand rewriting of an original text" 1984:84). There is no denying that Lin Shu took extreme liberties with the original text—even liberties to an alarming degree, partly because of his ignorance of his source languages and, perhaps more significantly, because of his irrepressible desire to demonstrate his erudition in the Chinese language. But if we judge Lin Shu's translation according to the tenets of translation studies that see translation as always involving manipulation, Lin Shu is no more than an extreme example of a textual manipulator. He was indisputably a pioneer in translating foreign literature into Chinese and as such was a person to set up norms for translation in China. Readers tended to accept his translations as epitomizing what literary translation should look like. His unsurpassed command of literary Chinese also contributed to consolidating the status of his translations as the norm of his time. Consequently his translations were well received, and they in turn influenced many great Chinese writers and translators, as we have seen.[9]

Lin Shu's translations presently face serious criticism in China, but his work must still be regarded as translation. Given the premise that all translations involve the process of manipulation, Lin Shu's translations differ from contemporary translations only in degree, not in kind. Moreover, norms constantly change with time. As norms change, so do approaches to translation. A norm is a product of its time and has a particular function to play. Although in China today no one is likely to translate following the norms of Lin Shu's time, no one can say for sure that at some time in the future, norms will not again favor Lin Shu's style of translation.

Although manipulation can be viewed as an ever-present aspect of translation, not all manipulations are necessary or welcome. During the 1950s, China saw its fourth wave of translation, a typical case of a translation movement characterized by the overmanipulation of source texts. Class struggle was imposed as the primary norm for categorizing and screening literary works during this period. Moreover, generally speaking, only literary works from the Soviet Union and other socialist countries, as well as former colonies of European countries, were deemed to be qualified for translation. Thus there was strict control of textual selection during this period, a control exercised in accordance with the predominant political orientation. As for Western literary works, particularly American and English literature, only those depicting class struggle and racial discrimination—that is, only those exposing the dark side of capitalist society—were deemed worthy of translation. Thus, for example, *Uncle Tom's Cabin* was selected for its delineation of racial oppression and *Oliver Twist* for its portrayal of capitalist exploitation. Many other masterpieces, James Joyce's *Ulysses* for one, were labeled as decadent and reactionary; they remained untranslated until the early 1990s when the norms of translation again changed in China.

The extreme manipulation of translation in the 1950s and thereafter in China not only manifested itself in what was selected for translation but also in how works were translated. The translation of Mao's works into English offers an example. As we have seen, Mao's works were regarded as sacred texts during the period; the saying "one word in Mao's works equals ten thousand in value" vividly reflects the power and value of Mao's sayings at the time. It is said that translators of his works during that period were required to follow the linguistic form of the original, strictly, and they were not allowed to break his long sentences into short clauses, even when it was necessitated by the grammar of the target language. Cheng Zhenqui, a veteran translator of Mao's works into English, commenting later on this absurd translation practice, has said that if there were something problematic with the translation of political classics, it was that translation of the period tended to be too rigid (1984:6). It has also been said that Qian Zhongshu, a famous Chinese scholar, was engaged as a consultant for a translation team of Mao's works. Qian made many suggestions, most of which were aimed at making freer versions of the translations, but his suggestions were by and large not accepted by cultural affairs officials.[10] This example shows how overmanipulation can adversely affect the quality of translation.

Manipulation is a natural occurrence in the process of translation. Every translator, according to his or her particular background, interests, experience, education, and preferences, manipulates the source text to a greater or lesser extent throughout the process of translation and the production of a target text. However, institutional manipulation—sometimes even taking the form of governmental or administrative decrees shaped by political motivations—is an extreme manifestation of the phenomenon and one that tends to do more harm than good. It sometimes imposes embargoes on the intellectual fruit of the world's civilizations, often violating linguistic principles such that the result is an awkward or an unfaithful translation. It must be pointed out that this excessive form of institutional manipulation of the act of translation has been widespread in world history, not at all limited to the Soviet-dominated wave of translation in China. Writing in 1995, Toury discusses a similar case in Israel: "Between the 1930s and the 1960s translation of German literature came to a virtual standstill, as an unofficial censorial reaction to the horrors of the Nazi regime. . . . The ban was gradually lifted in the late 1960s, but contacts between Hebrew and German literature have hardly been resumed, particularly when it comes to the selection of texts for translation" (144). German writers to be translated were selected on the basis of their status in the English-speaking world, especially in the United States, instead of on the basis of their own qualifications and the needs of the receptor culture. This example indicates the great and lasting influence that overmanipulation can produce in translation.

Now, at the start of the twenty-first century, overmanipulation is no longer the norm among Chinese translators, who are by and large free to translate what they like, as is indicated by the translation into Chinese of Rae Yang's autobiography, *Spider Eaters*, which is extremely critical of the Cultural Revolution and some practices of the government in the 1950s and thereafter. This is not to say that the cultural factors affecting translation have disappeared altogether. The balance of power has left its distinct marks on decisions about what to and what not to translate. In many ways Euro-American works, especially those from the United States, now dominate translation in China as Soviet works did in the 1950s, regulated by the market rule of supply and demand rather than institutional decree. Unlike the 1950s, the tipping of the balance, this time in favor of the West, is a natural outcome of China's policy of engagement with the West so as to introduce the world's most advanced technology and managerial expertise to China. The real problem currently facing the Chinese translation community is how to introduce a cultural approach to translation studies so as to keep pace with the world in understanding the role of translation in history and the role of power in translation. Without the cultural component, no study of translation can be considered complete.

I have sought to apply the current "cultural turn" of Western translation theory to examine and reexamine some of the major events in the history of translation in China. In the process it became obvious that translation study can be approached from three directions, namely, from those of experience, linguistics, and culture. These are complementary rather than conflicting approaches. Clearly, current Western translation theory can be applied productively in analyzing Chinese data.

Translation has played and will continue to play a vital role in promoting social change in China. Since the opening of China to the outside world in the late 1970s, China has been determined to introduce everything that is positive and conducive to the development of the country and the happiness of its people. In this process translation is indispensable.

It is also important for scholars in China to work hard to develop translation theory, an indispensable complement to the current wave of translation, offering different models of translation that will enrich the practice of translation in China. Many foreign theories have been introduced, principally linguistic theories that have greatly expanded the traditional Chinese views of translation. But the scope is not yet comprehensive enough—theories that challenge basic premises themselves must also be integrated into Chinese views of translation. Descriptive approaches, such as those used in this essay, promise to be particularly productive, despite the fact that, from a traditional Chinese approach to translation, such approaches may not even be seen as concerned with translation at all, because traditionally translation theory in China has been so closely integrated with concrete translation practice, providing a guide as to how to translate a particular word or sentence. Translation scholars in China have usually studied culture in order to seek more appropriate translation equivalents. Approaching translation from a macroscopic point of view, however—seeing translation in the context of politics, economics, history, and power—makes it possible to come to a better understanding of those components of society using translation for their own ends and to recognize the power of translation to change and transform society.

Notes

1. My most sincere and heart felt thanks to Maria Tymoczko and Edwin Gentzler for their encouragement, comments, and suggestions throughout the process of writing this essay. Without their help this essay would not have been possible.

2. *Wu shi ben*, 'five cases of infidelity', refers to (1) changing the inverted word order of the original Sanskrit to suit Chinese grammar; (2) translating beautifully to win favor of the populace because Sanskrit favors literalness while the Chinese like embellishments; (3) where Sanskrit favors detailed description, cutting them short in translation; (4) avoiding the translation of the summary at the end of a Sanskrit text; and (5) omitting in translation the summary at the end of a paragraph when the author changes topic. *San bu yi*, 'three difficulties', refers to (1) enabling the present-day reader to understand the old customs and habits; (2) making the great sayings by sages understood by common folk of a later generation; and (3) translating the sacred scriptures by laymen.

3. *Ba bei*, 'eight requirements for qualified translators', refers to (1) remaining faithful to Buddhism and being ready to help others; (2) having a clean record of behavior and being reliable; (3) being widely read and knowing everything; (4) knowing the history of Buddhism in China and in literature; (5) being tolerant and patient; (6) being dedicated to Buddhism and caring little about name and fame; (7) having a good command of Sanskrit and the skills of translation; and (8) having a good mastery of Chinese so as to achieve accuracy in translation.

4. The interpretation of *ya* has always been a difficult point, one that I take up later in this essay.

5. Yan Fu was also known as a famous educator. He was the first president of the prestigious Peking (now Beijing) University.

6. The three principles of translation put forward by Tytler are as follows: (1) the translation should give a complete transcript of the ideas of the original work; (2) the style and manner of writing should be of the same character as that of the original; and (3) the translation should have the same ease as the original composition.

7. Chinese characters usually enjoy more semantic density than parallel English words, and as a result it takes less space to convey the same content in Chinese than in English. Another reason for the change of title in translation is that Chinese audiences like to know the plot of a film or a literary work. Sometimes the one-word English titles fail to satisfy the curiosity of Chinese audiences.

8. I am indebted to Yu Feng for the description of the nature of Chinese and Indian culture here, which he presented in a lecture delivered at the University of Massachusetts Amherst on 27 February 1998.

9. Lin Shu's translations were appreciated by Westerners as well. Arthur Waley, an influential translator of Chinese literary works, spoke highly of Lin Shu

after comparing Lin's version with Charles Dickens's original work: "the humor is there, but is transmuted by a precise, economic style; every point [that] Dickens spoils by uncontrolled exuberance, Lin Shu makes quietly and effectively" (qtd. in Hsú 1995:425).

10. From personal communication with a former member of the translation team of Mao's work.

CAROL MAIER

Translation, *Dépaysement*, and Their Figuration

Perhaps we can make a domain of translation itself.

Octavio Armand, "Poetry as *Eruv*"

In his essay "Poetry as *Eruv*," Octavio Armand envisions the creation of an intriguing defense to be constructed through the poetry of exile, often a poignant expression of *dépaysement*.[1] He proposes the erection of a rampartlike fence that will not only separate and exclude but also foster community and collaboration. As he explains, the *eruv* is the "legal fiction" that, for Orthodox Jews, creates a domain within which certain items may be transported without breaking the laws of the Sabbath: "On Saturdays, Orthodox Jews designate an area of their neighborhood as a private domain by encircling it with a piece of wire" (1994:231).[2] When—and if—Armand returns to Cuba, he intends to "ask Christo to surround the entire island with an *eruv* . . . to wrap it like a present so that it finally belongs to everyone" (1994:223).

Referring to his wish for Cuba, from which his family was exiled twice when he was an adolescent (in 1958, under Batista, and in 1960, under Castro), Armand plays with the word *Jerusalem*, rewriting it as "J*eruv*salem" (emphasis in original). The poetry of exile could, and should, he states, function like the wire rampart that creates an *eruv* in Orthodox Jewish neighborhoods and makes possible the "transportation or conveyance of things from one domain to another" (1994:231). Armand clearly harbors no illusions about the difficulties of collaboration among exiles—exiles are themselves transposed beings—but he calls on them to act as translators. Using the Spanish noun *traslado* and recalling etymo-

logical and historical links between transposition, transfer, and translation, all of which prompt a "convergence of two unpaired domains"
(1994:231), he suggests that poets of exile might be able to "make a
domain of translation itself" (1994:232).

As the translator of Armand's essay, I find his analogy between *eruv*
and translation—and consequently the analogy between poets of exile
and translators—highly provocative. I also find it disquieting, because my
work with the essay has showed me that the "convergence of two unpaired domains" I experienced and occasioned was more contradictory
than I realized or liked to realize. In fact, my initial reactions to Armand's
analogy included both assent and disagreement, even to the point of
anger; and it has been only after rereading and revising the essay over
more than a decade that I have gradually formulated my own understanding of the translator's work with respect to Armand's *eruv* and the domain it creates. Translators do prompt convergences, but when translation occurs as fully as possible, the translator not only conveys or
communicates a "message" but may also experience the ambivalence, the
absence of ease, and even the abrasion that are no doubt inherent in any
dépaysement. To believe otherwise is to idealize the work of translators
and to disregard the binary oppositions—the feelings of separation and
foreignness—and the power struggle that the *eruv*, whether as concrete
place or as metaphor, can occasion. Let me explain by discussing first my
work with Armand's essay and poetics, and then experiences noted by
several other translators.

My work with Armand's essay began in the summer of 1985 when
he asked me to translate a talk he had written for a panel on "The Poetry
of Exile," to be held that fall at the Festival of New Latin American Poetry
in Durango, Colorado. When I read the piece for the first time, I was
struck by a marked alteration that I sensed in what I would call Armand's
principal or individual "gesture."[3] Replacing the defensiveness and alienation that so often characterized his address to the second person, particularly in his poems, with an apparently unqualified request that the
"ruins" of exile be affirmed as a possibility for collective dwelling, Armand
invited that second person to join him in a (re)construction endeavor.
This new stance prompted me to feel a distinct shift in my position with
respect to his (and my) reader, or in this case our audience. Whereas in
the past, I had often been called on to rewrite the words of a cagey,
elusive first person, this time I was extending a welcome, encouraging a

second person or persons to participate in an effort based on the condition of exile and disorientation they shared and, implicitly, to set aside
its very diverse causes.

Initially, the change in Armand's work pleased me. It seemed more
consistent with the generosity of spirit that, despite feelings of disagreement or even animosity, I had seen him exhibit on many occasions. It
also seemed more consistent with the way I had myself always thought
of both translation and exile. I had not yet reflected much on my own
first experiences with exile nor experienced the recognition of translation
as refuge or homecoming that several years later would be prompted by
the accounts of translators such as Suzanne Jill Levine (1991) or Donald
Keene (1996). In fact, many of my strongest memories of safety and
community were based in a situation of *dépaysement* and possibly one of
exile as well. In those memories, I am a child from birth to adolescence;
I am in a refuge, a dwelling that in many ways seemed more like home
to me than my parents' house, which seemed limited and narrow in comparison and to which I often returned with reluctance. More specifically,
I am in the corner of the living room of that refuge-dwelling, which also
served as the "study" that gave the room its particular ambience; or I am
in the kitchen, where a modern range sits next to a large (and operative)
wood stove, or in the garden, a small but intricate maze of meticulously
trimmed paths and carefully manicured rosebushes.

In each of those places, I lived the "convergence of unpaired domains" that, without my realizing it, provided my first exposure to translation. Especially until I was in my early teens, they were luminous zones,
familiar and devoid of abrasion for me. I heard conversations in German
and English, without feeling adrift or lost between the two languages.
The same grace could be said before meals in either language without
causing misunderstanding; the plum kuchen was never plum cake, but
neither did it impress me as something "hybrid," "foreign," or "exotic."
No doubt most important, the study and the garden were places that
gave rise to a convergence of the "Old Country" with the new (which I
later came to associate with Ramón del Valle-Inclán's definition of beauty
as the "intuition of unity" [1974:20]). For the uncle who created them,
those places were simultaneously sites of beauty and places of homesickness, retreat, and isolation—something I learned only after their impression on me had taken hold and I had grown to know them as places at
once intimate and open, where my uncle spoke with an animation and

intensity he never exhibited in other areas in or around his house, and certainly not outside the house.

Years later, when I began to visit Armand's family, I immediately felt comfortable. Neither the differences between the Armands' second-floor duplex in Queens, New York, and the house my uncle shared with my maternal grandparents and two aunts, one of whom was his wife, nor the difference between my uncle's emigration in the late 1920s and the Armands' forced exile overrode the ease with which I translated or transposed my previous experience to their home. On the contrary, that transposition actually increased my urge to translate—to convey or communicate—Octavio Armand's world to others. Nor did my disagreement with many of the Armands' attitudes and positions prevent me from experiencing an intuition akin to the one I had experienced repeatedly in my uncle's study. Although I was often troubled by the discrepancy between my understanding of the Cuban Revolution and the discussions I heard about it in Armand's home, I was drawn both to Armand's home and to his family and community by a familiar convergence of domains within myself, a sense of ease that held at bay—even suppressed—a simultaneous discomfort. In fact, although I did not reflect on the coincidence at the time, some years before I had begun to wonder and inquire about the reasons for my uncle's emigration, his relationship with the German community during the years of World War II, and the backgrounds of the many other family members and friends who gathered frequently in my grandmother's kitchen or on her back porch. My questions had not led to definitive answers, however. Most of the people who could have answered them were by then deceased, and those few who were not I felt reluctant to approach. Consequently, I had realized that I would most likely never feel totally comfortable with the ease I associated with my uncle's study when I was a child.

In the essay "Poetry as *Eruv*," Armand suggests that exile can become a site of joint refuge rather than the arena of comfort laced with conflict and competition from which he had been excluded as a Cuban, an arena about which his sentiments had become bitter. I initially felt great relief to assume the role, as a translator, of a genuinely hospitable "first person" instead of the crafty, deceptively welcoming one to which I had frequently given voice in his poems in English. After all, that person had caused me no small dis-ease both within Armand's words and without. In fact, I had gradually been growing impatient with the schizoid reality of the first person with whom I often felt imprisoned. For despite my awareness that as the translator of that voice I was identifying (improperly) with what one literary critic has defined as a "role craftily designed for us . . . by 'authorial' narrative address" (Spear 1990:139), it was often my impression that I was not only caressed but also insulted and ridiculed as the "you" Armand addressed in his poems and essays. (One of those poems, "Braille for the Left Hand," was even dedicated to me.) In those instances, I had felt that I was being battered by the first person's effort to challenge what that person assumed was my relative wholeness as a second person and to appropriate that wholeness as a way of healing its own fractured self. Moreover, some of my attempts to publish Armand's work in English were being met with a similar lack of hospitality. In the late 1970s and early 1980s, Cuban exile poets were not merely invisible in print (as Guillermo Cabrera Infante indicated about the same time), they were virtually banished from print, and at times both my translations and I were met with distrust, at best.[4] I was caught off guard, then, when I began to feel decidedly uneasy about Armand's suggestion in "Poetry as *Eruv*" that the condition or context of exile could serve as a meeting place.

At this point, however, I want to be honest and say that neither as I first translated "Poetry as *Eruv*," nor as I witnessed the mixed reception the essay received at the Festival of New Latin American Poetry, nor throughout its not untroubled journey into print, did I fully articulate my feelings about possible assault and imprisonment as the "you" in Armand's poems. In fact, I felt that the antagonism and ambivalence I did experience was "not turning me from Armand's work but freeing me in relation to it" (Maier 1985:7). Several years were to pass before whatever aspect of my translator's "I" identified with the second person in Armand's work actually rebelled against his first person, having become aware of the cunning and provocation inherent in his call for poets in exile to construct an *eruv* and to set aside the advantages some of them experienced by adopting exile "as a profession" open to some exiles but not to others (1994:227).

Exactly how and why that occurred must be discussed elsewhere, but in 1989 when I began to revise "Poetry as *Eruv*" for republication in *Refractions*, I was already feeling uncomfortable and disoriented when I thought about my work as a translator of Armand's texts. Although I did not think about my discomfort in terms of *dépaysement*, what I experienced at that time (and have often experienced since as I worked with other writers in exile besides Armand) was, I believe, a desire for *dépaysement*. My feelings, however, were not feelings of yearning for a country in which I no longer lived but for an area, a zone, where "two unpaired domains" converged in translation as I had first known it: exhilaration, ease, escape. In other words, what I yearned for was translation itself. And if I was angry as a "second person," this was because both the "first person" in his poems and the political context outside of them were making it impossible for me to experience translation as I envisioned it.

Rereading "Poetry as *Eruv*" and reviewing its history for my introduction to *Refractions*, I realized that my feelings of relief as I encountered what impressed me as a gesture of openness and inclusion had prevented me from recognizing the gesture of the piece as a whole. That gesture is provocative and contestatory, and it proposes a highly controversial collaboration in a situation where Armand knows he will have few sympathizers, in view of Cuba's exclusion from most North American discussions of exile and the fear then (and still) felt by many "rootless cosmopolites" whose work fails to "include the cause of exile" (Ilie 1995: 226, 247).[5] Although that understanding only served to strengthen my respect for and admiration of Armand's writing, it also brought my sense of *dépaysement* into sharp focus, and further translation of Armand's work seemed impossible. I felt the same affection for Armand and his family, but my role as the inevitable communicator of his dis-ease seemed intolerable. After all, in "Poetry as *Eruv*" Armand had suggested that poetry "could be a cure for some of the ills that affect our planet" (1994:227). In this case the ill was exile, which, like language, Armand believes is a "movable disease" (1994:227). This means, he suggests, that it could be cured by *translatio*, "a curious therapy whose roots go back to the days when castles were built" (1994:227). "This so-called cure," he continues, "has healing by sympathy, also known as magnetic transfer, transplanting, or translation. It was only applicable to movable diseases. Movable or transplantable" (1994:227). In other words, it could be cured by distancing if it could be transferred or passed to something—or someone— else "by way of a variation of one form of *translatio* known as *inescatio*, in which *magnes mumia* is fed to an animal passed to something—or someone—else" (1994:228). Armand explains that in the instance of *inescatio*, "nail clippings from the patient are tied to a crab that is then tossed to the current" (1994:228). Exiles, he goes on to suggest, are already implicated in such an effort, for they have all served as crabs, as agents of healing cast out from diseased continents. When he proposes that poetry, particularly by way of translation, could serve as an agent of healing, he is in fact proposing an intriguing reversal: in order to be cured (in this case of exile), poets must communicate it, something they might be able to achieve within the *eruv*-like sphere of transferal, of translation. A very clear, albeit potentially controversial proposal. What, though, does it imply for the agent of that agent, for a translator of those poets?[6]

This was a question that began to trouble me increasingly. As a translator, my task was to convey, to spread the condition of exile, which seemed more and more distant from, even contrary to, the *dépaysement*, the "melk en honing" to which I longed to be taken.[7] How to work in a sphere filled not only with the pleasurable associations of other sites but also with the polemical associations I knew to be present? To translate Armand's work was to pass on that duality, that dis-ease of simultaneous consolation and conflict, and I felt uncomfortable with his comments and jokes about exiles from countries other than Cuba, and also about other Cubans and other individuals in general whose sexual preferences differed from his. I decided that, at least for a while, I could not continue to translate, to serve as an agent for work about which I felt so ambivalent, work whose puns and spectacular feats with language implied a collective effort on the part of embittered individuals hoping to free themselves from dis-ease by infecting others not only with compassion but its contradictions.

Unexpectedly a recent request to reprint "Poetry as *Eruv*" as the prologue to Peter Bush's anthology of short stories by Cuban writers, *The Voice of the Turtle* (1997), necessitated that I reread the essay once more. Perhaps it was merely a question of coincidence with other work that involved the question of the translator's identity and expectations, but again I was led to rethink my involvement with Armand's writing. And again my reaction was different from what I had anticipated, because I realized that the discomfort I had experienced with respect to the *eruv* as an area of contention was not inconsistent with the dis-ease, even the ruins, I have come to affirm as integral to the activity of translation. Just as translating poetry by Chicana writer Ana Castillo,[8] studying the multiple mediations in Rigoberta Menchú's *testimonio* and the ways they might best be presented to North American university students,[9] or questioning a translator's allegiance to a particular gender or ideology has forced me to examine my own subjectivity and my own identifications,[10] so the translation of Armand's work led me to recognize the expectations—and the desire—with which I had originally approached translation. Albeit unknowingly, my expectations for translation had been every bit as high as Armand's. I had expected to return to, to recover, not only a convergence of unpaired domains but also an experience of unqualified beauty I once lived intensely but understood only minimally. For I had not even associated translation with the dislocation I experienced moving between the home of my uncle and his family on the one hand and the home of my parents on the other, not to mention the dislocation vis-à-vis one's language (and language itself) that, as a translator, I always considered integral and valuable to translation. This had meant that, despite my attraction to Armand's work, sooner or later I would be unable to identify with it unconditionally. Once I recognized, however, the need to acknowledge and, insofar as possible, suspend or at least monitor my own motivations and *dépaysement* as a translator, another convergence of our unpaired domains might be possible.

As I write that last sentence, I am reminded of the final lines in Seamus Heaney's "Remembered Columns": "I lift my eyes in a light-headed credo, / Discovering what survives translation true" (1996:45). "Nothing survives translation true," I wrote beside those lines when I first read them, and now (aware that I am also altering Heaney's "truth") what I discovered by working yet again with Armand's "Poetry as *Eruv*" is that what survives translation "true" is the messiness and the ambivalence of any convergence of unpaired domains and the impossibility of creating an uncomplicated passage between them. Indeed, I wonder increasingly if translators might not do well to discard the notion of moving "between" two discrete domains in favor of more complex, more vital, and more truthfully shared dwellings and dominions.[11]

Seen from this perspective, Armand's ruins and his J*eruv*salem offer provocative, truthful images of the condition of exile and the activity of translation. They also remind me of other recent representations of these concepts that I have found affecting and candid. It is worth noting, for example, that several years before Armand wrote his talk for the festival in Colorado, Naomi Lindstrom suggested that translators, particularly academics and novices, were really writers afraid to take the risk of affirming themselves as such and that "they should seriously consider making themselves the creative writers whom they nourish" (1989:586). And it is worth remembering that Lawrence Venuti's first call for an end to the translator's invisibility appeared not long after the festival occurred. I am thinking too of Eva Hoffman's comments about the perils of both exile and its current metaphorizations, many of which mask or even glamorize the suffering physical exile implies. Hoffman's remarks are especially pertinent here in view of similar comments made by Abraham B. Yehoshua, whose essay about the "neurosis" inherent in the Jewish *golah* solution Hoffman cites, and in the statement Armand makes about brandishing one's "exile as a profession" (1994:227). Other examples would include the dislocation Peter Bush experiences translating Juan Carlos Onetti (1999), the disorientation suffered by the writer-translators in Lydia Davis and Banana Yoshimoto's novels, the fight for authorial control in some of David Shapiro's poems (for example, "The Boss Poem," 1994:62), and the disappearances and "tearings" in the underbrush in Benjamin Hollander's *The Book of Who Are Was* (1997).

And last but perhaps most, current examples of translation and *dépaysement* would also include Barbara Wilson's fictional character Cassandra Reilly, a translator whose newest escapades in *The Death of a Much-Travelled Woman and Other Adventures* (1998) offer an engaging, albeit disturbing portrait of translation as a potential power struggle and of the translator as both collaborator and competitor. "Expatriate dyke detective" (13), Cassandra finds herself embroiled in contentious situations with one writer after another and finally resolves to become an author herself, even though she's never had much of an imagination. Having decided that she'll pretend "to translate the work of a Latin American writer who did not exist" (196), she lists herself as the other writer's translator. This leads to numerous conflicts, even with a woman in Madrid, a translator, who claims to have written the original Spanish work. The two meet and, after a heated argument, end up working together in a curious collaboration that is far more perilous but also far richer than the relationship Cassandra experiences with the "real" Latin American writer whose work she usually translates. One can deny the authenticity of such portraits, but to do so is to affirm and yearn for a purity that may prompt the translation of texts but will ultimately prevent translation, with all its complexity and competition, from truly taking place.

Notes

1. The first version of this essay was written for "Nature, Land, Dwelling, Home" a conference held 25–26 April 1997 at the State University of New York at Binghamton. I wish to thank Marilyn Gaddis Rose for her invitation to speak at the conference; Ronald Christ for the insightful, thought-provoking comments he made on the first version; and Octavio Armand for his consultations and collaboration.

My understanding of *dépaysement* is based largely on the definition of it as disorientation and feeling of strangeness (*Robert and Collins* 1978:193) and on the less formal definitions provided by two colleagues in the French Department at Kent State: "profound homesickness when one is among alien corn" (North American native); "disorientation experienced when customs are different from yours and you feel foreign with discomfort" (French citizen). I have used *dépaysement* throughout this essay rather than *exile* or other related words such as *expatriation, immigration,* or the *repatriation* Bharati Mukherjee discusses (1998:83–86), neither to equate the two situations nor to dismiss the differences between them, but instead to evoke a feeling that I sense is integral to them all.

2. With the exception of the word *domain* (*dominio*), all citations of "Poetry as *Eruv*" are from *Refractions*, where *dominio* is rendered as *spheres*. The change came about in the writing of this essay, and I believe it is explained, albeit implicitly, in the essay itself.

3. I am thinking here of Peter Schjeldahl's 1997 comments about Willem de Kooning's "mighty gesture" and of Ramón del Valle-Inclán's "gesto único" ('singular' or 'unique gesture', 1974:113).

4. See my "Note to 'Cuba is Not, But She Calls' " (1984).

5. See also Hoffman's more recent comments about the current "new nomadism" (1998:57–58).

6. In our discussions about "Poetry as *Eruv*," Armand mentioned Wayland D. Hand's essays as one of his primary sources for his discussion of *translatio*.

7. My reference here is to Willem Van Toorn's poem (1999:4). I am also thinking of Chana Bloch's written contribution to *Threepenny Review*'s "Symposium on Translation," in which she describes what seems to be an attraction to translation similar to my own. Recalling the "taste for language" she inherited from her parents, whose early lives contrasted sharply with the "American background" they had given her, she explains that she embraced translation, "longing for what I called real life . . . happy to be bereaved" (Bloch 1997:10).

8. See my "Notes After Words" (1989).

9. See Dingwaney and Maier 1995a:303–19.

10. See my "Issues in the Practice of Translating Women's Fiction" (1998).

11. For related discussions of "between," see the "compact" in my "Notes

After Words" (1989), Donald E. Pease's "visionary compacts" (1987), and the "interactive inversions" and the negativity that Sanford Budick discusses as the elements of "a manifold of mind" (1996:225). Those images seem far more appropriate—and accurate—than either the opposition in Anthony Pym's *Blendlinge* (1995) or the affirmation in Douglas Robinson's *Translation and Taboo* (1996).

EDWIN GENTZLER

Translation, Poststructuralism, and Power

In this essay I reflect on the engagement by translators and translation studies scholars in the United States with poststructural thought. I find that the use of deconstruction for causes such as feminism, postcolonialism, liberal humanism, and multiculturalism, for example, tends to be full of contradictions. After briefly looking at work by leading translation studies scholars in the United States, including Lawrence Venuti and Suzanne Jill Levine, I juxtapose their work against that of postcolonial feminist Gayatri Spivak. I find that poststructuralism in the United States tends to be used on a selective basis, often with a definite sociopolitical agenda in ways that are remote from the kind of double writing of continental scholars that challenges as well as opens up new avenues of interpretation. By way of closing I review poststructural translation practices by scholars in Canada and Brazil, suggesting that translation scholars in the United States could learn much from their neighbors.

In my earlier work I have discussed deconstructive strategies and the role of power in Foucauldian terms, showing how contemporary theories of translation challenge privileged concepts of the sanctity of the source text and the originality of the author. In *Language, Countermemory, Practice* (1977b), which contains the essay "What Is an Author?," Michel Foucault cites Jorge Luis Borges as saying, "The fact is that every writer creates his own precursors. His work modifies our con-

ception of the past, which will modify our conception of the future" (5).
Borges implies that every "original" work can be viewed as a re-creation
of a re-creation or, by extension, a translation of a translation (of a translation . . .), locating the writer/translator in the *mise en abîme* that erases
any sense of access to an "original" (Gentzler 1993:164–69). Such a
reassessment of "the author" has repercussions for translation studies
scholars, who now are increasingly required to make comparisons less to
a unified source text and more to a long chain of multiple meanings and
a plurality of languages, becoming involved in the proverbial Borgesian
labyrinth.

This paradigm shift in the field has led to translations being discussed increasingly in poststructuralist and postcolonial terms—for it is
often in translation and the affirmative play of language that repressed
meanings, sometimes by accident, resurface. Additionally, the analysis of
translated texts allows scholars to see subtle acts of repression of certain
meanings at work. The problem with repression, however, is that it is
often carried out at a subconscious level. Teachers, politicians, and religious leaders are often not aware of their own cultural, racial, and class
biases. Thus, illustrating such out-of-sight prejudices is quite difficult. Yet
in the analysis of translation, especially in the analysis of translations done
by Western-educated translators translating so-called Third World texts,
translation scholars can expose those often unconscious manipulations at
work—manipulations such as making changes in the translation so that
it better conforms to existing literary and cultural norms, smoothing out
religious and political differences to make a text more palatable to the
receiving audience, and constructing images of indigenous cultures that
reinforce cultural stereotypes in the West.

This scholarship in turn has exerted an influence on practicing translators: several North American literary translators, including Suzanne Jill
Levine, Carol Maier, and Douglas Robinson, have begun exploring more
resistant theories of translating. In translation studies, scholars such as
Lawrence Venuti have turned to theorists such as Sigmund Freud, Louis
Althusser, and Jean-Jacques Lecercle to explain symptomatic shifts in
translation, not as mistakes or subjective interpretations, but as shifts that
are culturally and socially determined by the discourses of the age. André
Lefevere has used Michel Foucault and Pierre Bourdieu to explain ideological factors inherent in the decision-making processes of practicing
translators. The intersection of ideas is multiple and growing, leading to

reverberating changes in both theory and practice. Practicing translators, using poststructural, feminist, and postcolonial theories, have become increasingly liberated—that is, less apt to uncritically adhere to source-text linguistic and semantic aspects—and more open to importing extra linguistic codes and cultural markers from the source culture. Some translators feel so empowered that they deliberately subvert traditional allegiances of translation, interjecting their own worldviews and politics into their work. Thus, one aspect of the "power turn" in translation studies involves the assertion of power by translators themselves.

Yet this business of interjecting a political stance into a translation is not without controversy. Consciously or not, translators invariably conform to certain standards and differ from others. What might be socially or politically progressive in one time and place may be the reverse in other situations. Often translators adopt different linguistic and political strategies depending on the type of text they are translating and the type of audience they have in mind, thus making translation analysis increasingly difficult. In addition, having power or translating for a powerful institution such as a church, a king, or a dominant racial group is not necessarily progressive or regressive in and of itself. Thus, it is becoming increasingly important to explore the specific situation in which institutions of power have had an impact on translation activity and the resulting impact that translations have had on the development of culture. With those ends in mind, I explore some of the deconstructive strategies employed by translators in the United States, beginning first with the politics of the translation of deconstruction in the United States.

Translating Poststructuralism

Though advocates of poststructuralism claim that deconstruction does not lend itself for use by any particular political group, its reception in the United States has always been charged with power relations. Some of the criticism is directed at its appropriation during the early years by conservative critics, especially a group of critics on the east coast of the United States known as the Yale School, including J. Hillis Miller, Harold Bloom, Geoffrey Hartman, and Paul de Man. More recently, however, deconstruction has been used by some of the more radical scholars on the left, including some progressive translation studies scholars.

Many Yale School critics were influenced in their early years by the

New Critics, who advocated studying literary texts and translations in and of themselves, totally divorced from extraliterary factors such as the social context in which the text was written. Deconstruction, in some minds, suggested that "there is nothing outside the text" and was occasionally adapted to serve New Critical tenets. Some of the early translators of Jacques Derrida have done fine work, giving us important "texts" by Derrida, but the lack of prefaces, footnotes, and supplementary material in these early translations constrains the dissemination of his ideas. Later translations of Derrida, such as those by Gayatri Spivak and Barbara Herrnstein Smith, which include extensive prefaces, notes, and commentary, help contextualize Derrida's work and open up tangential avenues that are suggested but not elaborated by Derrida, yet are nevertheless crucial to the project. For Derrida, that which is beyond the printed word, that which escapes and hides, is covered up by language and metaphysical concepts.

Derrida's later work, which includes his thinking on translation, particularly Walter Benjamin's essay "The Task of the Translator," has attracted many younger scholars with different ethnic backgrounds who are more open to cultural studies and postcolonial criticism. For them, Derrida has been appropriated for liberal causes, including, ironically, the deconstruction of New Criticism with all its humanistic premises. Recent translation scholars, such as Lawrence Venuti, who incorporate certain poststructuralist strategies, have turned to Derrida to justify some of their interventionist strategies. Deconstruction's "translation" in the United States might be characterized as one generation of scholars using Derrida's work to support a conservative criticism and a later generation using deconstruction to support a more radical, multicultural agenda, which is symptomatic not just of the cultural wars in the academy in the United States but also of the problem that may be inherent in the definition of the term *translation*.

Deconstruction itself, if done well, invariably escapes its own definition and its own appropriation. Derrida himself does not distinguish between original writing and translation; every act of writing is already a translation, or better said, a translation of a translation of a translation. Deconstruction advocates seldom distinguish between languages as translation scholars do; instead they see multiple languages, codes, discourses, and semiotic chains already embedded within any "single" language.

Therein lies the play, which makes reading and translating such texts fun on the surface; however, therein also lies the "threat" of poststructuralism, for in the play arises the theoretical challenge, one that also threatens the foundation of translation studies. Some of the deconstructive practices of writing include the activity of provoking from within, the use of graphic disorder, distorted words, crossed-out words, and altered single letters, all aimed to break down standardized, conventional usage. Additional practices include the element of play and polysemia—the use of language games, puns, and neologisms as an attempt to get beyond logical, serious, rational discourse—and the introduction of supplementary material such as notes, prefaces, afterwords, and tangential passages that disrupt the linear flow of the text and indicate that tangential ideas are as important as the main body.

Poststructural scholars have found thinking in that space between languages that occurs in the process of translation exceedingly fruitful—that space that occurs before the right word has crystallized—for the pursuit of such activities. In Freudian terms, that state has been characterized as a kind of dream state, occurring before conscious rational thought, and all its repressive, identity-preserving mechanisms (cf. Bassnett 1992). And it is in that space, often referred to by Derrida as the space of translation, that the elusive concept of *différance*, as close as might be possible, manifests itself. *Différance*, of course, is the neologism coined by Derrida to refer not to what is there in language, but to what is not there. Deriving his neologism from the Latin term *differre*, meaning both 'to defer' and 'to delay', Derrida, by introducing the letter *a*, creates a new word that does not exist in French, locating between a verb and a nonexistent noun something that has been lost in the evolution of language (cf. Gentzler 1993:158). The very translation into English as a concrete term *différance*, invariably italicized, further distorts its deferring quality and its inaudible presence in French.

Translators have found that elusive in-between space to be a kind of opening where new voices—alternative voices—can be heard. Yet that space is not without its dimension of power; even poststructural texts frequently presume knowledge about the structures and forms that predominate in Western literary and philosophical discourse. Translators, in their subversive play with language, implicitly refer to standard forms of expression, and those often efface alternative concepts as they surface.

Such is the power of metaphysical thinking and patterns of colonial domination. Even when the translator/reader seeks difference, the constraint of the past weighs heavily.

While the poststructuralist might welcome that lack, that nonpresence, and its power to disrupt conventional notions, at the same time the translator also *desires* the presencing of the perfect conceptual term. Indeed the practice of translation is constituted by that very task: finding the solution, a signifier that best represents those signifying elements of the source text. This desire locates the activity of translation in an always contradictory position, always trying to "make sense" out of a multifaceted and polyvalent original. The translator, unlike the deconstructionist, must stop the fertile and enjoyable play of the signifier between literary systems and take a stand. But in doing so, how does the translator avoid traditional metaphysical distinctions between sign and signified? How does the translator avoid neoliberal humanistic formulations about meaning and the author's intention? Or if the translator chooses a strategy of resistance to normative usage, how does the translator avoid binary oppositions that characterize most translation debates? Negotiating the in-between space between destabilizing play and taking a stand is indeed a rather tricky business, politically and theoretically.

Poststructuralism and Translation: Venuti and Levine

Perhaps the leading translation studies scholar in the United States is Lawrence Venuti, who has intellectually engaged poststructural theory as much as any translation studies critic. Though his theoretical basis is more Marxist, more Althusserian, than poststructuralist, to his credit he acknowledges his political and social aims. Nevertheless, he often uses deconstruction to reinforce his arguments. Here is an example from the introduction to *Rethinking Translation* (1992): "Poststructuralist textuality redefines the notion of equivalence in translation by assuming from the outset that the differential plurality in every text precludes a simple correspondence of meaning. . . . The heterogeneous textual work insures that the translation is transformative and interrogative as well: it sets a deconstruction of the foreign text" (8–9). Venuti asserts that all texts are heterogeneous, especially translations. If translators use too fluent a style of translation, they cover up the heterogeneous nature and erase the transformative, political qualities of the source text and its translation.

Venuti advocates an alternative translation practice, one that foregrounds foreign elements, one that resists dominant discursive modes and forms, and he refers to translating Derrida's "inventive and self-reflexive writing into English" (1992:11) to illustrate his thinking.

Venuti adopts deconstruction's disruptive practices, which he uses to destabilize translation strategies in which translators make themselves invisible; hence the title of his book, *The Translator's Invisibility* (1995). To his credit Venuti uses Derrida's deconstruction in order to demonstrate how discontinuous any text is, original or translation, and to show how the translator is involved in the production of culture, inviting critical analysis of the power relations behind the scenes. Venuti is particularly strong in analyzing those power structures in the United States, including legal, educational, and literary institutions, and in showing how they have marginalized translators and made them subservient and self-effacing (see in particular Venuti 1998). To combat such a cultural development, he advocates a strategy he calls "abusive fidelity," one that is "faithful" to the tone and tenor of the source text, but "abusive" to the literary norms of the target culture, therefore allowing more elements of the foreign culture to enter the target culture.

The term "abusive fidelity" is derived from Philip Lewis's essay "The Measure of Translation Effects" on Derrida's essay entitled "White Mythology" from *The Margins of Philosophy* (1982). The original French title of Lewis's essay is "Vers la traduction abusive" (1981); in it Lewis begins to consider in more theoretical terms a strategy that translators can use when translating Derrida and, by extension, other poststructural writing. In a translation of the essay into English in 1985 for Joseph Graham's anthology *Difference in Translation*, however, Lewis chose not to use the term *abuse* in his title in English, choosing instead "The Measure of Translation Effects." I suspect that Lewis avoided the term *abusive* in English for fear of its being misappropriated by English-speaking scholars as a theoretical concept. The French term *abuser* used by Lewis suggests "ab-use"—an un-usual, non-normative, mis-leading, or de-familiar form of writing. It also calls into association references to alternative usages, deception, tricks, chicanery, seduction—all references that Derrida would naturally be invoking in "La Mythologie blanche: La Métaphor dans le texte philosophique" (1971) and, moreover, that would participate in the tropes outlined above as characteristic of his discursive mode. In his essay Lewis attempts to outline what he calls "a new axiomatics of fidelity, one that requires attention to the chain of signifiers" (1985:42). Lewis's essay is carefully written, tentative in its claims, exploratory in its aim, trying to create new openings for theorizing translation in the age of poststructuralism.

In the English language, however, the word *abuse*, especially in to-day's climate, denotes something much stronger and more violent, moving into the realm of verbal insult and physical injury, thus perhaps explaining Lewis's hesitancy to use the term in the English version of his own essay. Venuti's appropriation of the term might be called the "violent turn" in translation studies (cf. Arrojo 1995a). When Derrida uses the term as in a "une 'bonne' traduction doit toujours abuser" ("a 'good' translation must always commit abuses"), he used it because of the *multiplicity of referents* associated with the term, including those creative, playful connotations in French, always pointing his form of deconstruction toward the positive, the affirmative, the life-giving. In a typical Derridean rhetorical strategy, there is a kind of double-writing manifest, with *abuser* here connoting both pleasure and pain, mixing destruction with construction. The playful use of language with multiple referents/allusions is one way in which Derrida attempts to create openings to allow alternative voices to be heard within the dominant discourse of Western (logocentric) philosophy, thereby allowing poststructuralist scholars to participate at least in certain micropolitics of the age.

Venuti, by contrast, misses the opportunity to incorporate such poststructuralist practices in his theory and, as he restores *traduction abusive* to English, he omits the play, connotations, tricks, and deception of the term in Lewis's context. He also fails to note the hesitancy and restraint of Lewis's translation as well as the openness to new theoretical terms for the field. Venuti writes in his forceful style, "Abusive fidelity clearly entails a rejection of fluency that dominates contemporary translation in favor of an opposing strategy that can aptly be called resistancy" (1992:12). This concept became the cornerstone of Venuti's book *The Translator's Invisibility* (1995), which was built around the thesis that the norms of literary translation in the United States favor faithful, fluent translations, and that it is difficult to publish translations that are strange sounding or estranging. Venuti documents his work well, drawing many examples from his own struggles to publish translations of the nineteenth-century Milanese bohemian (*scapigliatura*) Italian novelist Iginio Ugo

Tarchetti. Venuti prefers that translators preserve the foreign linguistic and cultural elements of the original, thereby producing translations that are "strange or estranging" (1992:13). He concludes the chapter entitled "Dissidence" in *Translator's Invisibility* this way: "Foreignizing translation is a dissident cultural practice, maintaining a refusal of the dominant by developing affiliations with marginal linguistic and literary values at home" (1995:148). Though I agree with Venuti in terms of the state of literary translation in the United States in the twentieth century, in terms of translation *theory*, in terms of this volume on translation and power, he seems to have simplified the complexity of the problem, and certain unanswered questions remain. Is this a new theory of translation? How are poststructuralist terms being used to support arguments for resistant theories of translation? To me, Venuti's theory sounds more modernist than postmodernist, more structuralist than poststructuralist. His argument also strikes me as particularly teleological, conforming to traditional either/or debates about identity politics, despite the poststructuralist terminology. What is covered up or erased by the adoption of such clearcut terms in English?

By contrast, in her book *The Subversive Scribe: Translating Latin America Fiction* (1991), Suzanne Jill Levine also uses poststructuralist strategies, but she seems to avoid the identity politics that Venuti so emphasizes. While she, too, adopts an abusive strategy, a strategy she calls *subversive*, her situation is slightly different from Venuti's. Whereas Venuti seems to be calling for his abusive strategy regardless of the text of the original, Suzanne Jill Levine seems to be applying her translation strategy to selected authors, for example, the Cuban novelist Guillermo Cabrera Infante, whose own prose is *already* subversive and abusive. Thus Levine seems to claim a certain poetic license to take such liberties with her translation because the original text also plays with language, especially dialects of Cuban Spanish, offering multiple referents and puns, making intersemiotic connections to movies, passages from the Bible, nonsense verse, and comics. Levine has also talked extensively with the author and has Cabrera Infante's blessing to take the liberties she does. And what abuses she commits. The translation *Three Trapped Tigers* (1971) by Donald Gardner and Suzanne Jill Levine is more than thirty pages longer than Cabrera Infante's *Tres tristes tigres* (1967), with Levine adding tangential material in her translation.

In terms of Levine's translation strategies, one can see many parallels to the strategies of deconstruction. Her creative approach to translating puns, sounds, alliteration, and word games gives one a sense of play and of polyvalence. Her use of the street jargon of metropolitan New York immigrant culture to simulate Havana's urban Spanish leads to cross-cultural connections and semiotic invention that is procreative and breaks down borders between languages. Her knowledge of and reference to Hollywood films matches Cabrera Infante's obsession with film. Her ability to let herself go, following the puns and double entendres of Cabrera Infante's language, adding to and elaborating rather than reducing and simplifying, enriches her texts in a Joycean fashion. Her ability to follow the sounds as well as the meaning gives the translation a kind of aural pleasure, one that Cabrera Infante clearly intended with his Havana Cuban nocturnal Spanish slang. Most scholars agree that Spanish tends to be a more polyvalent language than English is, but Levine has found a way to expand the boundaries of English to parallel the Spanish. Of all the translators in the United States, Levine comes the closest to using the rhetorical strategies of deconstruction. Yet her deconstruction has a strangely conservative ring to it. It should come as no surprise that two of her mentors included Gregory Rabassa at Columbia University, whose translation work generally has a humanistic agenda and privileges the author's original, and Emir Rodríguez Monegal from Yale, who was for a time closely affiliated with the conservative group of the Yale School during the early years of the reception of deconstruction in the United States.

With regard to questions of power, Suzanne Jill Levine's use of "authority," that is, the authority of the original author Cabrera Infante, to "legitimize" her translation choices is troubling. Without his authority, could she ever publish her work? Would a publisher accept a translation that has an additional thirty to forty pages not present in the original? Clearly the most abusive translators—Ezra Pound, Jorge Luis Borges, Augusto and Haroldo de Campos—are famous creative writers in their own right and already have enormous cultural prestige and power. If Venuti were more famous as a creative writer in his own right, could he have more easily placed his Tarchetti translations? Or if Tarchetti were alive and could legitimize the translations, would the publication have been facilitated? While the poststructuralist project has always been aimed at "deconstructing" the notion of author, of authority, Levine *uses* the fame of the author to legitimize her translation strategy.

As we have seen, Levine is suggesting a selective use of such subversive strategies: because Cabrera Infante is already a subversive original writer, the subversive translation strategy is the "correct" one in this case. Her strategy reinforces both literary style and ideological beliefs held by the writer. Given the fact that Cabrera Infante is an extremely conservative, male, and misogynist writer, what does the selection of a deconstructive translation strategy for the translation of this text say then about deconstruction? Levine seems to dance the dance of deconstruction but largely avoids participating in the politics surrounding such selectivity. In some of her recent thinking about translation, she, too, is clearly troubled by such a nonfeminist position in her work (Levine 1991:181).

In *What Is Translation?* (1997b), Douglas Robinson also raises a question with regard to the translation of already abusive texts, such as Tarchetti's or Cabrera Infante's. For example, referring to Levine's translation of Cabrera Infante, Robinson asks, in cases where the original text is already abusive, whether the abusive translator actually *conforms* to the source language usage by using a subversive strategy? Robinson finds that, ironically, translators such as Levine, Lewis, and Venuti are *more* faithful to foreign syntax and semantics than those translators whose work is more fluent. Robinson cites Marilyn Gaddis Rose, who has gone so far as to refer to theorists such as Venuti as "neo-literalists" (Rose 1993:266). Robinson questions Venuti's use of authority in his arguments, even going so far as to suggest an alliance with a cultural elite whose foreignizing translation strategy actually blocks popular access to their translated texts. Robinson writes: "Just how 'radical' or 'oppositional' a subject position does [Venuti] want [the translator] to inhabit? Proletarian, feminine, subaltern? Popular, populist, lay? Crazy, delirious, schizzed? How much hegemonic authority does he want to retain while adopting this 'resistant' or oppositional position?" (1997b:104). Robinson's questions provoke thinking about resistant translation strategies in an age of multiple, complex, often hybridized subject positions. Does a foreignizing approach work in all cases? One person's resistance might be another's conformity. Does Venuti's resistance, which appeals to feminists, rationalists and academics, oppress the popular, the populist, or people with diverse ethnic backgrounds?

In terms of theory, the most interesting part of Robinson's criticism of Venuti/Lewis, for me, is his question concerning who is perpetuating the abuse against whom. He writes: "[I]n an abusive translation as Lewis and Venuti imagine it, who is the abused? The source-language author, text, culture? The target-language reader, text, culture? Both, or in some combination of the various aspects of the two? . . . What social and psychological effects does it have on its victims and its perpetrators?" (Robinson 1997b:136–37). Venuti, who claims to be on the side of the oppressed and ethnically marginalized, clearly suggests that the abuse be committed against the hegemonic norms in the target culture. Yet often the strategy also abuses the source language culture and author, and Robinson suggests that this on occasion might be unfair, especially when the source language author has no way of fighting back.

Though useful for challenging certain literary conventions within the United States, when applied to other countries and cultural situations, Venuti's favored form of translation might appear to be perpetuating violent and abusive strategies that have served to oppress and colonize. Although Cabrera Infante may not mind seeing his texts man- or womanhandled in translation, such a strategy applied to writers from smaller countries may not be much appreciated. In deconstructive strategies, there is violence involved, but there is also affirmation and fun. Yet let us not lose sight of the fact that Derrida's term *abuser* involves a kind of double writing, including both play and pain, as is typical of his use of signifiers in his writing, such as his use of the word *pharamakon* to refer both to the poison and the cure (1981:97–98). In discussions of poststructuralism and translation in the United States, often the pleasure, the double meaning, and the trickery of deconstruction have been omitted in favor of some ideological agenda, or the play is preserved at the expense of political engagement.

Selective Essentialism: Spivak

As a tentative first step to find a way out of the dilemma of either poststructuralism without the politics, or politics without the poststructuralism, I turn to Gayatri Spivak, noted for her work as a translator of Derrida and of the Bengali peasant writer Mahasweta Devi. Perhaps better than anyone else, she has raised the question of how the "Third World" subject is represented in Western discourse, including in translation. Her work continually raises questions regarding whose interests are represented and what institutions of power are involved. In her essay "Can the Subaltern Speak?" (1988a), for example, she asks the question whether or not it is even possible for the subaltern to speak for themselves, in light of the colonization processes that they have undergone and especially in light of generations of intellectuals reporting what minorities say, as if they, the intellectuals, were some sort of transparent medium. Nowhere is this more apparent than in translation: the image of the Indian peasant (as well as African tribal, Native American, and so forth) as projected via translation has in turn been reproduced within Indian culture and impacts identity formation in that country. In her essay Spivak considers the margins of society—the illiterate peasants, the tribals, the lowest level of urban subproletariate—and discusses the findings of the subaltern studies group headed by Ranagit Guha in the 1980s in India and their search for the "subaltern consciousness."

Spivak's answer, though not completely encouraging, is that the Western scholar can only partially access the subaltern condition, not through what is specifically said by either the subaltern group or by the intellectuals (or translators) representing them, but by reading what is not said—reading the gaps, the silences, and the contradictions symptomatically. Here I find her project close to Venuti's concept of reading the "remainder"—that which is left over or exceeds the transparent use of language (Venuti 1995:216). And if this sounds like deconstruction, it is close to it. Deconstruction, Spivak argues, is useful in order to analyze and measure such silences and to intervene. In order for the subaltern and mute to speak, Spivak suggests that it is necessary to *unlearn* and to *mark our position* as investigating subjects clearly before being able to learn again. There is also a Marxist impulse underlying her strategy; unlike Derrida's deconstruction, which dismantles texts and opens the way for random connections and unlimited semiosis, Spivak's deconstruction moves toward affirmative production. The attempt is less an uncovering of the "true" or "essential" or "original" subaltern consciousness, which she would argue is impossible, and more a coming to an understanding of the *effects* of colonization on the subaltern consciousness in *specific* historical situations. She calls this approach a kind of "strategic essentialism." In an interview with Ellen Rooney in the first chapter of *Outside in the Teaching Machine* (1993a), Spivak addresses the issues of subaltern studies and essentialism in a footnote:

Reading the work of Subaltern Studies from within but against the grain, I would suggest that elements in their text would warrant a reading of the project to retrieve the subaltern consciousness as an attempt to undo a massive historiographic metalepsis and *"situate"* *the effect of the subject as subaltern.* I would read it, then, as a strategic use of positive essentialism in a scrupulously visible political interest. This would put us in line with the Marx who locates fetishization . . . ; the Nietzsche who offers us genealogy in the place of historiography; the Foucault who plots the construction of "counter-memory"; the Barthes of semitropy; the Derrida of "affirmative deconstruction." This would allow them to use the critical force of antihumanism, in other words, even as they share its constituting paradox: that the essentializing moment, the object of their criticism, is irreducible. (286, my emphasis)

The use of essentialism to support an antiessentialist project, the use of memory to construct a counter-memory, the use of the explicit to chart the implicit, is a complex and rather controversial move. For Spivak, however, there is no other recourse in order to get beyond the nihilism of deconstruction, in order to arrive at some form of post-poststructuralist theory. Here translation theorists could learn from Spivak's theory. Rather than using translation to access some sort of originary being, all we can ever access is the developing subject in specific situations; if that subject is "subaltern," then the location of that subject is always already within a colonized situation, implicated in the web of discursive and linguistic codes of the colonizer.

A notable feature of Spivak's statement here is also the use of the term *metalepsis*, a rhetorical figure that the *Oxford English Dictionary* defines as "the metonymical substitution of one word for another which is itself figurative." Metonymic substitution, as Maria Tymoczko has argued, is characteristic of all translation: because it is impossible to translate every literary and linguistic feature contained in the original, translators have to make choices, whether consciously or unconsciously, and must substitute a part for the whole, implicating them in the long intersemiotic chain of signification (Tymoczko 1999: chapters 2, 10; see also the introduction to this volume). This "partiality" also enables translators to engage in the dialectics of power, which, as Spivak argues above, has traditionally served to cover up subaltern consciousness. Spivak urges translators to deconstruct the chain of signification and to expose the metaleptical/metonymical process of figuration. Only by undoing this "massive historiographic metalepsis" can one begin to locate the conditions and effects of oppression. This use of "affirmative deconstruction"— or in Spivak's words "positive essentialism"—to expose repressive conditions and allow for new openings is both overtly political and also one of the few means of power that language minorities and oppressed societies have at their disposal. We see our present volume, *Translation and Power*, as a contribution to this project.

To further complicate matters, Spivak also claims that deconstruction needs to be applied to ourselves as well as to the historical situation situating the subjects to be translated. The example Spivak gives in "Can the Subaltern Speak?" has to do with suicides, specifically Hindi widow sacrifice. She demonstrates how British male colonial rulers tried to abolish this practice as barbaric from their civilized worldview; yet Spivak also raises an eyebrow at the fact that no white women ever developed an alternative analysis of the practice, implicating white Western women in the colonial project. After giving a history of the practice in India, including examples from self-immolation as a stage of enlightenment, a stage of freedom, she asks several questions. What is the correct form of resistance? Are all widow sacrifices the result of patriarchal cultures oppressing women? Are all widow sacrifices the same? How is a Western translator or feminist scholar, given what they have "learned," supposed to know when one suicide might be liberating and another perpetuating male dominance?

Showing how important translation is to her feminist, postcolonial theorizing, Spivak demonstrates her theory through the translation of three stories by Mahasweta Devi collected in *Imaginary Maps* (1995). Spivak uses her knowledge of Indian and Bengali culture to help Western readers "imagine" (hence the title) not an abstract, politically correct Other, but real cultural difference in its specific forms. Spivak refuses to make claims for any metafictional construction of the indigenous Indian life. She does this by providing, in addition to the translated story, contextual information in the form of a translator's preface, an interview with the author, and an afterword. The interview not only allows the author to speak but also positions the translator as involved in the mediation to follow. Marking one's position as a translator, as a mediating subject, is an important part of postcolonial translation.

The prefatory matter allows Spivak to set the scene of the situation in India for the tribal communities that Devi portrays in her fiction. "Facts" are introduced, such as the facts that tribals make up one-sixth of the population of India and that many tribal groups are older than the Indo-European groups that migrated to Europe. The preface also allows Spivak to introduce certain specific community practices, such as the tribals' communal ownership of land. She also introduces linguistic differences—indicating, for example, that there is no word for *orphan* in most tribal languages, nor is there a word for *rape*. Finally, importantly, she sets the contemporary political scene for Devi's writing. There has been a price paid for decolonization in India, and many communities have not been decolonized in this "postcolonial world." Devi's tribal community, for example, still uses a caste system in which "untouchables" persist; the tribe has been forced onto worthless land; many tribal customs have been criminalized by the postcolonial Indian government; bonded labor still exists; and, importantly, many women are still sold as merchandise, especially into marriage. Spivak's technique of including prefatory material and historical background—supplementary material in a Derridean sense—with the translated text is increasingly becoming an important technique used by postcolonial translators.

The translations themselves continue the strategies outlined in the preface. To take just one example, the story "The Hunt" presents a woman named Mary Oraon, whose mother is a Bhikni tribal woman and whose father is an Australian Christian immigrant (hence Mary's first name). Mary works as a housecleaner for a wealthier Indian named Prasadji; Mary is portrayed as a tough woman—she carries around a machete for protection; she is a capable household manager; and she negotiates well at the market. Mary is trying to save money to marry the man she loves, a tribal named Julim. An Indian developer named Tehslidar Singh comes to town, who sees the attractive Mary and wants to "possess" her in more ways than one. Mary resists, further demonstrating her toughness, but a lot of pressure is applied to her by her family and community to consummate her relationship with Singh for the economic benefit of the community. Without giving away the end of the story, I will say that a traditional spring festival arrives that includes the ritual of "The Hunt" (hence the story's name), a ritual Mary adapts to her current hunted situation.

What is Spivak trying to accomplish with her translation of Devi's story? First, while she discusses a tribal situation, there is no exoticization of the tribe—work, play, rich, poor, love, sexism, family structures, old rituals, and resistance are all depicted as part of everyday life. Mary herself has a hyphenated identity—half tribal and half white. She is independent, a strong woman in her own situation, perhaps stronger than some Western feminists care to admit. Though Mary is an individual within a tribal collective, it seems that Spivak chose this story precisely because Mary is *not* a representative of that collective, but a woman with specific problems in a specific cultural situation. The plot that drives the story is the question of how will Mary solve her problem, how will she act in this specific situation? Western standards of feminism or political correctness do not apply. Spivak suggests that the goal of the postcolonial translator is not to describe again master-slave relations, not to revive to age-old dichotomies, but instead to measure the differences, to *stage* specific angers, loves, despairs, and resolutions under specific circumstances, so that we all can learn from them.

Spivak's translation strategy also participates in ongoing discussions regarding Third World feminism, showing how translation studies can and does participate in theoretical debates in other fields such as feminism, ethnic studies, and cultural studies. In an earlier essay, "The Politics of Translation" (1993b), Spivak is particularly damning of Western feminist translators and their analysis of writing by Third World women: according to Western feminists, Spivak claims, all writing by Third World women sounds the same. Women writers from India end up sounding like male writers from Taipei. It is not enough, she argues, to have some sort of liberal commitment to politics; attention must also be paid to the forms, the language, and the specific contexts of texts. Translation, thus, becomes a key component of Spivak's theory. The demands made on the translator as mediator are correspondingly high: the translator must be familiar with the "history of the language, the history of the author's moment, the history of the language-in-translation" (1993b:186).

If all of this sounds like what we teach in translation studies, it is quite close. Regarding the standards of translation, in addition to knowing the history of the language and the history of the language-in-translation, Spivak also asks that the translator have graduated into speaking of "intimate matters in the language in the original" (1993b:187).

For the translation studies scholar, however, these are all precepts developed by translation studies years ago; I am reminded of André Lefevere's *Translating Poetry: Seven Strategies and a Blueprint* (1975), in which he argued that the translator not only has to be fluent in the language but also has to grasp the time, place, and tradition of the source text, rendering all elements in an equivalent target culture language, time, place, and tradition (1975:99). Many rigorous translation-training programs are equally demanding. But to cultural studies scholars, who have generally not engaged translation studies, many of whom do not speak foreign languages well at all, these ideas seem new.

Spivak uses foreignizing strategies as an attempt to deconstruct normative thinking in the United States, and her translation strategy closely resembles Venuti's in terms of politics and method, yet what differs between Spivak and Venuti, for example, is that she seems more hesitant to draw conclusions in terms of the politics of her translations. Rather, she suggests that her translations are a *first step* in what she calls "attentive reading," one that opens a space for "learning from below," which is earned by "slow effort at ethical responding—a two way road—with the compromised other as teacher" (1995:202). Her heroine Mary in the story "The Hunt" is not representative of the collective, but a single individual in a particular situation who chooses a specific ritual to stage her resistance in her own way. Spivak suggests that the task of the translator is to articulate cultural differences in specific cultural historical situations. She uses poststructuralist strategies selectively to *measure* those differences. The language she prefers is distinctly unliterary, stark, and angular (cf. Simon 1996:146), incorporating Brechtian defamiliarization devices. For example, in the title of one story, Spivak chooses "The Breast-Giver" instead of the more familiar "Wet-Nurse" used by a previous translator, a choice which Devi suggests better reflects her signature style (1993b:182). Spivak also uses North American rather than British English in her translations, perhaps to alienate the Indian reader educated in British English, and she sprinkles her prose with American slang terms, further interrupting the smooth flow of the English.

Much of this sounds *less* abusive to source or target cultures, however, and it seems that there may be a kind of reversal going on here: that Spivak's translation is *more accurate* than previous versions, versions that added softening, exoticization, and Western literary-like phrases. Indeed, Spivak's selective essentialist strategy can lead to a win-win situation, good for both the source and target language cultures. Spivak accomplishes a kind of double writing in her translation, critiquing West metaphysical, humanist thinking, and at the same time creating openings to imagine real cultural differences at work.

Connections

This essay has focused on translation studies scholars practicing in the United States, but clearly their work is followed closely in other parts of the world. In Canada, it connects to a group of feminist translators who have adopted thinking by Jacques Derrida, Hélène Cixous, and Luce Irigaray in their thinking about translation. Writers/translators Nicole Brossard, Barbara Godard, Susanne de Lotbinière-Harwood, and others have used a kind of selective essentialism in their work, a mix of Mikhail Bakhtin with Derrida, which has led to creative openings and allowed them to think about women's writing in an affirmative, inventive fashion. Many of Derrida's rhetorical strategies are visible in their translation work, including the play, the chance, the lack of telos, and the polysemia. Rather than to fall into the trap of gains and losses, fluent or foreign, within their translations, there is deconstruction and construction of something else, for which they have coined the term *écriture au féminin*, something that is not characterized by binary oppositions. Distinctions blur between male/female writing, between standard French and Quebec French, between English and French, between poetry and prose, between presence and memory. Similar to Levine's work, images, pictures, and sounds allow the imagination to make new associations and meanings that are beyond normative, rational equivalents. Reason is destabilized; fantasy and memory are opened up. As Barbara Godard has argued in "Theorizing Feminist Discourse/Translation" (1990), women's discourse is always double, always already referring to the Other and inscribed within Western logocentric discourse. Susanne de Lotbinière-Harwood in *Re-belle et Infidèle/ The Body Bilingual* (1991) raises the variables of the equation exponentially, arguing that feminist translation is a *quadraphonic site*, the Self/ Other coming at you simultaneously in two languages from four sites. And as one enters the age of post-poststructuralism, with increasing gender, ethnic, and class distinctions, the discourses multiply further, increasing exponentially again, approaching a kind of unlimited semiosis in a Derridean sense.

The Canadian feminist translators are well aware of relations of power to their work. The women translators make it clear that their inventions are intended to subvert the patriarchal language and culture that dominates the cultural space of Quebec. They hope that by deconstructing the male space, space will be opened up for women. The contribution of translation to the increased popularity of the Bloc Québécois and its success politically (now the second largest party in Canada) demonstrates to scholars of emerging communities the power of translation. Questions remain, however. Once a space is opened for women, what in turn is covered up? If Québécois French becomes more centralized, what happens to other minority languages, such as Haitian Kreoyl or Native American languages? In fact, many women in Quebec have reached that position of power and find it troubling. Though writers such as Nicole Brossard and her translators do now enjoy unprecedented prestige in Canadian cultural and political circles, many seem more hesitant than ever to exercise their newly found power.

In essays such as "Feminist 'Orgasmic' Theories of Translation and Their Contradictions" (1995a), Brazilian translation theorist Rosemary Arrojo has criticized some of the essentialist claims that seem to underlie much feminist writing and theorizing about translation, especially arguments that feminist translation attempts to recuperate lost and covered-up meanings, or that through translation translators can access some sort of essential feminine language. Arrojo has been especially critical of the use by some of the Canadian translators of the rhetoric of deconstruction to substantiate their claims. She also raises concerns about the violent metaphors used by some feminist translators to express their strategies, such as "womanhandling" the text (Godard 1990:91). Arrojo's criticism would apply to metaphors such as "abusive fidelity" as used by contemporary male scholars, including Venuti, as well as earlier metaphors used by theorists such as George Steiner. Despite such a critique, the discourse in Quebec on translation, women's writing, identity politics, and the future, not just of the field of translation studies but also of the state of Quebec itself, is at an exceptionally rich level for all those interested in the theory and practice of alternative politics.

Arrojo's essay on Quebec translators is indicative of the engagement with theory ongoing in Brazil, where many of the debates on translation, poststructuralism, and power predate discussions in North America and

Europe. The translation strategies, for example, of the brothers Haroldo and Augusto de Campos also approach the double writing characteristic of deconstruction. Clearly the metaphors they use to talk about translation expand the boundaries of critical thinking about translation. In his essay "Transblanco" (1987), for example, Haroldo de Campos talks of translation in terms of "re-creation," "transcreation," "re-imagination," "transillummination" and, more famously, "mefistofaustican transluciferation" (1981:179, 1987:150; my translation). In his introduction to *Verso, reverso, e controverso* (1978), Augusto de Campos, in a deconstructionist move, talks of translation as "intraduçao," a neologism suggestive of a kind of translation from within, an implosion.

In the translation practice of the de Campos brothers, the inventions, juxtapositions, creation of new terms and neologisms, experiments with form, and interplay of voices come as close to the affirmative Derridean semiosis as I have seen. Their translations of John Donne, Stéphane Mallarmé, James Joyce, Octavio Paz, and Goethe destabilize Eurocentric concepts of the original and elevate translation to an equal plane with creative writing. The metaphors for translation used by the de Campos brothers are more provocative than those used by Derrida, yet their metaphors contain similar organic elements of growth and of love. Resurrecting the modernist term *cannibalism* coined by Oswald de Andrade in his *Manifesto Antropófago* (1928), the de Campos brothers redefine the term *cannibalism* as a devouring with love, a nourishing act. Their translations retain a kind of reverence for the author, spirit, tone, and culture of the original, and a language of intimacy, to use Spivak's terms. While a clear rejection of logical rational solutions in favor of more intuitive and emotional forms of connection can be sensed, it is a rejection that also suggests new ways of seeing and thinking. Unlike some theories in the United States that retreat into dualistic categories, often ones that reject or reinforce European ideas and forms of thinking, the de Campos brothers seem to *combine positive aspects* of both European texts and indigenous ideas and forms. The translations by the de Campos brothers seem to enact a double affirmation at play, one of which poststructuralists would approve.

Yet the de Campos brothers' translation work does not avoid power relations. As Randal Johnson has pointed out in his "Tupy or not Tupy: Cannibalism and Nationalism in Contemporary Brazilian Literature and

Culture" (1987), this cannibalism is very much connected to rejecting images of passive, submissive Native Americans in favor of more aggressive images of the cannibal. Johnson writes, "Rather than having the colonizer absorb the values of the defeated foe, Oswald [de Andrade] valorizes the cannibalization of the colonizer by the Indian. Initially then cannibalism is a form of resistance. Metaphorically speaking, it represents a new attitude toward cultural relations with hegemonic power" (49). This new relation, however, seems less aimed at either/or solutions than at the creation of a new national identity with its own artistic forms. This kind of poststructural translation is thus also connected to a selective essentialism. By reversing the power relations between the Old World and New, it reassesses the image of the indigenous peoples of America, which largely has been constructed through translation and which now needs to be reconstructed again through retranslation. This sort of translation both resonates with oppositional politics and satirizes those very oppositional categories.

By way of conclusion, let me emphasize two points. First, the translator has never been a neutral party in the translation process but, rather, an individual with linguistic and cultural skills and her or his own agenda. Ideology works in funny ways—some of it conscious and some of it unconscious. Contemporary translators tend to be increasingly sensitive to their own worldviews and realize how such views might color the translation process. Many no longer subscribe to the notion of the self-effacing translator; instead they are increasingly aware of their involvement in the process of textual production, exploring and interpreting the contemporary world in all its conflictual guises. Many authors realize this, too—Nicole Brossard, author of *Le Désert mauve* (1987), for example, views her translators as coauthors, actively involved in the production and staging of the translated text. Poststructural translation thus can be viewed as a creative act, the representation of the text, participating in the creation of knowledge and, by extension, power. Translation does not simply offer a window onto some unified, exotic Other; it participates in its very construction. The process of staging translation is a process of gathering and creating *new information* that can be turned to powerful political ends, including resistance, self-determination, and rebellion.

Second, poststructural translation is having an impact on our very definitions of translation. Theorists can no longer think in terms of an uncritical transfer from a monolithic language A to a similar monolithic language B; rather, translation takes place across a multilingual and multicultural environment A into an often equally multicultural environment B. Postcolonial translation does not mean some sort of return to an essentialist, precolonial state; rather, it involves complex encounters with new situations, and contemporary translators are increasingly open to mixing textures, beliefs, materials, and languages. Similarly in postructural translation, hybrid sites of new meaning open up; new borders are encountered and crossed, often with surprisingly *creative* results. Translation in this context is fun, with puns, neologisms, archaisms, jokes, and parodies part of the play, further illustrating the creative aspects of poststructural translation. Homi Bhabha has discussed this space in *The Location of Culture* (1994) as a transnational/translational hybrid location, which he sees not as an anomaly characteristic of certain cultures of the world, but in fact as more indicative of the postcolonial, postmodern condition of *all* cultures. Bhabha looks at the space in which émigrés gather at the edge of foreign cultures—in the cafés, ghettos, and city centers—all sites that are multilingual and multicultural, and that include migrants, minorities, colonials, and postcolonials. Translation, according to Bhabha, is one of the tools *best* suited to access and understand this space. Translation in his mind is viewed as a form of re-writing, reinterpreting, trans-lating, and trans-valuing.

In such spaces translation breaks certain silences and can be liberating, a form of repetition that can lead to social change. Foucault again continues to be helpful on this point: "Difference is transformed into that which must be specified within a concept, without overstepping its bounds. And yet above the species, we encounter the swarming of individualities. What is this boundless diversity, which eludes specification and remains outside the concept, if not the resurgence of repetition?" (1977a: 182). In this poststructuralist age, translation exemplifies this resurgence of repetition, exposing hidden cultural data, repressed images, and marginalized worldviews. Thus translation is increasingly becoming one of the central tools at our disposal for better understanding how cultures are interconnected as well as fragmented. There are still huge ideological and cultural differences that need to be analyzed and thousands of texts that await their translators. Translation can help reveal the complexity of the labyrinth and point to some ways out of our closed conceptual spaces. Translation today is not considered a mindless activity reflecting cultural struggle but, rather, one that brings real differences to the fore, thereby providing a powerful tool in the construction of culture. Through translation, in Borges's terms, we re-create once again our precursors, thereby producing new modes of articulation for the future.

Bibliography

Adams, Peter William Trelawney (1977) *Fatal Necessity: British Intervention in New Zealand 1830–1847.* Auckland: Auckland University Press.

Aijmer, Göran (1992) "Comment on an Article by P. Steven Sangren" *Current Anthropology* 33:296–97.

Alonso Tejada, Luis (1977) *La represión sexual en la España de Franco.* Barcelona: Caralt.

Altman, Janet (1998) "Association Internationale des Interprètes de Conférence" in Mona Baker (ed.) *Routledge Encyclopedia of Translation Studies.* London: Routledge, 16–17.

Álvarez, Román, and M. Carmen-África Vidal (1996) *Translation, Power, Subversion.* Clevedon: Multilingual Matters.

Amin, Shahid (1988) "Gandhi as Mahatma" in Ranajit Guha and Gayatri Chakravorty Spivak (eds.) *Selected Subaltern Studies.* Oxford: Oxford University Press, 288–342.

Anderson, Benedict (1991) *Imagined Communities.* London: Verso.

Anderson, R. Bruce W. (1976) "Perspectives on the Role of Interpreter" in Richard W. Brislin (ed.) *Translation: Applications and Research.* New York: Gardner Press, 208–28.

Andrade, Oswald de (1928) "Manifesto antropófago," *Revista de antropofagia* 1:1.

——— (1991) "Cannibalist Manifesto," trans. Leslie Bary. *Latin American Literary Review* 19:38.

Appadurai, Arjun (1996) *Modernity at Large: Cultural Dimensions of Globalization.* Minneapolis: University of Minnesota Press.

Arambel-Güiñazú, Maria Cristina (1993) *La escritura de Victoria Ocampo: Memorias, seducción, collage.* Buenos Aires: Edicial.

Arblaster, Anthony (1993) Democracy. Buckingham: Open University Press. First edition 1987.

Ariane (1957) Expediente de Censura 16411. Madrid: Ministerio de Educación y Cultura. Unpublished.

Armand, Octavio (1994) Refractions, trans. Carol Maier. New York: SITES/Lumen Books.

Arnold, Matthew (1962) Democratic Education, ed. R. H. Super. Ann Arbor: University of Michigan Press.

———— *(1993) Culture and Anarchy and Other Essays,* ed. Stefan Collini. Cambridge: Cambridge University Press.

Arnold, Thomas (ed.) (1835) The History of the Peloponnesian War by Thucydides, 3 vols. Oxford: James Parker.

Arrojo, Rosemary (1984) "Jorge Luis Borges's *Labyrinths* and João Guimarães Rosa's *Sertão:* Images of Reality as Text." Dissertation, Johns Hopkins University.

———— *(1993) Tradução, desconstrução e psicanálise.* Rio de Janeiro: Imago.

———— *(1994)* "Fidelity and the Gendered Translation" *TTR* 7:2.147–63.

———— *(1995a)* "Feminist 'Orgasmic' Theories of Translation and Their Contradictions" *Tradterm* 2:67–75.

———— *(1995b)* "Translation and Postmodernism in Calvino's *Se una notte d'inverno un viaggiatore*" in *La traduzione: Saggi e documenti II, Libri e riviste d'Italia.* Ministero per i Beni Culturali e Ambientali, Divisione Editoria, 41–56.

Baker, Mona (1997) "Non-Cognitive Constraints and Interpreter Strategies in Political Interviews" in Karl Simms (ed.) *Translating Sensitive Texts.* Amsterdam: Rodopi, 111–30.

Bakhtin, Mikhail (1981) The Dialogic Imagination, ed. Michael Holquist, trans. Caryl Emerson and Michael Holquist. Austin: University of Texas Press.

Bann, Stéphane (1997) "Théorie et pratique de la traduction au sein du Groupe de Coppet" in Simone Balayé and Jean-Daniel Candaux (eds.) *Le Groupe de Coppet: Actes de documents du deuxième Colloque de Coppet.* Geneva: Librairie Slatkine, 217–33.

Barsky, Robert F. (1996) "The Interpreter as Intercultural Agent in Refugee Hearings" *The Translator* 2:1.45–63.

Bassnett, Susan (1992) "Writing in No Man's Land: Questions of Gender and Translation" in Malcolm Coulthard (ed.) *Studies in Translation.* Special issue of *Ilha do desterro* 28:63–73.

———— *(1993) Comparative Literature.* Cambridge: Blackwell.

———— *(1996)* "The Meek or the Mighty: Reappraising the Role of the Translator" in Román Álvarez and M. Carmen-África Vidal (eds.) *Translation, Power, Subversion.* Clevedon: Multilingual Matters, 10–24.

Bassnett, Susan, and André Lefevere (1990a) "Proust's Grandmother and the Thousand and One Nights: The 'Cultural Turn' in Translation Studies" in

Susan Bassnett and André Lefevere (eds.) *Translation, History and Culture*. London: Pinter, 1–13.

—— *(eds.) (1990b) Translation, History and Culture*. London: Pinter.

Bassnett, Susan, and Harish Trivedi *(eds.) (1999) Post-colonial Translation: Theory and Practice*. London: Routledge.

Beebee, Thomas *(1994a)* "The Fiction of Translation: Abdelkebir Khatibi's *Love in Two Languages*" *Sub/stance* 73:63–78.

—— *(1994b) The Ideology of Genre: A Comparative Study of Generic Instability*. University Park: Pennsylvania State University Press.

Beer, Gillian *(1996) Open Fields: Science in Cultural Encounter*. Oxford: Clarendon Press.

Behdad, Ali *(1994) Belated Travellers: Orientalism in the Age of Colonial Dissolution*. Cork: Cork University Press.

Belton, John *(ed.) (1996) Movies and Mass Culture*. London: Athlone.

Benjamin, Walter *(1969)* "The Task of the Translator" in *Illuminations*, trans. Harry Zohn. New York: Schocken Books, 69–82.

Berman, Antoine *(1984) L'Epreuve de l'étranger: Culture et traduction dans l'Allemagne romantique*. Paris: Gallimard.

—— *(1988)* "De la translation à la traduction" *TTR* 1:1.23–40.

Bhabha, Homi K. *(1992)* "Postcolonial Criticism" in Stephen Greenblatt and Giles Gunn (eds.) *Redrawing the Boundaries: The Transformation of English and American Literary Studies*. New York: Modern Language Association, 437–65.

—— *(1994) The Location of Culture*. London: Routledge.

Black, Gregory D. *(1994) Hollywood Censored: Morality Codes, Catholics, and the Movies*. Cambridge: Cambridge University Press.

Bloch, Chana *(1997)* "Remarks: A Symposium on Translation" *Threepenny Review* (Summer) 18:2.10.

Bloomfield, S. T. *(trans.) (1829) The History of Thucydides: Newly Translated into English and Illustrated with Very Copious Annotations, Exegetical, Philological, Historical and Geographical*. London: Longman, Rees, Ormen, and Brown.

Boletín oficial del estado (BOE) *(1936–1975)*. Madrid: Ministerio de la Presidencia.

Borges, Jorge Luis *(1952)* "El escritor argentino y la tradición" in *Discusión*. Buenos Aires: Emecé.

—— *(1956)* "La muerte y la brújula" in *Ficciones*. Buenos Aires, Emecé, 147–64.

—— *(1980)* "Las versiones homéricas" in *Discusión: Prosa completa*, vol. 1. Barcelona: Editorial Bruguera, 181–86.

—— *(1994a) Ficciones* in *Obras completas*. Buenos Aires: Emecé, 1.425–530.

—— *(1994b) Obras completas*, 3 vols. Buenos Aires: Emecé.

Bouvier, Nicolas *(1992) L'Usage du monde*. Paris: Payot.

Bowen, Margareta, David Bowen, Francine Kaufmann, and Ingrid Kurz *(1995)*

"Interpreters and the Making of History" in Jean Delisle and Judith Woodsworth (eds.) *Translators through History*. Amsterdam: John Benjamins, 245–77.

Braidotti, Rosa (1994) *Nomadic Subjects: Embodiment and Sexual Difference in Contemporary Feminist Theory*. New York: Columbia University Press.

Brisset, Annie (1990) *Sociocritique de la traduction: Théâtre et alterité au Québec (1968–1988)*. Longueil: La Préambule.

—— (1996) *A Sociocritique of Translation: Theatre and Alterity in Quebec, 1968–1988*, trans. Rosalind Gill and Roger Gannon. Toronto: University of Toronto Press.

Brossard, Nicole (1987) *Le Désert mauve*. Montreal: L'Hexagone.

Budick, Sanford (1996) "Cross-Culture, Chiasmus, and the Manifold of Mind" in Sanford Budick and Wolfgang Iser (eds.) *The Translatability of Cultures: Figurations of the Space Between*. Palo Alto: Stanford University Press, 224–44.

Bury, Emmanuel (1995) "Postface" in Roger Zuber (ed.) *Les "Belles infidèles" et la formation du goût classique*. Paris: Albin Michel, 495–505.

Bush, Peter (ed.) (1997) *The Voice of the Turtle: An Anthology of Cuban Stories*. New York: Grove.

—— (1999) "Translating Juan Carlos Onetti for Anglo-American Others" in Gustavo San Román (ed.) *Onetti and Others: Comparative Essays on a Major Figure in Latin American Literature*. Albany: State University of New York Press, 177–86.

Buzard, James (1993) *The Beaten Track: European Tourism, Literature and the Ways to "Culture" 1800–1918*. Oxford: Clarendon Press.

Cabrera Infante, Guillermo (1967) *Tres tristes tigres*. Barcelona: Editorial Seix Barral.

—— (1971) *Three Trapped Tigers*, trans. Donald Gardner and Suzanne Jill Levine. New York: Harper and Row.

Caminha, Pedro Vaz de (1947) "The Discovery of Brazil" in Charles David Ley (ed.) *Portugese Voyages*. London: J. M. Dent, 41–59.

Campos, Augusto de (1978) *Verso, reverso, e controverso*. São Paulo: Perspectiva.

Campos, Haroldo de (1981) *Deus e o diablo no Fausto de Goethe*. São Paulo: Perspectiva.

—— (1987) "Transblanco: Reflexión sobre la transcreación de 'Blanco' de Octavio Paz, con una digresión sobre la teoría de la traducción del poeta mexicano" in Lisa Block de Behar (ed.) *Diseminario: Otro descubrimento de América*. Montevideo: XYZ Editores, 147–58.

Carré, Jean-Marie (1947) *Les Écrivains français et le mirage allemand 1800–1940*. Paris: Marcel Didier.

Castillo, B. Díaz del (1926) *The True History of the Conquest of New Spain*, trans. Alfred Percival Maudslay. London: Hakluyt Society.

Cebollada, Pascual (ed.) (1963) La censura de cine en España. Madrid: Centro Español de Estudios Cinematograficos.

Chambers, Iain, and Lidia Curti (1996) The Post-Colonial Question: Common Skies, Divided Horizons. London: Routledge.

Charles, Michel (1985) L'Arbre et la source. Paris: Éditions du Seuil.

Chatterjee, Partha (1993) The Nation and its Fragments: Colonial and Postcolonial Histories. Princeton: Princeton University Press.

Chen Fukang (1992) Zhongguo yi xue li lun shi gao [*A History of Translation Theory in China*]. Shanghai: Foreign Languages Publishing House.

Chen Yugang (1989) Zhongguo fan yi wen xue shi gao [*A History of Translated Literature in China*]. Beijing: Publishing House of Foreign Languages Teaching and Research.

Cheng Zhenqiu (1984) "Tantan Zhou Enlai xuanji (shangjuan) ying yi ben" [Review of *Selected Works of Zhou Enlai, Vol.1*] *Fanyi tongxun* [*Translators' Notes*] 5.69–73.

Cheyfitz, Eric (1997) The Poetics of Imperialism: Translation and Colonization from "The Tempest" to "Tarzan." Expanded edition. Philadelphia: University of Pennsylvania Press.

Clarke, Martin Lowther (1959) Classical Education in Britain 1500–1900. Cambridge: Cambridge University Press.

Clifford, James (1986) "Introduction: Partial Truths" in James Clifford and George E. Marcus (eds.) *Writing Culture: The Poetics and Politics of Ethnography.* Berkeley: University of California Press, 1–26.

—— *(1988) The Predicament of Culture: Twentieth-Century Ethnography, Literature, and Art.* Cambridge: Harvard University Press.

Clifford, James, and George E. Marcus (eds.) (1986) Writing Culture: The Poetics and Politics of Ethnography. Berkeley: University of California Press.

Colenso, William (1890) Signing of the Treaty of Waitangi. Wellington: Government Printer.

Cortázar, Julio (1963) Rayuela. Madrid: Cátedra.

—— *(1966)* "Las babas del Diablo" *Las armas secretas,* 4th ed. Buenos Aires: Sudamericana, 77–98.

—— *(1967a)* "Blow-Up" *End of the Game and Other Stories* (later retitled *Blow-Up and Other Stories*), trans. Paul Blackburn. New York: Pantheon, 114–31.

—— *(1967b) Hopscotch,* trans. Gregory Rabassa. New York: Signet.

—— *(1972) 62: A Model Kit,* trans. Gregory Rabassa. New York: Pantheon.

—— *(1973) Libro de Manuel.* Buenos Aires: Sudamericana.

—— *(1976)* "Del sentimiento de no estar de todo" *La vuelta al día en 80 mundos,* 10th ed. Madrid: Siglo XXI, 32–42.

—— *(1978) A Manual for Manuel,* trans. Gregory Rabassa. New York: Pantheon.

———— *(1980)* "Apocalypse at Solentiname" *A Change of Light and Other Stories,* trans. Gregory Rabassa. New York: Alfred Knopf, 119–28.

———— *(1981)* "Apocalipsis de Solentiname" *Alguien que anda por ahí,* 3d ed. Madrid: Bruguera, 77–88.

———— *(1986)* "On Feeling Not All There" *Around the Day in Eighty Worlds,* trans. Thomas Christensen. San Francisco: North Point Press, 17–20.

———— *(1994) 62—Modelo para armar,* 5th ed. Buenos Aires: Sudamericana.

Crawley, Richard *(trans.) (1876) History: The History of Herodotus; The History of the Peloponnesian War [by] Thucydides,* 2 vols. London: J. M. Dent.

Cronin, Michael *(1996) Translating Ireland: Translation, Languages, Cultures.* Cork: Cork University Press.

Dahl, Roald *(1982) The Twits.* London: Penguin.

Dale, Henry *(trans.) (1848) The History of the Peloponnesian War by Thucydides: A New and Literal Version.* London: Henry Bohn.

Darwin, Charles *(1986) Journal of Researches into the Geology and Natural History of the Various Countries visited by the H.M.S. "Beagle," The Works of Charles Darwin,* ed. Paul Barrett and R. B. Freeman, vol 2. London: J. M. Dent.

Davis, Lydia *(1995) The End of the Story.* New York: Farrar.

Dawson, Paul Martin Stuart *(1993)* "Poetry in an Age of Revolution" in Curran Stuart (ed.) *The Cambridge Companion to British Romanticism.* Cambridge: Cambridge University Press, 44–73.

Delabastita, Dirk *(1991)* "A False Opposition in Translation Studies: Theoretical versus/and Historical Approaches" *Target* 3:2.137–52.

Deleuze, Gilles, and Félix Guattari *(1987) A Thousand Plateaus,* trans. Brian Massumi. Minneapolis: University of Minnesota Press.

Delisle, Jean *(1987) La Traduction au Canada: Translation in Canada: 1534–1984.* Ottawa: Les Presses de l'Université d'Ottawa.

Delisle, Jean, and Judith Woodsworth *(eds.) (1995) Translators through History.* Amsterdam: John Benjamins.

Derrida, Jacques *(1971)* "La Mythologie blanche: La Métaphor dans le texte philosophique" *Poetique* 5:1–52.

———— *(1981)* "Plato's Pharmacy" *Dissemination,* trans. Barbara Johnson. Chicago: University of Chicago Press.

———— *(1982) Margins of Philosophy,* trans. Alan Bass. Chicago: University of Chicago Press, 207–72.

———— *(1985)* "Des Tours des Babel" in Joseph F. Graham (ed.) *Difference in Translation.* Ithaca: Cornell University Press, 165–248.

Devi, Mahasweta *(1995) Imaginary Maps,* trans. Gayatri Chakravorty Spivak. London: Routledge.

Dingwaney, Anuradha, and Carol Maier *(1995a)* "Translation as a Method for Cross-Cultural Teaching" in Anuradha Dingwaney and Carol Maier (eds.) *Between Languages and Cultures: Translation and Cross-Cultural Texts.* Pittsburgh: University of Pittsburgh Press, 303–19.

———— eds.) (1995b) *Between Languages and Cultures: Translation and Cross-Cultural Texts*. Pittsburgh: University of Pittsburgh Press.

Dyson, Ketaki Kushari (1988) *In Your Blossoming Flower Garden: Rabindranath Tagore and Victoria Ocampo*. New Delhi: Sahitya Akademi.

Elyot, Thomas (1883) *The Boke Named The Governour*, ed. Henry Herbert Stephen Croft, 2 vols. London: Kegan Paul. First edition 1531.

Escarpit, Robert (1954) *L'Angleterre dans l'oeuvre de Madame de Staël*. Paris: Marcel Didier.

Even-Zohar, Itamar (1990) *Polysystem Studies*. Special issue of *Poetics Today* 11: 1. Tel Aviv: Porter Institute for Poetics and Semiotics.

Fairclough, Norman (1989) *Language and Power*. Singapore: Longman.

Fanyi chuban waiguo gudian wenxue zhuzuo mulu 1949–1979 [*A Catalogue of Foreign Classical Literary Works in Translation, 1949–79*] (1986). Nanjing: Jiangsu People's Publishing House.

Fanyi chuban waiguo wenxue zhuzuo mulu he zhaiyao 1949–1979 [*Foreign Literary Works Translated and Published between 1949 and 1979: List and Précis*] (1980). Beijing: Zhonghua Press.

Fanyi yanjiu lunwen ji (1894–1948) [*A Collection of Papers on Translation (1894–1948)*] (1984) compiled by the Association of Chinese Translators and the Editorial Board of *Translators' Notes*. Beijing: Publishing House of Foreign Languages Teaching and Research.

Felski, Rita (1997) "The Doxa of Difference" *Signs* 23:1.1–21.

Foster, Finley Melville Kendall (1918) *English Translations from the Greek: A Bibliographical Survey*. New York: Columbia University Press.

Foucault, Michel (1977a) *Language, Counter-memory, Practice*, ed. and trans. Donald F. Bouchard and Sherry Simon. Ithaca: Cornell University Press.

———— (1977b) "What Is an Author?" *Language, Counter-memory, Practice: Selected Essays and Interviews*, ed. and trans. Donald F. Bouchard and Sherry Simon. Ithaca: Cornell University Press, 113–38.

———— (1990) *The Will to Knowledge*. Vol. 1. of *The History of Sexuality*. Harmondsworth: Penguin.

Freud, Sigmund (1983) "Creative Writers and Daydreaming" in Edith Kurzweil and William Phillips (eds.) *Literature and Psychoanalysis*. New York: Columbia University Press, 24–28.

Gadamer, Hans-Georg (1989) *Truth and Method*, trans. Joel Weinsheimer and Donald G. Marshall. London: Sheed and Ward. First edition 1975.

Geertz, Clifford (1973) "Thick Description: Toward an Interpretative Theory of Culture" *The Interpretation of Cultures: Selected Essays*. London: Fontana, 3–30.

Gentzler, Edwin (1993) *Contemporary Translation Theories*. London: Routledge.

Gile, Daniel (1995) *Regards sur la recherche en interprétation de conférence*. Lille: Presses Universitaires de Lille.

Gillies, John (trans.) (1778) The "Orations" of Lysias and Isocrates, 2 vols. London: J. Murray.

———— *(1792) The History of Ancient Greece, Its Colonies, and Conquests from the Earliest Accounts till the Division of the Macedonian Empire in the East Including the History of Literature, Philosophy, and the Fine Arts*, 3d ed., 2 vols. London: A Strahan and T. Cadell. First edition 1786.

———— *(trans.) (1813) Aristotle's Ethics and Politics Comprising His Practical Philosophy*, 2 vols. London: T. Cadell and W. Davies. First edition 1797.

Glotz, Gustave (1929) The Greek City and Its Institutions trans. N. Mallison. London: Kegan Paul.

Godard, Barbara (1990) "Theorizing Feminist Discourse/Translation" in Susan Bassnett and André Lefevere (eds.) *Translation, History and Culture*. London: Pinter, 87–96.

Goldar, Ernesto (1992) Buenos Aires: Vida cotidiana en la década del 50. Buenos Aires: Plus Ultra.

Grote, George (1888) A History of Greece from the Earliest Period to the Close of the Generation Contemporary with Alexander the Great, 12 vols. London: John Murray. First edition 1846–56.

Guha, Ranajit (1983) Economic Aspects of Peasant Insurgency in Rural India. Oxford: Oxford University Press.

Gutiérrez Lanza, Camino (1999a) "El poder del doblaje censurado en la España franquista: *Esmeralda la Zíngara o El Jorobado de Nuestra Señora de París*" *Proceedings of the VI Simposio Internacional de Comunicación Social: Centro de Lingüística Aplicada*. Santiago de Cuba: Editorial Oriente, 25–28.

———— *(1999b)* "Traducción y censura de textos cinemotagráficos en la España de Franco: Doblaje y subtitulado inglés-español (1951–1975)." Dissertation, University of León.

Hagège, Claude (1985) L'Homme de paroles. Paris: Fayard.

Hamilton, Alexander, James Madison, and John Jay (1970) The Federalist or The New Constitution. London: J. M. Dent. First edition 1787–88.

Hand, Wayland D. (1980) "The Magical Transference of Disease" *Magical Medicine: The Folkloric Component in the Folk Belief: Custom and Ritual of the Peoples of Europe and America: Selected Essays of Wayland D. Hand*. Berkeley: University of California Press, 17–39.

Hanson, Russell L. (1985) The Democratic Imagination in America: Conversations with Our Past. Princeton: Princeton University Press.

Hazard, Paul (1921) "L'Invasion des littératures du nord dans l'Italie du XVIIIᵉ siècle" *Revue de littérature comparée* 1:1.30–67.

Heaney, Seamus (1996) "Remembered Columns" *The Spirit Level*. London: Faber and Faber, 45.

Held, David (1996) Models of Democracy, rev. ed. Cambridge: Polity Press and Blackwell.

Hermans, Theo (ed.) (1985) *The Manipulation of Literature: Studies in Literary Translation*. London: Croom Helm.

—— (1991) "Translational Nouns and Correct Translations" in Kitty M. van Leuven-Zwart and Ton Naaijkens (eds.) *Translation Studies: The State of the Art*. Amsterdam: Rodopi, 155–69.

—— (1999) *Translation in Systems: Descriptive and System-oriented Approaches Explained*. Manchester: St. Jerome.

Hobbes, Thomas (trans.) (1843) *The History of the Grecian War, Written by Thucydides, Translated by Thomas Hobbes*, in William Molesworth (ed.) *The English Works of Thomas Hobbes of Malmesbury*, vols. 8–9. London: John Bohn. First edition 1629.

—— (1968) *Leviathan*, ed. Crawford Brough Macpherson. Harmondsworth: Penguin. First edition 1651.

Hoffman, Eva (1998) "The New Nomads" in André Aciman (ed.) *Letters of Transit: Reflections on Exile, Identity, Language, and Loss*. New York: New Press, 35–63.

Hollander, Benjamin (1997) *The Book of Who Are Was*. Los Angeles: Sun and Moon.

Hsü, Immanuel C. Y. (1995) *The Rise of Modern China*. London: Oxford University Press.

Hung, Eva (1996) "The Introduction of Dickens into China (1906–1960): A Case Study in Target Culture Reception" *Perspectives: Studies in Translatology* 1:29–42.

Ilie, Paul (1995) "Exolalia and Dictatorship: The Tongues of Hispanic Exile" in Hernan Vidal (ed.) *Fascismo y experiencia literaria: Reflexiones para una recanonización*. Minneapolis: Institute for the Study of Ideologies and Literature, 222–52.

Isbell, John Claiborne (1994) *The Birth of European Romanticism: Truth and Propaganda in Staël's "De l'Allemagne," 1810–1813*. Cambridge: Cambridge University Press.

Jackson, Donald (1973) "The Irish Language and Tudor Government" *Éire-Ireland* 8:1.21–28.

Jaeger, Werner (1965) *Paedeia: The Ideals of Greek Culture*, trans. Gilbert Highet, 3 vols. Oxford: Blackwell. First edition 1939.

Jin Di and Eugene Nida (1984) *On Translation: With Special Reference to Chinese and English*. Beijing: China Publishing Corporation of Translations.

Johnson, Randal (1987) "Tupy or not Tupy: Cannibalism and Nationalism in Contemporary Brazilian Literature," in John King (ed.) *Modern Latin American Fiction: A Survey*. London: Faber and Faber.

Jowett, Benjamin (trans.) (1881) *Thucydides Translated into English with Introduction, Marginal Analysis, Notes and Indices*, 2 vols. Oxford: Clarendon Press.

Kafka, Franz (1971) "The Burrow" *The Complete Stories,* ed. Nahum N. Glatzer, trans. Willa and Edwin Muir. New York: Schocken Books, 325–59.

Kálmán, György C. (1986) "Some Borderline Cases of Translation" *New Comparison* 1:117–22.

Kawharu, Ian Hugh (ed.) (1995) Waitangi: Maori and Pakeha Perspectives of the Treaty of Waitangi. Auckland: Oxford University Press.

Keene, Donald (1996) On Familiar Terms: To Japan and Back: A Lifetime across Cultures. New York: Kodansha International.

King, John (1983) " 'A Curiously Colonial Performance': The Ec-centric Vision of V. S. Naipaul and J. L. Borges" *The Yearbook of English Studies* 13:228–43.

Koelb, Clayton (ed.) (1990) Nietzsche as Postmodernist: Essays Pro and Contra. Albany: State University of New York Press.

Kofman, Sarah (1993) Nietzsche and Metaphor, trans. Duncan Large. Stanford: Stanford University Press.

Kosztolányi, Dezso (1996) "O tradutor cleptomaníano" in *O tradutor cleptomaníano e outras histórias de Kornél Esti,* trans. Ladislao Szabo. Rio de Janeiro: Editora 34, 7–11.

Lambert, José (1975) "La traduction en France à l'époque romantique: À propos d'un article récent" *Revue de littérature comparée* 46:3.396–412.

Lambert, José, and Clem Robyns (forthcoming) "Translation" in Roland Posner, Klaus Robering, and Thomas A. Sebeok (eds.), *Semiotics: A Handbook on the Sign-Theoretic Foundations of Nation and Culture.* Berlin: de Gruyter.

Larkosh, Christopher (1996) "Limits of the Translatable Foreign: Fictions of Translation, Migration, and Sexuality in 20th-Century Argentine Literature." Dissertation, University of California at Berkeley.

Lecercle, Jean-Jacques (1990) The Violence of Language. London: Routledge.

Lefevere, André (1975) Translating Poetry: Seven Strategies and a Blueprint. Assen: Van Gorcum.

—— *(ed. and trans.) (1977) Translating Literature: The German Tradition from Luther to Rosenzweig.* Assen: Van Gorcum.

—— *(ed.) (1992) Translation/History/Culture: A Sourcebook.* London: Routledge.

Levine, Suzanne Jill (1991) The Subversive Scribe: Translating Latin American Fiction. St. Paul: Graywolf Press.

Lewis, Philip E. (1981) "Vers la traduction abusive" *Les Fins de l'homme.* Paris: Galilée, 253–61.

—— *(1985)* "The Measure of Translation Effects" in Joseph F. Graham (ed.) *Difference in Translation.* Ithaca: Cornell University Press, 31–62.

Lindstrom, Naomi (1989) "Translation and Other Academic Endeavors" *Hispania* 72:3.585–86.

Locke, John (1988) Two Treatises of Government. Cambridge: Cambridge University Press. First edition 1690.

Lotbinière-Harwood, Susanne de (1991) Re-Belle et infidèle: La Traduction comme pratique de réécriture au féminin/The Body Bilingual: Translation as a Rewriting in the Feminine. Toronto: The Women's Press and Montreal: Les Éditions de Remue-ménage.

Ludmer, Josefina (1988) El género gauchesco: Un tratado sobre la patria. Buenos Aires: Editorial Sudamericana.

Ma Zuyi (1984) Zhongguo fanyi jian shi [*A Brief History of Translation in China up to the May Fourth Movement of 1919*]. Beijing: China Publishing Corporation of Translations.

Macpherson, Crawford Brough (1966) The Real World of Democracy. Oxford: Oxford University Press.

—— *(1977) The Life and Times of Liberal Democracy.* Oxford: Oxford University Press.

Maier, Carol (1984) "Note to 'Cuba Is Not, But She Calls' " *Spectacular Diseases* 7:73–74.

—— *(1985)* "Woman in Translation, Reflecting" *Translation Review* 17:5–8.

—— *(1989)* "Notes After Words: Looking Forward Retrospectively at Translation and (Hispanic and Luso-Brazilian) Criticism" in Hernan Vidal (ed.) *Cultural and Historic Grounding for Hispanic and Luso-Brazilian Feminist Literary Criticism.* Minneapolis: Institute for the Study of Ideologies and Literature, 625–53.

—— *(1998)* "Issues in the Practice of Translating Women's Fiction" *Bulletin of Hispanic Studies* 75:95–108.

Malherbe, Michel (1983) Les Langages de l'humanité. Paris: Seghers.

Martínez Bretón, Juan Antonio (1988) Influencia de la Iglesia Católica en la cinematografía española (1951–1962). Madrid: Harofarma.

Masiello, Francine (1992) Between Civilization and Barbarism: Women, Nation, and Literary Culture in Modern Argentina. Lincoln: University of Nebraska Press.

Matamoro, Blas (1986) Genio y figura de Victoria Ocampo. Buenos Aires: Eudeba.

Mattelart, Armand (1994) Mapping World Communication: War, Progress, Culture, trans. Susan Emanuel and James A. Cohen. Minneapolis: University of Minnesota Press.

Maura Gamazo, G. (1988) Lo que la censura se llevó (1938–54): Crítica política del movimiento. Madrid: Giner, Fundación Antonio Maura.

Mendelson, Edward (1985) "Baedeker's Universe" *Yale Review* 74:386–403.

Mill, John Stuart (1978) Essays on Philosophy and the Classics, in J. M. Robson (ed.) *Collected Works of John Stuart Mill,* vol. 11. Toronto: University of Toronto Press.

Mills, Sara (1997) Discourse. London: Routledge.

Mirandé, Alfredo, and Evangelina Enríquez (1979) La Chicana: The Mexican-American Woman. Chicago: University of Chicago Press.

Mitford, William (1835) *History of Greece*, rev. ed., 10 vols. London: T. Cadell. First edition 1778.
Molloy, Sylvia (1991) *At Face Value: Autobiographical Writing in Spanish America*. Cambridge: Cambridge University Press.
Montaigne, Michel de (1978) *Essays*, trans. J. M. Cohen. Harmondsworth: Penguin.
———— (1988) *Les essais*, vol 1. Paris: Quadrige/Presses Universitaires de France.
Morley, Vincent (1995) *An Crann ós Coill: Aodh Buí Mac Cruitín c. 1680–1755*. Dublin: Coiscéim.
Mukherjee, Bharati (1998) "Imagining Homelands" in André Aciman (ed.) *Letters of Transit: Reflections on Exile, Identity, Language, and Loss*. New York: New Press, 65–86.
Mukherjee, Sujit (1991) *The Book Review* 15:2. 30–31.
Murphy, Dervla (1990) *Muddling Through in Madagascar*. London: Arrow.
Nietzsche, Friedrich (1968) "Expeditions of an Untimely Man" *Twilight of the Idols and The Antichrist*, trans. R. J. Hollingdale. Harmondsworth: Penguin, 67–104.
———— (1969) "On the Genealogy of Morals" *On the Genealogy of Morals and Ecce Homo*, trans. Walter Kaufmann. New York: Vintage, 3–198.
———— (1973) "On Truth and Falsity in Their Ultramoral Sense" *Early Greek Philosophy and Other Essays*, trans. Maximilian A. Mugge. London: T. W. Foulis, 173–92.
———— (1979) "Thoughts on the Meditation: Philosophy in Hard Times" *Philosophy and Truth: Selections from Nietzsche's Notebooks of the Early 1870s*, ed. and trans. Daniel Breazeale. Atlantic Highlands, N.J.: Humanities Press, 101–23.
———— (1986) *Human, All Too Human: A Book for Free Spirits*, trans. R. J. Hollingdale. Cambridge: Cambridge University Press.
Niranjana, Tejaswini (1992) *Siting Translation: History, Post-structuralism, and the Colonial Context*. Berkeley: University of California Press.
Normanby to Hobson 14, 15 Aug. 1839, PRO, CO 209:4.251–82.
"Normas de censura" (1963) *Film ideal* 117:1.
"La nueva reglamentación legal del cine en España" (1963) *Revista Internacional del Cine* 42:73–92.
Ocampo, Victoria (1926) *De Francesca a Beatrice à traves la "Divine Comédie."* Paris: Bossard.
———— (1963) "Un regalo de Sarmiento" *Testimonios: Sexta serie 1957–1962*. Buenos Aires: Ediciones SUR, 24–26.
———— (1963) "El reinado de las institutrices" *Testimonios: Sexta serie 1957–1962*. Buenos Aires: Ediciones SUR, 37–51.
———— (1980a) *Autobiografía*, vol. 2. Buenos Aires: Ediciones SUR.
———— (1980b) *Soledad sonora*. Buenos Aires: Editorial Sudamericana.

———— *(1981a)* "Babel" *Testimonios: Primera serie 1920–34.* Buenos Aires: Ediciones SUR, 33–39.

———— *(1981b)* "Carta a Virginia Woolf" *Testimonios: Primera serie 1920–34.* Buenos Aires: Ediciones SUR, 7–14.

———— *(1982) Autobiografía,* vol 4. Buenos Aires: Ediciones SUR.

Ong, Walter J. *(1988) Orality and Literacy: The Technologizing of the Word.* London: Routledge. First edition 1982.

Orange, Claudia *(1987) The Treaty of Waitangi.* Wellington: Allan and Unwin.

———— *(1989) The Story of the Treaty of Waitangi.* Wellington: Allan and Unwin.

———— *(1990) An Illustrated History of the Treaty of Waitangi.* Wellington: Allan and Unwin.

Oxford English Dictionary *(1989)* 2d ed. Oxford: Claredon Press.

Pagano, Adriana *(1996)* "Percursos críticos e tradutórios da nação: Brasil e Argentina." Dissertation, Universidade Federal de Minas Gerais.

Pease, Donald E. *(1987) Visionary Compacts: American Renaissance Writings in a Cultural Context.* Madison: University of Wisconsin Press.

Pezzoni, Enrique *(1986) El texto y sus voces.* Buenos Aires: Editorial Sudamerica.

Piglia, Ricardo *(1986) Crítica y ficción.* Santa Fe: Universidad Nacional del Litoral.

———— *(1991)* "Memoria y tradición" *Anais do II Congresso da Associação Brasileira de Literatura Comparada.* Belo Horizonte: Universidade Federal de Minas Gerais, 60–66.

Pöckhacker, Franz *(1998)* "Unity in Diversity? The Case of Interpreting Studies" in Lynne Bowker, Michael Cronin, Dorothy Kenny, and Jennifer Pearson (eds.) *Translation Studies: Unity in Diversity.* Manchester: St. Jerome, 169–76.

Porter, Dennis *(1983)* "Orientalism and Its Problems" in Francis Barker, Peter Hulme, Margaret Iversen, and Diane Loxley (eds.) *The Politics of Theory.* Proceedings of the Essex Sociology of Literature Conference. Colchester: University of Essex, 179–93.

Porter, Francis *(1974) Turanga Journals 1840–1850.* Wellington: n.p.

Pratt, Mary Louise *(1992) Imperial Eyes: Travel Writing and Transculturation.* London: Routledge.

Pratt, T. M. *(1985)* "Madame de Staël and the Italian Articles of 1916" *Comparative Literature Studies,* 22:4.444–54.

Prawer, Siegbert Salomon *(1973) Comparative Literary Studies.* New York: Barnes and Noble.

Pym, Anthony *(1995)* "Schleiermacher and the Problem of *Blendlinge*" *Translation and Literature* 4:1.5–29.

Quart, Leonard, and Albert Auster *(1984) American Film and Society since 1945.* London: Macmillan.

Rafael, Vicente L. *(1993) Contracting Colonialism: Translation and Christian*

Conversion in Tagalog Society under Early Spanish Rule, rev. ed. Durham: Duke University Press.

"*Report of the House of Commons Committee of Aborigines in British Settlements*" *(1837)* Extract, Great Britain Parliamentary Papers 1837–1838 (26 June): 40.544–623.

Robert and Collins Dictionnaire Français-Anglais/English-French Dictionary (1978) London: Collins.

Roberts, Jennifer Tolbert (1994) Athens on Trial: The Antidemocratic Tradition in Western Thought. Princeton: Princeton University Press.

Robinson, Douglas (1996) Translation and Taboo. Dekalb: Northern Illinois University Press.

——— *(1997a) Translation and Empire: Postcolonial Theories Explained.* Manchester: St. Jerome.

——— *(1997b) What Is Translation?* Kent: Kent State University Press.

Rock, David (1987) Argentina 1516–1987: From Spanish Colonization to Alfonsín. Berkeley: University of California Press.

Rogers, Lawrence M. (ed.) (1961) The Early Journals of Henry Williams. Christchurch: Pegasus Press.

——— *(1973) Te Wiremu: A Biography of Henry Williams.* Christchurch: Pegasus Press.

Rose, Marilyn Gaddis (1993) "Foreignizing or Domesticating: Debating Norms Goes with the Territory" in Edith F. Losa (ed.) *Keystones of Communication: Proceedings of the 34th Annual Conference of the American Translators Association.* Medford, N.J.: Learned Information, 265–71.

Rossini, Gigliola (1987) "The Criticism of Rhetorical Historiography and the Ideal of Scientific Method: History, Nature and Science in the Political Language of Thomas Hobbes" in Anthony Pagden (ed.) *The Languages of Political Theory in Early-Modern Europe.* Cambridge: Cambridge University Press, 303–24.

Ruffinelli, Jorge (1987) "Julio Cortázar: Adiós a un gran escritor" *Julio Cortázar: Al término del polvo y el sudor.* Montevideo: Biblioteca de Marcha, 254–65.

Rushdie, Salman (1984) "Outside the Whale" *Granta* 11:123–38.

Sangren, P. Steven (1992) "Rhetoric and the Authority of Ethnography: 'Postmodernism' and the Social Reproduction of Texts" *Current Anthropology* 33:277–96.

Santiago, Silviano (1978) Uma literatura nos trópicos. São Paulo: Perspectiva.

Schjeldahl, Peter (1997) "Blue Stroke" *Village Voice* (8 April): 93.

Schrift, Alan D. (1990) Nietzsche and the Question of the Interpretation: Between Hermeneutics and Deconstriction. London: Routledge.

Sebreli, Juan José (1992) "Prológo" in Ernesto Goldar *Buenos Aires: Vida cotidiana en la década del '50.* Buenos Aires: Plus Ultra, 7–13.

Sengupta, Mahasweta (1990) "Translation, Colonialism, and Poetics: Rabindran-ath Tagore in Two Worlds" in Susan Bassnett and André Lefevere (eds.) *Translation, History and Culture*. London: Pinter, 56–63.

—— *(1995)* "Translation as Manipulation: The Power of Images and Images of Power" in Anuradha Dingwaney and Carol Maier (eds.) *Between Languages and Cultures: Translation and Cross-cultural Texts*. Pittsburgh: University of Pittsburgh Press, 159–74.

Shapiro, David (1994) After a Lost Original. Woodstock, N.Y.: Overlook Press.

Shen Suru (1998) Lun xin da ya [On xin, da, and ya: A Study of Yan Fu's Translation Theory]. Beijing: Commercial Publishing House.

Simon, Sherry (1989) "Conflicts de juridiction: La Double signature du texte trad-uit." *Meta* 34:2.195–209.

—— *(1992)* "The Language of Cultural Difference: Figures of Alterity in Ca-nadian Translation" in Lawrence Venuti (ed.) *Rethinking Translation*. Lon-don: Routledge, 159–76.

—— *(1996) Gender in Translation: Cultural Identity and the Politics of Trans-mission*. London: Routledge.

Simon, Sherry, and Paul St-Pierre (eds.) (2000) Changing the Terms: Translating in the Postcolonial Era. Ottawa: University of Ottawa Press.

Simpson, Paul (1993) Language, Ideology and Point of View. London: Routledge.

Sinclair, Keith (1991) A History of New Zealand. London: Penguin.

Sinclair, Robert K. (1988) Democracy and Participation in Athens. Cambridge: Cambridge University Press.

Smith, Charles Forster (trans.) (1956) Thucydides, *History of the Peloponnesian War*, vol. 1. Loeb Classical Library. Cambridge: Harvard University Press.

Smith, William (trans.) (1831) History of the Peloponnesian War by Thucydides, 2 vols. London: Valpy. First edition 1753.

Snell-Hornby, Mary (1988) Translation Studies: An Integrated Approach. Am-sterdam: John Benjamins.

Sopeña Monsalve, Andrés (1994) El florido pensil: Memoria de la escuela nacion-alcatólica. Barcelona: Crítica.

Spear, Thomas C. (1990) "The Imprisoned Narratee in Celine and Genet" *French Literature Series* 17:138–42.

Spivak, Gayatri Chakravorty (1988a) "Can the Subaltern Speak?" in Cary Nelson and Lawrence Grossberg (eds.), *Marxism and the Interpretation of Culture*. Urbana: University of Illinois Press, 271–313.

—— *(1988b) In Other Worlds: Essays in Cultural Politics*. London: Routledge.

—— *(1992)* "The Politics of Translation" in Michèle Barrett and Anne Phillips (eds.) *Destabilizing Theory*. Oxford: Polity Press, 177–200.

—— *(1993a) Outside in the Teaching Machine*. London: Routledge.

—— *(1993b)* "The Politics of Translation" in *Outside in the Teaching Machine*. London: Routledge, 179–200.

—— *(trans.) (1995)* Mahasweta Devi, *Imaginary Maps*. London: Routledge.

Staël, Germaine de *(1821)* "De l'Esprit des traductions" *Oeuvres complètes*, 17 vols. Paris: Treuttel et Wurtz, 17:387–92. First edition 1816.

—— *(1958–60) De l'Allemagne*, ed. Jean de Parge, 5 vols. Paris: Hachette.

—— *(1959) De la Littérature considérée dans ses rapports avec les institutions sociales*, ed. Paul Van Tieghem. Geneva: Droz.

Steiner, George *(1996)* "What is Comparative Literature?" *No Passion Spent*. New Haven: Yale University Press, 142–59.

St-Pierre, Paul *(1995)* "Être jeune de langue à l'âge classique" *Circuit* (Spring): 16–17.

Sturge, Kate *(1997)* "Translation Strategies in Ethnography" *The Translator* 3: 1.21–38.

Sussman, Henry *(1979) Franz Kafka: Geometrician of Metaphor*. Madison, Wisc.: Coda Press.

Szmurlo, Karyna *(1991)* "Introduction" in Madelyn Gutwirth, Avriel Goldberger, and Karyna Szmurlo (eds.) *Germaine de Staël: Crossing the Borders*. New Brunswick: Rutgers University Press, 1–10.

Thucydides *(1956) History of the Peloponnesian War*, trans. Charles Foster Smith, 4 vols. Loeb Classical Library. Cambridge: Harvard University Press.

Toury, Gideon *(1980) In Search of a Theory of Translation*. Tel Aviv: Porter Institute for Poetics and Semiotics.

—— *(1995) Descriptive Translation Studies and Beyond*. Amsterdam: John Benjamins.

"Treaty of Waitangi," 1840.

Turner, Frank M. *(1981) The Greek Heritage in Victorian Britain*. New Haven: Yale University Press.

Tylor, Edward *(1920) Primitive Culture: Researches into the Development of Mythology, Philosophy, Religion, Language, Art and Custom*. London: J. Murray.

Tymoczko, Maria *(1990)* "Translation in Oral Tradition as a Touchstone for Translation Theory and Practice" in Susan Bassnett and André Lefevere (eds.) *Translation, History and Culture*. London: Pinter, 46–55.

—— *(1999) Translation in a Postcolonial Context: Early Irish Literature in English Translation*. Manchester: St. Jerome.

—— *(2000)* "Translation and Political Engagement: Activism, Social Change and the Role of Translation in Geopolitical Shifts" *The Translator* 6:1.23–47.

Valle-Inclán, Ramón del *(1974) La lámpara maravillosa*, 3d ed. Madrid: Austral.

Van Toorn, Willem *(1999)* "Translation," trans. Craig Raine. *Times Literary Supplement* (1 January):4.

Venuti, Lawrence *(1986)* "The Translator's Invisibility" *Criticism* 28:2.179–212.

—— *(1991)* "Genealogies of Translation Theory: Scheiermacher" *TTR* 4: 2.125–50.

———— *(ed.) (1992) Rethinking Translation: Discourse, Subjectivity, Ideology.* London: Routledge.

———— *(1995) The Translator's Invisibility: A History of Translation.* London: Routledge.

———— *(1998) The Scandals of Translation: Towards an Ethics of Difference.* London: Routledge.

Vieira, Else Ribeiro Pires (1994) "A Postmodern Translation Aesthetics in Brazil" in Mary Snell-Hornby, Franz Pöchhacker, and Klaus Kaindl (eds.) *Translation Studies: An Interdiscipline.* Amsterdam: John Benjamins, 65–72.

———— *(1995)* "(In)visibilidades na tradução: Troca de olhares teóricos e ficcionais" *Com Textos* 6:50–68.

———— *(1996)* "El ser en visible: El espejo en Guimarães Rosa" *Estudios: Revista del Centro de Estudios Avanzados* 6:21–27.

———— *(1998)* "Towards a Paradigm Shift for Translation in Latin America" in Peter Bush and Kirsten Malmkjær (eds). *Rimbaud's Rainbow: Literary Translation in Higher Education.* Amsterdam: John Benjamins, 171–96.

Walker, Ranginui (1972) "The Treaty of Waitangi" in *Extension Seminar Papers.* Wellington: Victoria University.

Warner, Rex (Trans.) (1972) Thucydides, *History of the Peloponnesian War*, rev. ed. London: Penguin.

Wilden, Anthony (1980) The Imaginary Canadian. Vancouver: Pulp Press.

Williams, Raymond (1988) Keywords: A Vocabulary of Culture and Society, rev. ed. London: Fontana.

Wilson, Barbara (1998) The Death of a Much-Travelled Woman and Other Adventures with Cassandra Reilly. Chicago: Third Side Press.

Xiong Yuezhi (1996) "An Overview of the Dissemination of Western Learning in Late-Qing China" *Perspectives: Studies in Translatology* 3:13–28.

Yang, Rae (1997) Spider Eaters. Berkeley: University of California Press.

Yehoshua, Abraham B. (1996) "Exile as a Neurotic Solution" in Etan Levine (ed.) *Diaspora: Exile and the Contemporary Jewish Condition.* New York: Shapolksy Books, 15–35.

Yoshimoto, Banana (1994) N.P.: A Novel, trans. Ann Sherif. New York: Grove.

Contributors

Rosemary Arrojo teaches translation studies at the Universidade Estadual de Campinas in Brazil, where she also directs graduate students. She is author of two books, *Oficina de tradução: A teoria na prática (Translation Workshop: Theory and Practice)* (São Paulo: Ática, 1986) and *Traduçao, desconstrução e psicanálise (Translation, Deconstruction, and Psychoanalysis)* (Rio de Janeiro: Imago, 1993), and many articles. She is currently working on a book provisionally entitled *A aceitação de Babel: A tradução passada a limpo na pós-modernidade (The Acceptance of Babel: Translation in Postmodern Times)*.

Michael Cronin is director of the Centre for Translation Studies at Dublin City University. Founding member, professional member, and former president of the Irish Translators Association, he is author of *Translating Ireland: Translation, Languages, Identities* (Cork University Press, 1996) and *Crossing the Lines: Travel, Language and Translation* (Cork University Press, 2000), and coeditor of *Unity in Diversity: Current Trends in Translation Studies* (Manchester: St. Jerome, 1998).

Sabine Fenton directs the Centre for Translation and Interpreting Studies at the University of Auckland. She is involved in translation and interpreting at a national and international level as teacher, researcher, practitioner, and consultant.

Edwin Gentzler is associate professor of comparative literature and director of the Translation Center at the University of Massachusetts Amherst. He is author of *Contemporary Translation Theories* (rev. ed. Clevedon: Multilingual Matters, 2001), which has recently been translated into Italian as *Theorie della traduzione:*

Tendenze contemporanee (Torino: UTET Libreria, 1998). He serves as coeditor (with Susan Bassnett) of the Topics in Translation Series for Multilingual Matters (Clevedon, U.K.).

Camino Gutiérrez Lanza is a lecturer at the University of León in Spain in the Department of Modern Philology. Her special field of expertise is media translation and censorship, particularly as it pertains to television and cinema. She is author of several articles and conference papers on the subject, and her dissertation topic focused on the influence of autocensorship in cinema script translation.

Christopher Larkosh is an independent scholar working on issues of literature and culture in the context of multilingualism and global migration. He has held a number of academic positions pertaining to Latin American and Polish literature, most recently visiting assistant professor of Latin American literature and culture in the Spanish department at Emory University. He received his Ph.D. in Comparative Literature from the University of California at Berkeley; his dissertation focused on the role of literary translation in the formation of national identity in Argentine literature. In 1998 he held a Rockefeller postdoctoral fellowship for research on Brazilian literature and urban space at the Universidade Federal de Minas Gerais in Belo Horizonte, Brazil.

Alexandra Lianeri is a research fellow at the Institute of Hellenic and Roman Studies in the Department of Classics at the University of Bristol. She has studied linguistics and Greek literature at the University of Athens and translation studies at the University of Warwick, where she completed her doctorate in 2001. Her research has focused on the political meanings and functions of English translations of the ancient Greek concept of *democracy* during the nineteenth century.

Lin Kenan is professor of translation studies at Tianjin Foreign Studies University, where he directs the M.A. program in the theory and practice of translation. One of the first Chinese scholars to absorb contemporary Western translation theories, he has since worked to introduce them to China and find ways to use such theories in the Chinese context by integrating them with traditional Chinese approaches. Author of more than thirty papers on the subject in major Chinese academic journals, he was a visiting scholar at the University of Massachusetts in 1997–98.

Carol Maier is professor of Spanish at Kent State University, where she is also affiliated with the Institute for Applied Linguistics. In addition to her work with Octavio Armand, she has translated the writing of Rosa Chacel, Severo Sarduy, and María Zambrano. She has also written about contemporary Hispanic literature and translation theory, practice, and pedagogy. Her translation of Sambrano's *Delirio y destino, Delirium and Destiny,* appeared in 1999 (State University of

New York Press); her current projects include translations of Rosa Chacel's *La sinrazón* (*Unreason*) and Nivaria Tejera's *El barranco* (*The Ravine*).

Paul Moon was born in Auckland, New Zealand, of English and Serbian parents. His degrees are in history, political studies, and development studies. Author of *Hobson: Governor of New Zealand 1840–1842* (Auckland: David Ling, 1998), he is presently a senior lecturer in development studies at Te Ara Poutama, the Faculty of Maori Development, at the Auckland University of Technology.

Adriana S. Pagano is associate professor of English in the Department of Germanic Languages and Literatures at the Universidade Federal de Minas Gerais, Belo Horizonte, Brazil. Her specialities include translation studies and nation building in Latin America. She was a visiting scholar at the Department of Spanish and Latin American Studies in Nottingham, England, and a visiting scholar at the Translation Center at the University of Massachusetts in 1999–2000. She is currently investigating translation in the 1950s in North and South America.

Sherry Simon directs the Ph.D. in Humanities Programme at Concordia University, Montreal. She has published *Le Trafic des langues* (Montreal: Boréal, 1994) and *Gender in Translation* (London: Routledge, 1996), in addition to editing a collection of essays by Canadian translators entitled *Culture in Transit* (Montreal: Véhicule Press, 1995). In collaboration with Paul St-Pierre, she has edited *Changing the Terms: Translating in the Postcolonial Era* (Ottawa: University of Ottawa Press, 2000). Her current work focuses on the aesthetics of cultural hybridity and includes research on translation and multilingualism in India.

Maria Tymoczko is professor of comparative literature at the University of Massachusetts Amherst, where she teaches literature and translation studies. Her translations of early Irish literature into English, supported by a translation grant from the National Endowment for the Humanities, were published as *Two Death Tales from the Ulster Cycle* (Dublin: Dolmen, 1981). She has published a book on James Joyce entitled *The Irish "Ulysses"* (Berkeley: University of California Press, 1994). Her most recent study, *Translation in a Postcolonial Context: Early Irish Literature in English Translation* (Manchester: St. Jerome, 1999), was awarded the Michael J. Durkan Prize for the best book on Irish language or cultural studies by the American Conference for Irish Studies.

Index